ENGLISH
At Your Command!

Curriculum Consultants

Nancy Alexander   Kristi Lichtenberg   Ellie Paiewonsky

Elizabeth Buckley   Lourdes Lopez   Wilma Ramírez

HAMPTON-BROWN

About the Curriculum Consultants

Nancy Alexander
ESL Teacher, Grades 6, 7, 8
Nichols Middle School
Community Consolidated SD 65
Evanston, Illinois

Elizabeth M. Buckley
ESL Teacher, Grades K–8
Lincoln, Emerson, Whittier,
Mann Schools
Oak Park SD 97
Oak Park, Illinois

Kristi M. Lichtenberg
Bilingual 3rd Grade Teacher
Williams Elementary School
Garland ISD
Garland, Texas

Lourdes A. Lopez
ESOL Grade 3 Teacher
Citrus Grove Elementary School
Miami-Dade County Public Schools
Miami, Florida

Ellie Paiewonsky
Director, Nassau BOCES BETAC
Bilingual/ESL Technical
Assistance Center
Seaford, New York

Wilma Ramírez
Instructional Coach for
Curriculum-Based ELD
Alisal Community and Chavez
Elementary Schools/Alisal USD
Salinas, California

Hampton-Brown
P.O. Box 223220
Carmel, California 93922
(800) 333-3510

Printed in the United States of America
0-7362-0192-0
98 99 00 01 02 03 04 9 8 7 6 5 4 3 2 1

ACKNOWLEDGMENTS

Every effort has been made to secure permission, but if any omissions have been made, please let us know. We gratefully acknowledge permission to reprint the following material:

Alphabet Font Copyright © 1996 Zaner-Bloser
p71, From CINDER-ELLY by Frances Minters. Copyright © 1994 by Frances Minters, text. Used by permission of Viking Penguin, a division of Penguin Putnam Inc.
p72, RICHIE'S ROCKET by Joan Anderson. Illustrations by George Ancona. Text Copyright © 1993 by Joan Anderson. Illustrations Copyright © 1993 by George Ancona. Used by permission of Morrow Jr. Books, a division of William Morrow & Company, Inc.
p73, Cover illustration from SUBWAY SPARROW by Leyla Torres. Copyright © 1993 by Leyla Torres. Reprinted by permission of Farrar, Straus & Giroux, Inc.
pp76 –77, From TOAD IS THE UNCLE OF HEAVEN by Jeanne M. Lee, © 1985 by Jeanne M. Lee. Reprinted by permission of Henry Holt and Company, Inc.
p94, Courtesy of Pleasant Company Publications
p97, Used by permission of Galeria de ArteMexicano.
p98, Cover, from THE LOST LAKE by Allen Say.

Copyright © 1989 by Allen Say. Reprinted by permission of Houghton Mifflin Co. All rights reserved.
pp99 and **105**, Extensive unsuccessful attempts were made to contact the copyright holder of these works.
pp99, 11, and **135** Copyright © 1997 by Highlights for Children, Inc., Columbus, Ohio.
p113, Adapted excerpt from THE INNER WORLD OF THE IMMIGRANT CHILD (p89) by Christina Igoa, 1995. New York: St. Martin's Press. Copyright 1995 by St. Martin's Press, Inc. Adapted by permission of Lawrence Erlbaum Assoc., Inc.
p115, Copyright 1998 American Online, Inc. All Rights Reserved.
p124, Reprinted with permission of the publisher, Children's Book Press, San Francisco, CA.
p136, From SNAKE POEMS by Francisco Alarcón. © 1992. Published by Chronicle Books, San Francisco.
p137, "Today is Very Boring" from THE NEW KID ON THE BLOCK by Jack Prelutsky. Copyright © 1984 by Jack Prelutsky. By permission of Greenwillow Books, a division of William Morrow & Company, Inc.
p142, Adapted from DEAR AMERICA: THE WINTER OF RED SNOW, THE REVOLUTIONARY WAR DIARY OF ABIGAIL STEWART VALLEY

FORGE PENNSYLVANIA, 1977 by Kristiana Gregory. Copyright © by Kristiana Gregory. Reprinted by permission Scholastic Inc. DEAR AMERICA is a trademark of Scholastic Inc.
p143, Excerpt from JUMANJI by Chris Van Allsburg. Copyright © 1981 by Chris Van Allsburg. Reprinted by permission of Houghton Mifflin Co. All rights reserved.
p144, © 1997 Time Inc. Reprinted by permission. Photo from Reuters/Stringer/ Archive Photos.
p146, From PAUL BUNYAN by Steven Kellogg. Copyright © 1984 by Steven Kellogg by permission of Morrow Jr. Books, a division of William Morrow and Company, Inc.
p194, "Icy", from STORIES TO BEGIN ON by Rhoda W. Bacmeister. Copyright 1940 by E.P. Dutton, renewed © 1968 by Rhoda W. Bacmeister. Used by permission of Dutton Children's Books, a division of Penguin Putnam Inc.
pp218, 222, and **247**, Map © 1998 by Rand McNally R.L. #98-S-90.
pp218, 223, 225, and **244 –245**, Reprinted with permission from THE WORLD ALMANAC FOR KIDS 1998. Copyright © 1997 PRIMEDIA Reference Inc. All rights reserved.

Acknowledgments continued on pages 335–336.

Welcome!

In this book, you'll find all kinds of ways to communicate what you're thinking, feeling, and imagining. You can use this book to find out just what you want to know about words and writing. You'll learn how to organize your ideas and how English works. You can also learn how to do research—not just in the library, but on the Internet, too! At the back, you'll find fascinating facts about life in the U.S.A.

Whenever you have a question about English, you can look here first. This book will put **English At Your Command!**

Table of Contents

Chapter 1
Just the Right Word

Chapter 2
Picture It!

Chapter 3
Put It in Writing!

Chapter 4
Grammar Made Graphic

Chapter 5

Look It Up!

Chapter 1
Just the Right Word

shiny

spectacular

hundreds

enormous

like gold

stunning

Patrick and Carla love looking at the sky at night. They are looking for just the right words to describe it. Patrick admires the starry sky. Carla likes how the stars shine like gold.

This chapter will help you find just the right word, too. You'll find color words, number words, time words and more. Turn the pages to find hundreds of words that will help you say exactly what you mean.

Describing Words

Some **describing words** tell what something is like.
Others tell how many, how you or someone else feels,
or where something is.

Color Words

- red
- pink
- crimson
- purple
- lavender
- maroon

- blue
- turquoise
- teal
- royal blue
- sky blue
- navy blue
- green
- lime green
- forest green
- emerald green
- yellow
- gold
- orange
- brown
- tan
- black
- gray
- silver
- white

This cat mask has **red** lips and **white** teeth.

Size Words

small

medium

large

Go To **Synonyms** on pages 33 and 35 to find more size words.

Shape Words

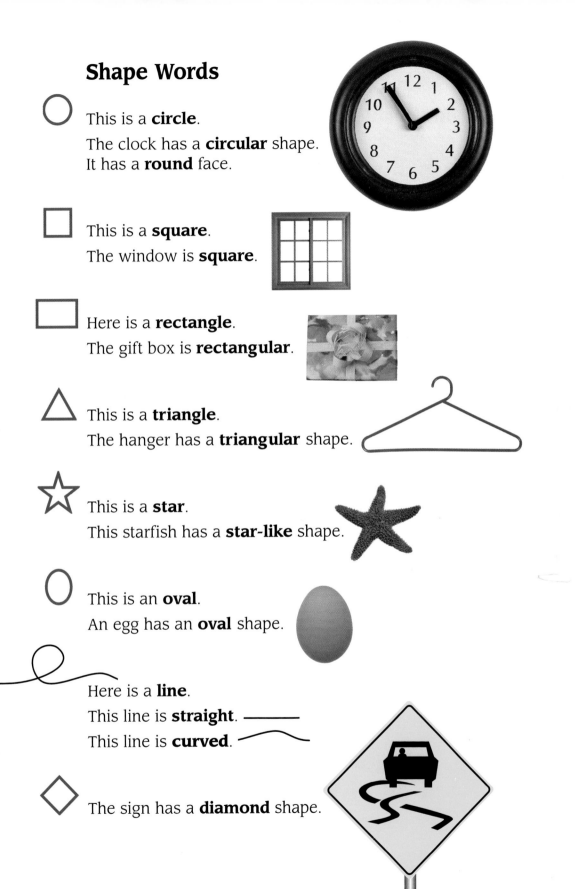

This is a **circle**.
The clock has a **circular** shape.
It has a **round** face.

This is a **square**.
The window is **square**.

Here is a **rectangle**.
The gift box is **rectangular**.

This is a **triangle**.
The hanger has a **triangular** shape.

This is a **star**.
This starfish has a **star-like** shape.

This is an **oval**.
An egg has an **oval** shape.

Here is a **line**.
This line is **straight**. ———
This line is **curved**. ⌒

The sign has a **diamond** shape.

Number Words

0	zero	26	twenty-six
1	one	27	twenty-seven
2	two	28	twenty-eight
3	three	29	twenty-nine
4	four	30	thirty
5	five	40	forty
6	six	50	fifty
7	seven	60	sixty
8	eight	70	seventy
9	nine	80	eighty
10	ten	90	ninety
11	eleven	100	one hundred
12	twelve	500	five hundred
13	thirteen	1,000	one thousand
14	fourteen	5,000	five thousand
15	fifteen	10,000	ten thousand
16	sixteen	100,000	one hundred thousand
17	seventeen	500,000	five hundred thousand
18	eighteen	1,000,000	one million
19	nineteen		
20	twenty		
21	twenty-one		
22	twenty-two		
23	twenty-three		
24	twenty-four		
25	twenty-five		

She came in **first** to win the race.

Order Words

1st	first
2nd	second
3rd	third
4th	fourth
5th	fifth
6th	sixth
7th	seventh
8th	eighth
9th	ninth
10th	tenth
11th	eleventh
12th	twelfth
13th	thirteenth
14th	fourteenth
15th	fifteenth
16th	sixteenth
17th	seventeenth
18th	eighteenth
19th	nineteenth
20th	twentieth
21st	twenty-first
22nd	twenty-second
23rd	twenty-third
24th	twenty-fourth
25th	twenty-fifth
26th	twenty-sixth
27th	twenty-seventh
28th	twenty-eighth
29th	twenty-ninth
30th	thirtieth
40th	fortieth
50th	fiftieth
60th	sixtieth
70th	seventieth
80th	eightieth
90th	ninetieth
100th	one hundredth

More Words That Tell How Many

a **pair** of eggs

a **couple** of eggs

a **few** eggs

several eggs

some eggs

a lot of eggs

many eggs

all the eggs

Describing Words, continued

Sensory Words

Look at the **red** apples.

An apple has **smooth** skin.

How It Looks

beautiful sunset

dark shadow

fluffy clouds

gloomy day

 **red** pepper

round ball

shiny medal

tiny ants

How It Feels

bumpy road

dry chalk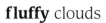

hard rock

hot soup

rough wood

slimy worm

smooth grapes

soft cotton

It has a **fresh** smell.

It sounds **crisp**.

The apple tastes **delicious**!

How It Smells

fragrant rose

fresh pepper

rotten garbage

musty closet

sweet perfume

How It Sounds

blaring siren

crisp celery

crunchy carrot

loud drums

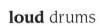

noisy music

quiet footsteps

soft whisper

How It Tastes

bitter herb

delicious food

fresh vegetables

salty pretzel

sour lemon

spicy mustard

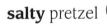

sweet cake

tangy orange

Describing Words, continued

Feeling Words

Jason is **afraid** of the bee.

Is Jason **bored**?

Jason is **sad**.

Jason is **angry**.

What is Jason **happy** about?

Jason is **surprised**.

He's **puzzled**.

Words That Tell Where

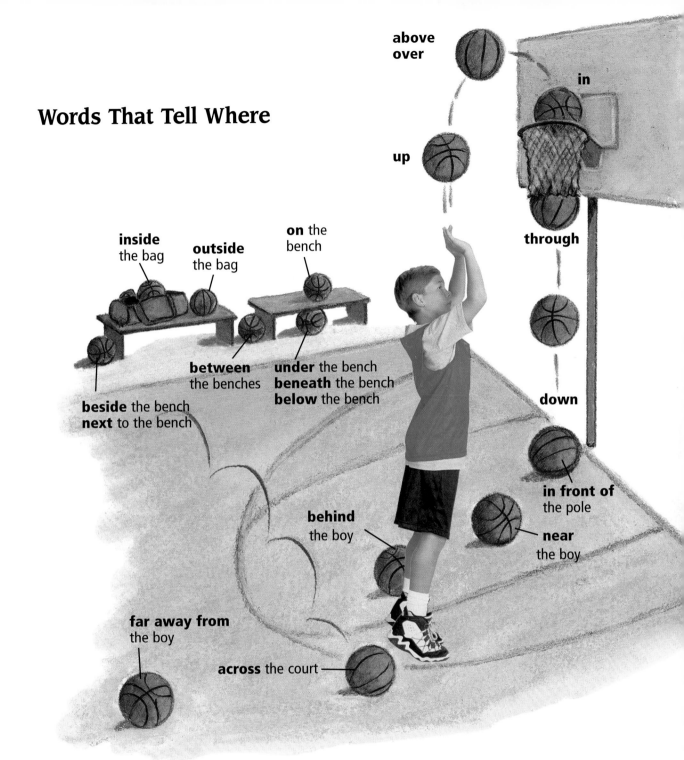

above
over

in

up

through

inside the bag

outside the bag

on the bench

between the benches

under the bench
beneath the bench
below the bench

down

beside the bench
next to the bench

in front of the pole

behind the boy

near the boy

far away from the boy

across the court

Greetings and Good-byes

There are many ways to say **hello** and **good-bye.** When you say hello and good-bye to your friends, you can be informal. When you say hello and good-bye to teachers and other adults, you need to be formal.

Informal

Hello

Hi!
Hi, there!
Hello, there!
Hey!
Howdy!
How's it going?
What's up?
What's new?
What's happening?

Good-bye

Bye!
Bye-bye!
See you later!
See you later, alligator.
So long!
Take care!
Take it easy!

Formal

Hello

Good morning!
Good afternoon!
Good evening!
How are you?
It's nice to see you.

Good-bye

It was nice talking to you.
Good night!
Good-bye!
Have a good day.
I hope you have a good afternoon.
It was good to see you.

Multiple-Meaning Words

Multiple-meaning words look the same but have different meanings. They can have two or more different meanings.

address

noun
1. My **address** is 231 South Elm Street.

verb
2. The speaker will give a report today.
He will **address** the group.

bark

noun
1. A dog makes a short, loud sound called a **bark**.

noun
2. Bark covers the outside of a tree trunk.

bat

noun
1. Use a **bat** to hit a baseball.

noun
2. A **bat** is a small, flying animal.

country

noun
1. The United States of America is a big **country**.

noun
2. Farms are found in the **country**.

Multiple-Meaning Words, continued

current

adjective
1. When something is **current**, it is happening now.

noun
2. Strong winds and the ocean **current** moved the sailboat farther out to sea.

directions

noun
1. The **directions** on a test tell you what to do to answer the questions.

Directions:
Please fill in the space next to the correct answer.

noun
2. The **directions** on a map are north, south, east, and west.

fair

noun
1. A **fair** is a place that has rides and games.

adjective
2. You're being **fair** if you treat everyone the same way.

adjective
3. When the weather is clear and sunny, it's **fair**.

fan

noun
1. They love sports. They are sports **fans**.

noun
2. Turn on the **fan** to make the air move.

float

noun
1. Our **float** for the parade was colorful.

verb
2. An inner tube can **float** in water.

foot

noun
1. Put the shoe on your **foot**.

noun
2. A **foot** is 12 inches long.

ground

noun
1. The corn is growing in the **ground**.

adjective
1. Use **ground** corn to make tortillas.

jam

noun
1. Jam is a sweet food. It is made with fruit and sugar.

verb
2. I tried to **jam** too many clothes into my small suitcase.

key

noun
1. Press the delete **key** to erase a word.

noun
2. You need a **key** to open the lock.

last

adjective
1. The person at the end of the line is **last**.

verb
2. If you take good care of something, it will **last** a long time.

left

verb
1. He is not here. He has **left** the room.

verb
2. Part of the cookie is **left**.

adjective
3. She wore a ring on her **left** hand.

letter

noun
1. My friend wrote me a **letter**.

noun
2. The first **letter** in the English alphabet is <u>A</u>.

Aa Bb Cc

light

adjective
1. Something that is not heavy is **light**.

noun
2. Turn on the **light** so you can see.

miss

verb
1. When my mother is gone, I **miss** her.

verb
2. When you don't hit your target, you **miss** it.

noun
3. She is called **Miss** Kratky because she is not married.

pen

noun
1. A **pen** is a fenced-in area for animals.

noun
2. You can write a letter with a **pen**.

pitcher

noun
1. The **pitcher** is a baseball player who throws the ball to a catcher.

noun
2. Mix the juice in a **pitcher**. Then pour some into a glass.

plant

noun
1. My dad works at the **plant**.

noun
2. A tree is one kind of green **plant**.

verb
3. **Plant** tomato seeds two inches apart.

Multiple-Meaning Words, continued

point

verb
1. Point to the place on the map.

A

noun
2. A **point** is a dot on a line.

noun
3. She made a good **point** in the debate.

pupil

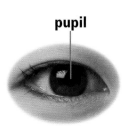

pupil

noun
1. The **pupil** is the center part of the eye.

noun
2. Another word for *student* is **pupil**.

pound

noun
1. The vegetables weigh one **pound**.

verb
2. Use a hammer to **pound** a nail into wood.

ring

noun
1. A **ring** is a piece of jewelry. You wear it on your finger.

verb
2. When you hear the telephone **ring**, someone is calling you.

noun
3. Draw a **ring**, or a circle, around the answer.

scale

noun
1. You can use a **scale** to find out how much something weighs.

noun
2. A map **scale** shows how many inches on the map are equal to real miles.

inch = 1 mile

noun
3. Each **scale** on a fish's body is thin and flat.

space

noun
1. Words in a sentence are separated by a blank **space**.

noun
2. An astronaut works in outer **space**.

state

noun
1. Illinois is a **state** in the United States.

verb
2. I heard him **state** that he wanted to go to Illinois.

table

noun
1. I use a multiplication **table** in math class.

3 x 1 = 3
3 x 2 = 6

noun
2. We put our food on the **table**.

Similes

A **simile** compares one thing to another. Sometimes it uses the word *as*. Other times it uses the word *like*.

1. His hands were **as cold as ice**.

2. Dad's hat is **as flat as a pancake**.

3. My sister can sing **like a bird**.

4. That balloon is **as light as a feather**.

5. Her hair shines **like gold**.

6. Cora and Tara are **like two peas in a pod**.

Sound Words

How does a bee sound? What sound do you hear when a person sneezes? To name those sounds, you can use **sound words**.

Animal Sounds

baa

buzz

cock-a-doodle-do

meow

moo

neigh

oink

quack

woof

People Sounds

ah-choo

ha-ha

hmmm

ooh

waa

whee

yum

Machine Sounds

beep

clang

r-r-ring

tick-tock

zoom

Hitting Sounds

boom

crash

splat

splash

More Sounds

crackle

crunch

fizz

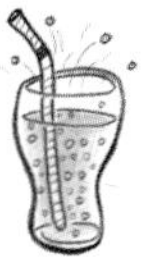

glug

pop

sizzle

whoosh

zip

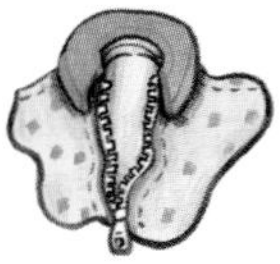

Sound-Alike Words

Many words like *flour* and *flower* sound alike, but have different spellings and different meanings. Be sure to choose the right meaning for the word you want to use.

flour   **flower**

ant
noun
An **ant** is a tiny insect.

aunt
noun
My **aunt** is my mother's sister.

ate
verb
I **ate** a sandwich.

eight
noun
The number **eight** comes after seven.

be
verb
What time will you **be** there?

bee
noun
A **bee** is an insect that makes honey.

blew
verb
The girl **blew** out the candles.

blue
noun
Her shirt is **blue**.

buy
verb
When you **buy** something, you pay money for it.

by
preposition
The ball is **by** the paddle.

noun

cent   A penny is one **cent**.

noun

scent   When something smells, it has a **scent**.

verb

sent   She **sent** a letter to her cousin in Peru.

preposition

for   What's **for** dinner?

noun

four   The number **four** comes after three.

verb

hear   You **hear** with your ears.

adverb

here   Please come **here**.

noun

hour   One **hour** is sixty minutes.

adjective

our   She took **our** picture.

noun

one   The number **one** comes before two.

verb

won   The fifth grade **won** the geography contest!

Sound-Alike Words, continued

noun
pair   A **pair** is two of something.

verb
pare   When you **pare** an apple, you peel it.

noun
pear   A **pear** is a kind of fruit.

verb
read   We **read** that book last year.

noun
red   **Red** is a bright color.

adjective
right   **Right** is the opposite of left.

verb
write   **Write** your name on the paper.

verb
see   Glasses help you **see** better.

noun
sea   The **sea** is home for lots of fish.

verb
threw   She **threw** a ball across the field.

preposition
through   I like to walk
through the woods.

Synonyms and Antonyms

Synonyms

A **synonym** is a word that has the same or almost the same meaning as another word.

afraid

The cat is **afraid** of the dog.

frightened
scared
fearful
alarmed
terrified

big

What a **big** dinosaur!

large
huge
enormous
gigantic
colossal

cold

It's **cold** today.

chilly
brisk
frosty
wintry
icy
freezing

bad

A monster!
Is it **bad**?

mean
naughty
unkind
awful
terrible
horrible
rotten
cruel

brave

The **brave** dog saved its puppy from drowning.

courageous
fearless
heroic

cry

Don't **cry**.
You'll be okay.

weep
whimper
whine
sob
bawl
wail

Synonyms, continued

eat

How many cookies
did you **eat**?

nibble on
bite into
chew up
dine on
consume
gobble up
feast on
devour

go

Come on! Let's **go**!

Ways to go fast:
run
scamper
scurry
gallop
jog
hurry
rush
dash
race
scramble
sprint

Ways to go slow:
walk
meander
stroll
ramble
trudge
hobble

Other ways to go:
crawl
hop
jump
leap
march
skip

good

That was **good**!

fine
pleasing
enjoyable
delightful
agreeable
wonderful
great
super
excellent
marvelous
terrific
awesome
splendid
top-notch
perfect
tremendous
spectacular

happy

We're so **happy**! We won!

glad
pleased
cheerful
joyful
delighted
thrilled

like

They **like** their grandmother.

enjoy
appreciate
admire
adore
love
cherish
treasure

mad

Why is he **mad**?

annoyed
cranky
irritated
cross
upset
angry
furious
enraged

laugh

My little brother likes to **laugh** when he's happy.

smile
grin
giggle
chuckle
cackle
howl

little

The flea is **little**.

small
slight
tiny
wee
miniature
minute
microscopic

noisy

Oh! That's too **noisy**!

loud
clamorous
shrill
booming
blaring
thunderous

Synonyms, continued

pretty

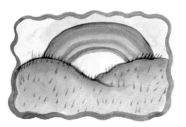

What a **pretty** rainbow.

attractive
lovely
beautiful
gorgeous
stunning

sad

He's **sad**. His toy is broken.

unhappy
blue
down
cheerless
disappointed
gloomy
miserable

talk

Everyone's **talking**!

Ways to talk loudly:
cheering
calling out
crying out
shouting
hollering
yelling
screaming

Ways to talk softly:
murmuring
whispering
mumbling

Ways to say said:
added
answered
asked
blurted
declared
exclaimed
explained
inquired
replied
reported
responded
stated
suggested
told

quiet

This is such a **quiet** place.
I can't hear a thing.

still
hushed
tranquil
silent
soundless

strong

The elephant is **strong**.

sturdy
tough
powerful
mighty
brawny

ugly

Ugh! All the trash on
the beach is **ugly**!

homely
unattractive
unappealing
unsightly
disgusting

warm

Boy! It's **warm** today!

hot
roasting
steaming
scorching
sweltering
sizzling
boiling

worried

You're late.
I was **worried**.

uneasy
concerned
upset
troubled
fretful
anxious
disturbed
distressed

wet

My shoes are **wet**.

damp
moist
soggy
soaked
drenched

Antonyms

Antonyms are words that have opposite meanings.
All kinds of words can have antonyms.

Nouns

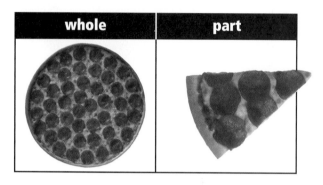

whole	part

male	female

Verbs

add	subtract

$$2 + 1 = 3 \qquad 3 - 2 = 1$$

float	sink

give	receive

enter	exit

start	finish

Adjectives

wild	tame

tiny	huge

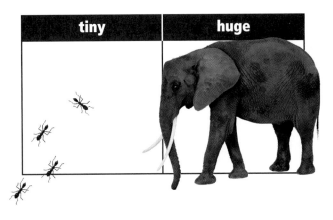

clean	dirty

empty	full

broken	fixed

beautiful	ugly

dull	bright

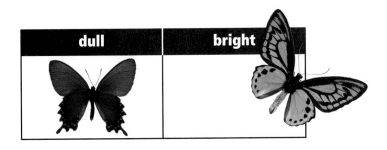

Time and Measurement

Time words tell you when things happen.
Measurement words tell how much of something you have.

Instruments Used for Measuring Time

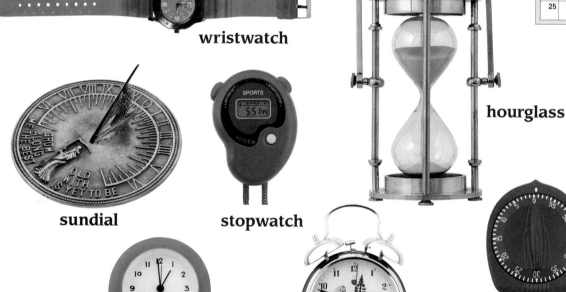

wristwatch

calendar

January

Sunday	Monday	Tuesday	Wednesday	Thursday	Friday	Saturday
				1	2	3
4	5	6	7	8	9	10
11	12	13	14	15	16	17
18	19	20	21	22	23	24
25	26	27	28	29	30	31

hourglass

sundial

stopwatch

clock

alarm clock

timer

Words for Telling Time on a Clock

o'clock

second

minute

hour

half hour
half past

quarter hour
quarter past

Short Periods of Time

instant   moment   second   nanosecond   split-second

Long Periods of Time

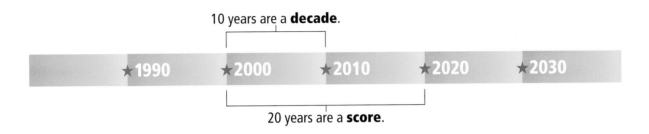

10 years are a **decade**.

★1990 ★2000 ★2010 ★2020 ★2030

20 years are a **score**.

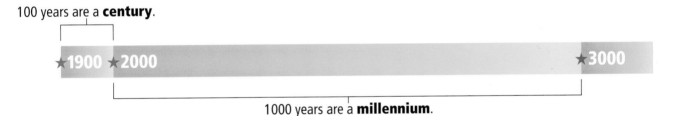

100 years are a **century**.

★1900 ★2000   ★3000

1000 years are a **millennium**.

Times of the Day

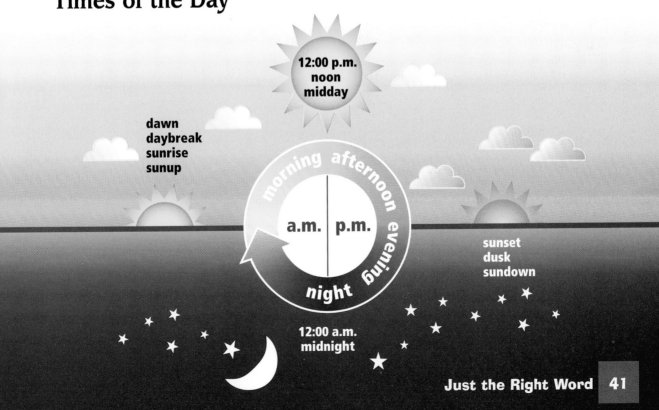

12:00 p.m.
noon
midday

dawn
daybreak
sunrise
sunup

morning afternoon evening night

a.m. | p.m.

sunset
dusk
sundown

12:00 a.m.
midnight

Seasons and Months of the Year

fall or **autumn**	**winter**	**spring**	**summer**
September	December	March	June
October	January	April	July
November	February	May	August

Days of the Week

Sunday   Monday   Tuesday   Wednesday   Thursday   Friday   Saturday

More Words That Tell When

first

next

then

finally

last

before   **after**

never

once in awhile

sometimes

occasionally

frequently

always

daily — every day

weekly — every week

biweekly — every two weeks

monthly — every month

quarterly — four times in a year

semiannually — two times in a year

annually — one time in a year

Length

inch

millimeter   centimeter

12 inches	= 1 foot	10 millimeters	= 1 centimeter
3 feet	= 1 yard	100 centimeters	= 1 meter
5,280 feet	= 1 mile	1,000 meters	= 1 kilometer

Weight

ounce
pound
ton

milligram
centigram
gram
kilogram

Volume

teaspoon   tablespoon   cup

pint   quart   gallon

Word Building

Word building is what you do when you make new words.

Compound Words

You can put two or more small words together to make one word. The new word is called a **compound word**.

backpack =
back + pack

fingernail =
finger + nail

backyard =
back + yard

flashlight =
flash + light

basketball =
basket + ball

headphones =
head + phones

bathtub =
bath + tub

hotdog =
hot + dog

bookshelf =
book + shelf

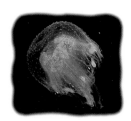

jellyfish =
jelly + fish

keyboard =
key + board

seashells =
sea + shells

lighthouse =
light + house

shoelaces =
shoe + laces

motorcycle =
motor + cycle

sunflower =
sun + flower

pineapple =
pine + apple

sweatshirt =
sweat + shirt

popcorn =
pop + corn

toothbrush =
tooth + brush

rainbow =
rain + bow

videocassette =
video + cassette

Suffixes

A **suffix** is a word part that comes at the end of a word.
When you add a suffix, you change the word's meaning.

-able, -ible means "can be"

A **breakable** vase can be broken.

A **reversible** coat can be reversed,
or turned inside out.

-en means "to make" or "made of"

She **sharpens** the pencil
to make the point sharp.

Is the mask made of wood?
Yes, it is **wooden**.

-er means "a person who"

A **runner** is a person who
runs in a race.

A **baker** is a person who bakes.

-ful means "full of

Some spider bites can be **harmful.**

An umbrella can be **useful**.

-less means "without"

A butterfly is **harmless.**

A broken umbrella is **useless**.

-ward means "in the direction of"

To go **forward** means to go in the direction in front of you.

To go **backward** means to go in the direction in back of you.

Prefixes

A **prefix** is a word part that comes at the beginning of a word. When you add a prefix, you change the word's meaning.

bi- means "two" or "twice"

A **bicycle** has two wheels.

A **biplane** has two sets of wings.

dis- means "the opposite of"

First she connected the cars. Then she **disconnected** them.

im-, in- mean "not"

Imperfect clothes are not completely right. These sneakers have holes in them.

Inexpensive items are ones that do not cost a lot.

mini- means "small" or "little"

The little globe is called a **miniglobe**.

pre- means "before"

I **precut** the vegetables before putting them in the soup.

re- means "again" or "back"

When you use something again, you **reuse** it.

When you put something back in its place, you **replace** it.

semi- means "half"

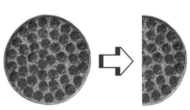

A **semicircle** is half of a circle.

Words Used in Special Ways

Idioms

Idioms are colorful ways to say something. Usually, a few words combine, or go together, to make up an idiom. In combination, these words mean something different from what the words mean by themselves.

What you say:	**What you mean:**
Skating is **a piece of cake**.	Skating is easy.
I'm **all thumbs**.	I'm clumsy.
Stop **beating around the bush**.	Stop talking about things that don't matter.

Pam always **bends over backwards**.

Pam always does whatever she can to help.

Don't **blow your top**.	Don't get angry.
Break a leg!	Good luck!
Juan is as **cool as a cucumber**.	Juan is very calm.
That car **costs an arm and a leg**.	That car is very expensive.
Cut it out.	Stop what you're doing.
My friend is **down in the dumps**.	My friend is feeling very sad.
Mr. Meyers is **down to earth**.	Mr. Meyers is easy to talk to.
I'll **drop you a line**.	I'll write you a letter.
It's as **easy as pie**.	It's very simple.

What you say:	**What you mean:**
I had to **eat my words**.	I had to say, "I'm sorry."
My **eyes were bigger than my stomach**.	I took more food than I could eat.
Now you have to **face the music**.	Now you have to take responsibility for what you did.
She **gave him the cold shoulder**.	She didn't pay any attention to him.
I'll **give it my best shot**.	I'll try my hardest.
Give me a break!	That's ridiculous!
Go fly a kite!	Go away!
I **got cold feet**.	I became unsure about doing something.
Tim **got up on the wrong side of the bed today**.	Tim is in a bad mood today.
Mom has a **green thumb**.	Mom is a good gardener.
Hang on.	Wait.

Daniel **has a heart of gold**.

Daniel is kind and generous.

I need to **hit the books**.	I need to study.
My mom **hit the ceiling**.	My mom got mad.

Idioms, continued

What you say:	What you mean:
Hold your horses.	Wait a minute.
I am walking around **in a fog**.	I am confused.
I'm **in a jam**.	I'm in trouble.
My brother's **in hot water**.	My brother's in trouble.
Don't **jump down my throat**.	Don't yell at me.
Keep your shirt on.	Wait a minute. Be patient.
Knock it off!	Stop it!

Will you **lend me a hand**?

Will you help me?

Her car runs **like clockwork**.	Her car runs smoothly.
We'd better **make tracks**.	We'd better hurry.
You're **off the hook**.	You're out of trouble.
My dad is **out of shape**.	My dad needs to exercise.
You're **out of the woods**.	You're safe.
Don't be a **pain in the neck**.	Don't bother me.
Pat yourself on the back.	Tell yourself you did a good job.

What you say:	**What you mean:**
He's **playing with fire**.	He's doing something dangerous.
Stop **pulling my leg**.	Stop kidding me.
I always **put my best foot forward**.	I always do my best.
Let's **put our heads together**.	Let's work together.
We don't **see eye to eye**.	We don't agree with each other.
My dog is as **smart as a whip**.	My dog is very quick and clever.
Please don't **spill the beans**.	Please don't tell my secret.
Don't **spread yourself too thin**.	Don't try to do too much.
That car can **stop on a dime**.	That car can stop quickly.
I **turned the room upside down**.	I looked everywhere in the room.
Jasmine is **under the weather**.	Jasmine is not feeling well.
You bet!	Yes, I agree!

Zip your lips!

Be quiet!

Two-Word Verbs

Sometimes a little word like *in*, *up*, or *out* can make a big difference in meaning. A **two-word verb** often includes one of these little words. Look at how they change a verb's meaning.

break

1. break — *to split into pieces*

Don't drop the plate! It will **break**.

2. break down — *to stop working*

My old car **breaks down** every week.

3. break up — *to come apart*

The ice on the lake will **break up** in the spring.

bring

1. bring — *to take or carry something with you*

Bring a salad to the picnic.

2. bring out — *to take out things you have in another place*

She **brings out** the pies.

3. bring up — *to suggest*

She **brings up** the idea to her friends.

check

1. check — *to make sure what you did is right*
Always **check** your work.

2. check in — *to stay in touch with someone*
My grandmother phones to **check in** with me every week.

3. check off — *to mark off a list*
Tom **checked off** the chores he had done.

4. check up — *to see if everything is okay*
The cowboy **checks up** on the cattle.

fill

1. fill — *to put as much as possible into a container or space*
Fill the pail with water.

2. fill in — *to color or shade in a space*
Please **fill in** the circle

3. fill out — *to complete*
Marcos **fills out** a form to order a book.

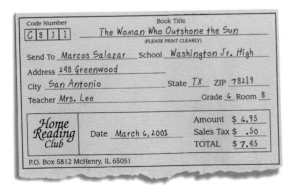

Code Number | Book Title
C 8 3 1 — *The Woman Who Outshone the Sun*
(PLEASE PRINT CLEARLY)
Send To *Marcos Salazar* School *Washington Jr. High*
Address *248 Greenwood*
City *San Antonio* State *TX* ZIP *78219*
Teacher *Mrs. Lee* Grade *6* Room *8*

Home Reading Club Date *March 6, 2001*
Amount $ *6.95*
Sales Tax $ *.50*
TOTAL $ *7.45*

P.O. Box 5812 McHenry, IL 65051

Two-Word Verbs, continued

get

1. **get** — *to go after something*
   Get the keys, please.

2. **get through** — *to finish*
   I can **get through** this book tonight.

3. **get ahead** — *to go beyond what is expected of you*
   She worked hard to **get ahead** in her math class.

4. **get out** — *to leave*
   The students **get out** at the bus stop.

5. **get over** — *to feel better*
   She'll **get over** her cold soon.

give

1. **give** — *to hand someone something*
   I will **give** you some cake.

2. **give back** — *to return*
   She **gives back** the CD she borrowed.

3. **give up** — *to quit*
   Never **give up**!
   Practice until you get it right!

go

1. go — *to move from one place to another*

I will **go** to the movies on Saturday.

2. go away — *to leave*

Tomorrow the rain will **go away**.

3. go back — *to return*

Every spring, the geese **go back** north.

4. go on — *to keep happening*

I hope the music will **go on** forever.

5. go out — *to go someplace special*

They like to **go out** to breakfast.

look

1. look — *to see or watch*

Look at the stars.

2. look forward — *to be excited about something that will happen*

I **look forward** to the parade every year.

3. look out — *to watch for danger*

Look out! The ball is coming right at you!

4. look over — *to review*

She needs to **look over** her test.

5. look up — *to hunt for and find*

You can **look up** a word in the dictionary.

Two-Word Verbs, continued

pick

1. pick — *to choose*
I always **pick** red clothes.

2. pick on — *to bother or tease*
If you **pick on** someone, you're asking for trouble.

3. pick out — *to choose*
I always **pick out** red clothes.

4. pick up — *to gather*
My class project is to **pick up** trash.

5. pick up — *to go faster*
When the wind **picks up**, you'll need your jacket.

run

1. run — *to move quickly on foot*
He had to **run** to catch the bus.

2. run into — *to see someone you know when you weren't expecting it*
Sometimes I **run into** my neighbor on the street.

3. run out — *to suddenly have nothing left*
If you use all of the milk, we'll **run out**.

stand

1. stand — *to be in a straight up and down position*
We **stand** in line to buy movie tickets.

2. stand for — *to represent*
The stars on the U.S. flag **stand for** the 50 states.

3. stand in — *to take the place of*
While our team pitcher is gone, Jerry will **stand in** for him.

4. stand out — *to make easier to see*
Highlight the words so they **stand out**.

turn

1. turn — *to change direction*
Turn right at the next corner.

2. turn in — *to give back*
She has to **turn in** her library book before it is due.

3. turn off — *to stop using*
Please **turn off** the lights when you leave.

4. turn up — *to appear*
I lost my favorite socks. I hope they **turn up.**

5. turn over — *put something on its opposite side*
He **turns over** the pot.

Chapter 2
Picture It!

Janet has a lot of bright ideas. She's using a story map to help her "picture" some of them before she starts to write a story. This chapter has all kinds of useful ways to picture ideas and details in clusters, story maps, graphs, time lines, and more. You can use these graphic organizers to make a picture of things you've read and to get organized before you write.

Clusters

A **cluster** is a picture that shows how words or ideas go together. Sometimes a cluster is called a **map**. Sometimes it is called a **web** because it looks a little like a spider web! Here are some examples.

Word Web

This **word web** groups words related to baseball.

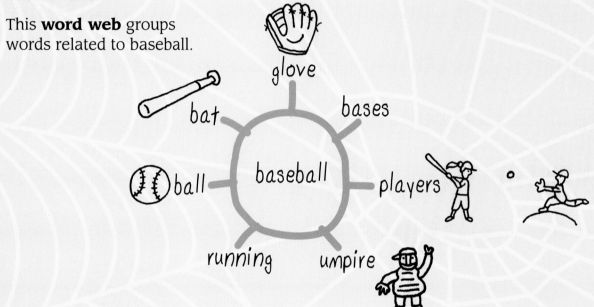

Character Map

A **character map** shows what a person in a story is like.

Event Cluster

The girl who made this **event cluster** was getting ready to write about a special celebration. She organized her ideas so she could tell what happened.

rice cakes

taro soup

foods

fruit

Circle Dance

Farmer's Dance

dances

Festival of the Harvest Moon

honored ancestors

family activities

at night looked at full moon

visited relatives

Main Idea Cluster

This **cluster** shows how details are related to a main idea.

very sharp
claws, can
be four
inches long

special
eyelids keep
eyes clean

large eyes

Detail:
strong claws
hooked beaks

Detail:
good
eyesight

beaks good for
tearing prey

Main Idea:
Eagles are strong predators.

prey is too
slow to
get away

Detail:
fly fast
and high

prey can't see
the eagle
coming

Diagrams

A **diagram** is a drawing that shows where things are, how something works, or when something happens. Most diagrams have words, or labels, that tell more about the drawing. Look at these examples.

Floor Plan

A **floor plan** is a diagram that shows where things are in a room or in a building. It shows what a room looks like as if you were above it looking down. Here is a floor plan for a museum.

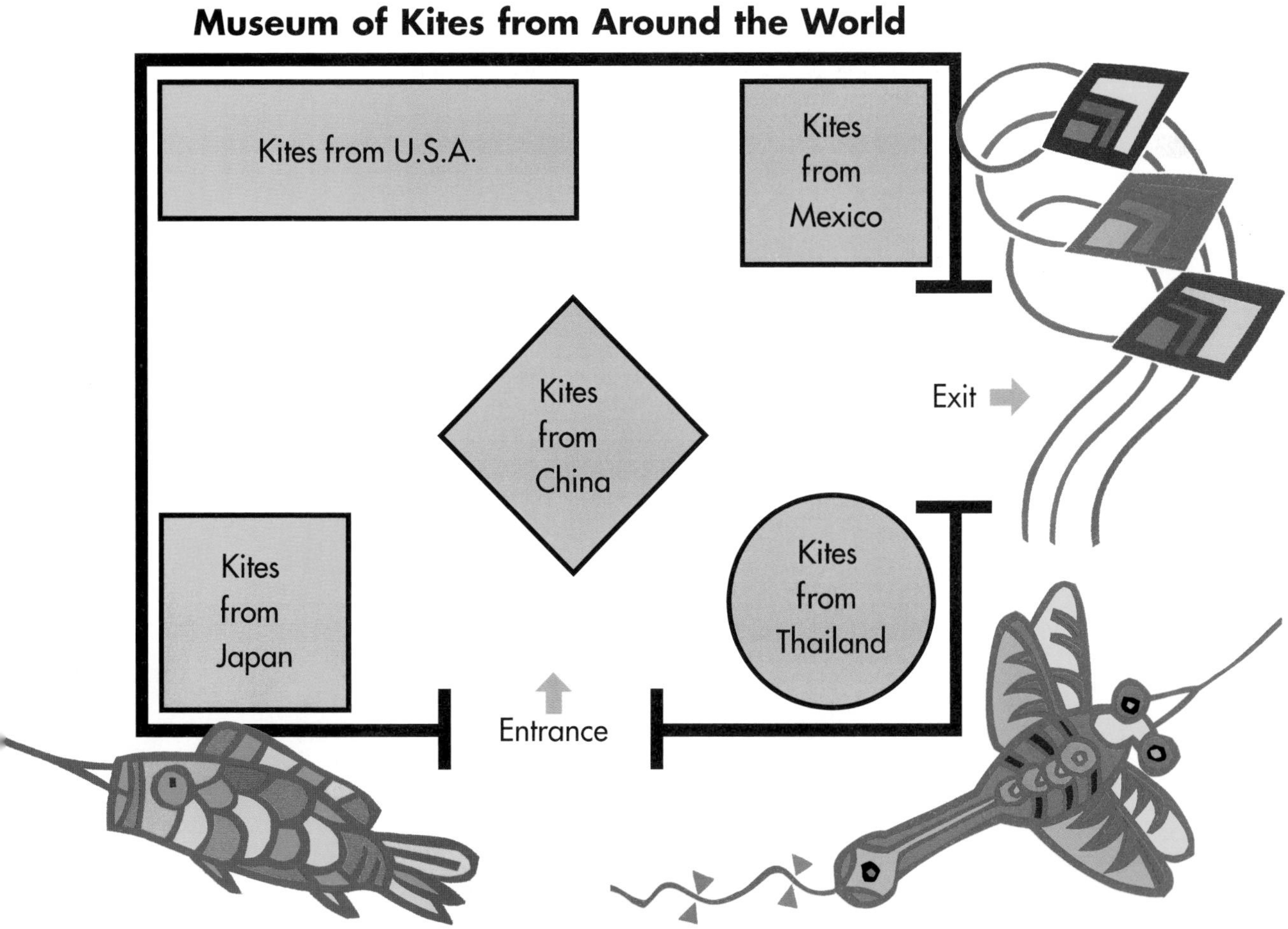

Museum of Kites from Around the World

Kites from U.S.A.

Kites from Mexico

Kites from China

Kites from Japan

Kites from Thailand

Exit ▶

▲ Entrance

Diagrams, continued

Parts Diagram

This diagram helps you know how a guitar works.

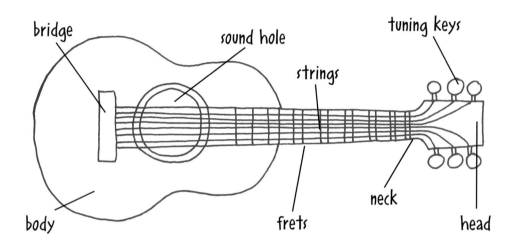

Scientific Diagram

Follow the arrows in this diagram to see how a beetle grows and changes over time.

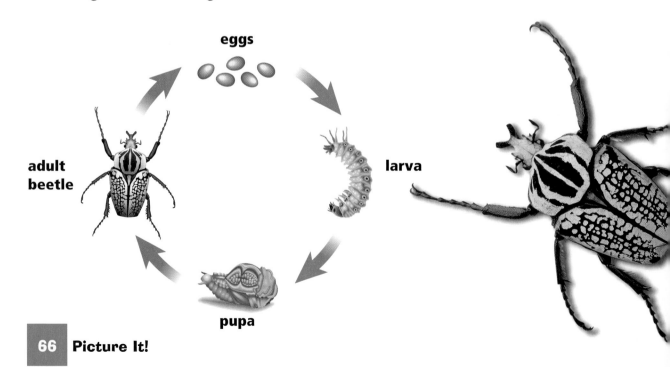

Venn Diagram

A **Venn diagram** compares and contrasts two things. It shows how two things are the same and how they are different.

Tell about one thing here.   **Tell about the other thing here.**

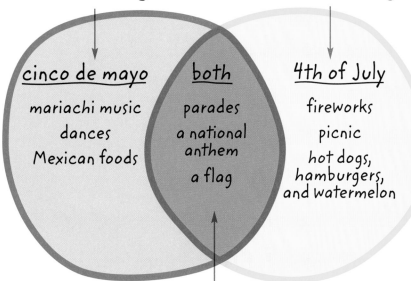

__cinco de mayo__

mariachi music
dances
Mexican foods

__both__

parades
a national anthem
a flag

__4th of July__

fireworks
picnic
hot dogs, hamburgers, and watermelon

Tell how both things are the same here.

Main Idea Diagram

This diagram shows how details are related to a main idea.

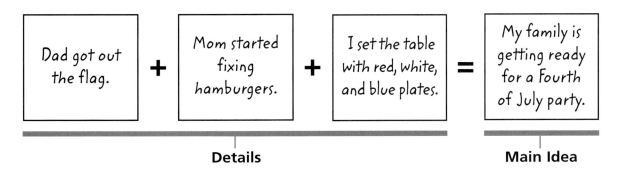

| Dad got out the flag. | **+** | Mom started fixing hamburgers. | **+** | I set the table with red, white, and blue plates. | **=** | My family is getting ready for a Fourth of July party. |

Details   Main Idea

Graphs

A **graph** is a picture that compares mathematical information, or data.

Bar Graph

One kind of graph has bars that go from left to right or up and down to give information. That's why it's called a **bar graph**.

- Each bar shows one kind of information.
- The length or height of the bar shows another kind of information.

In this graph, look at the bars to see which family sold the most tickets.

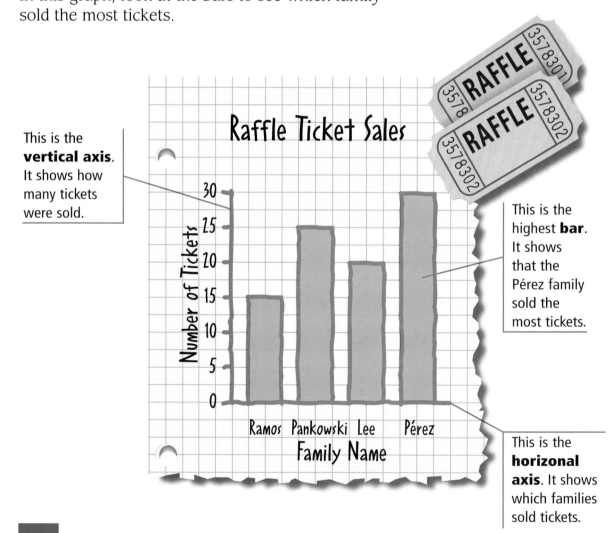

This is the **vertical axis**. It shows how many tickets were sold.

This is the highest **bar**. It shows that the Pérez family sold the most tickets.

This is the **horizonal axis**. It shows which families sold tickets.

Raffle Ticket Sales

Number of Tickets

30
25
20
15
10
5
0

Ramos Pankowski Lee Pérez

Family Name

Line Graph

This kind of graph has points, or dots, that show the data. It's called a **line graph** because lines are used to connect the points.

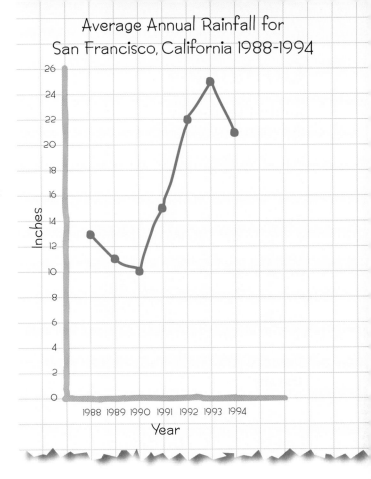

Average Annual Rainfall for San Francisco, California 1988-1994

Pie Graph

A **pie graph** looks a lot like a pie! It has a circular shape and is divided into parts. Each part of a pie graph is a percentage of the whole circle. All parts added together equal 100 percent.

Medals Won by the Top 10 Countries in the 1998 Winter Olympics

Russia 11%
Norway 16%
Austria 11%
Canada 9%
Germany 18%
United States 8%
8%
7%
6%
6% Italy
Finland
Japan
Netherlands

Outlines

An **outline** uses words to show the most important information about a topic. It groups the main ideas and details related to the topic.

Topic

Ways to Protect the Environment

Main Idea

I. Cut down on air pollution

Details

   A. Walk
   B. Ride a bicycle
   C. Share rides

Related Details

     1. Take turns riding with others
     2. Ride the bus or train

II. Reduce garbage
   A. Reuse
     1. Use paper and plastic bags more than once
     2. Share your newspaper with a neighbor
   B. Recycle

III. Save water
   A. Turn off the water while brushing teeth
   B. Fill the bathtub less than halfway when you take a bath
   C. Use less water when you wash your car
   D. Water the grass only in the morning or evening on every other day

Story Maps

A **story map** is a picture that tells what happens in a story. There are many different kinds of story maps because there are so many different kinds of stories. You can use a story map to plan a story you will write or to show what happened in a story you read.

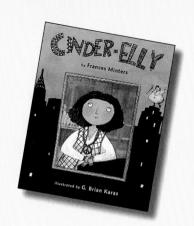

Beginning, Middle, and End

This kind of story map tells what happens in each main part of a story.

Title: _____Cinder-Elly_____

Author: _____Frances Minters_____

Beginning

Cinder-Elly and her sisters won free tickets to a basketball game. Elly's mean sisters and her mother wouldn't let her go.

↓

Middle

1. Elly's godmother helped Elly. She used a magic cane to give Elly glass shoes, new clothes, and a bike.

2. Elly went to the basketball game and met Prince Charming.

3. Elly stayed too late so her new clothes and bike disappeared. She lost a glass shoe.

4. Prince Charming tried to find Elly, but he only found her shoe.

5. Prince Charming wrote a note asking the shoe's owner to call him.

↓

End

Elly's mean sisters tried on the glass shoe, but it didn't fit. It only fit Elly.
The sisters said they were sorry for being mean.
Cinder-Elly and Prince Charming lived happily ever after.

Circular Story Map

Sometimes a story ends at the same place it begins.
Use a **circular story map** for this kind of story.

Richie's Rocket
Author: Joan Anderson

Event 6:
Richie's rocket
landed safely on
the roof of his
apartment building.

Event 1:
Richie was in his
home-made rocket
on the roof when it
blasted off into
outer space.

Event 5:
The rocket soared
back through space
toward Earth.

Event 2:
Richie met some
astronauts from
another spacecraft.
They towed his rocket
to the moon.

Event 4:
The astronauts
came back. Their
spacecraft lifted
Richie's rocket off
the moon.

Event 3:
The rocket landed on
the moon. Richie
walked on the moon
and wrote his name
in moon dust.

Problem-and-Solution Map

In some stories, there is a problem that has to be solved. A **problem-and-solution map** will help you show the problem, the ways the characters try to solve it, and the solution.

Title: _____ Subway Sparrow _____

Author: _____ Leyla Torres _____

Characters: Four passengers on a subway train

Setting: Atlantic Avenue subway station in Brooklyn, New York

↓

The **problem** gets the story started.

Problem: A sparrow flies inside a subway car. The doors close and the bird can't get out.

↓

The **events** tell what happens.

Event 1: A girl tries to catch the sparrow, but it flies away from her.

Event 2: A man tries to help by catching the sparrow with his hat, but he misses.

Event 3: A boy wants to help, too, but he's afraid that he might hurt the sparrow.

Event 4: The man starts to use an umbrella to catch the bird, but a woman stops him. She's afraid the umbrella will hurt the bird.

Event 5: Finally, the sparrow lands on the floor of the train and the woman covers it gently with her scarf.

↓

The **solution** tells how the problem is solved.

Solution: The girl picks up the sparrow and takes it out of the subway car. Outside the station, the four passengers watch the bird fly away.

Goal-and-Outcome Map

Some stories tell what characters do to get what they want, or to reach their goals. Use a **goal-and-outcome map** for these stories.

Title: _How Spider Got His Thin Middle_

The **goal** tells what the character in a story wants.

Goal
Two villages were having feasts at the same time. Spider, who loved to eat, wanted to go to both of them.

The **events** tell what happens.

Event 1	Event 2	Event 3	Event 4
Spider stood in the forest between the villages. He tied a rope around his middle.	He gave one end of the rope to a friend that was going to one feast. Then he asked him to pull the rope when the feast began.	He gave the other end to a friend who was going to the other feast and asked him to do the same thing.	Both friends started pulling on the rope at the same time. The rope kept getting tighter and tighter.

The **outcome** tells if the character gets what he or she wants.

Outcome
Spider didn't get to go to either feast. Spider's middle became thin, and that's how he is today.

Map for Rising and Falling Action

This kind of story map looks like a mountain. The most important part of a story, or the **climax**, is at the top of the mountain. Follow the arrows to find out what happens before and after the climax.

Caught in a Hurricane!

4. The hurricane hits! Wind, rain, and waves pound the town.

3. The Center announces a hurricane warning. Rosa and her family leave their house.

5. The electricity and phones go out.

2. Rosa's family hangs storm shutters and gathers emergency supplies.

6. Finally, the storm passes. Over the radio, people hear they can return home.

1. The National Hurricane Center announces a hurricane watch.

7. Rosa and her family go home to check for damage.

8. The people of the town begin to clean up after the storm.

Setting:
Early morning in a small town in Florida

Characters:
Rosa and her grandparents, Hector and Inez Santos, are eating breakfast.

Story Staircase Map

This story map looks like the steps in a staircase. Start at the bottom "step" and move up to the top to show when things happen.

"Toad is the Uncle of Heaven"
A Vietnamese Folk Tale retold and
illustrated by Jeanne M. Lee

The toad tried to ask for rain, but the King ordered his guards to capture the toad. The bees stung the guards.

When the animals found the King, the toad jumped into his lap by mistake. That made the King angry.

A very thirsty tiger joined them.

A sad rooster joined the toad and the bees.

There was a drought on Earth, so a toad went to see the King to ask for rain.

Some bees decided to go with the toad.

The toad tried to ask again, but the King told the Thunder God to make the toad be quiet. The rooster screeched and scared the Thunder God.

The King's hound tried to scare the toad, bees, and rooster away. The tiger fought the hound.

The King asked "Uncle Toad" to save his hound. The toad stopped the tiger because the King treated the toad with respect by calling him "Uncle."

Then the toad asked the King for rain.

The King ordered rain. He said that anytime Earth needed rain, all the toad had to do was croak.

The toad is a symbol of rain in Vietnam. When Uncle Toad croaks, rain will soon follow.

Tables and Charts

Tables and **charts** present information in rows and columns. Read across the rows and down the columns to compare information.

Number of Books Read During the October Read-a-thon

The **rows** go from left to right ➡.

	Class 1	Class 2	Class 3
Grade 1	47	35	62
Grade 2	33	85	102
Grade 3	75	95	88
Grade 4	78	93	82
Grade 5	96	96	95
Grade 6	102	107	65

The **columns** go from top to bottom ⬇.

Comparison Tables

Some tables show how two things are the same and how they're different.

Life in the United States and Russia

These tell how Russia and the U.S. are the same.

Life in the United States	Life in Russia
go to school Monday through Friday	go to school Monday through Friday
participate in many different sports	participate in many different sports
don't learn to swim at school	learn to swim at school in Kindergarten
cable television with hundreds of channels	television with only a few channels
can learn another language	must learn another language

These tell how Russia and the U.S. are different.

Cause-and-Effect Chart

This chart shows how one event can cause another event to happen. That's why it's called a **cause-and-effect chart**.

How a Volcano Erupts

Cause	Effect
The temperature is very hot below the earth's surface.	The rock melts to form a pool of magma in a magma chamber.
Solid rock around the magma chamber puts pressure on the magma.	The hot magma makes a conduit, or tunnel, up through the earth.
The magma forces its way out of the conduit.	The volcano erupts!

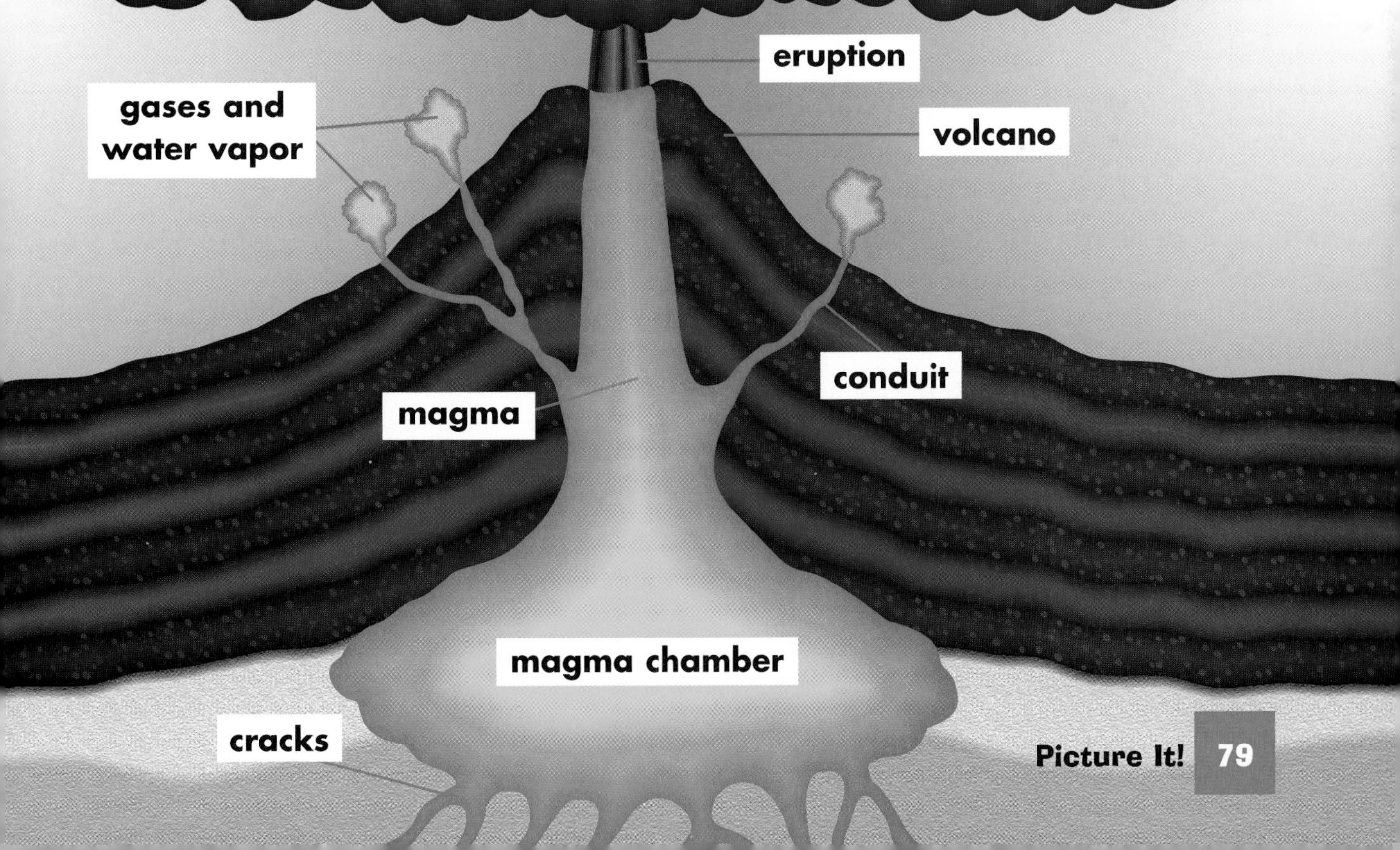

gases and water vapor

eruption

volcano

magma

conduit

magma chamber

cracks

KWL Chart

A **KWL Chart** helps you think about something you are studying. Read the question at the top of each column. It tells you how to complete the chart.

Topic: Basketball

K What Do I Know?	W What Do I Want to Learn?	L What Did I Learn?
• It takes two teams to play a game.	• How many players are on each team?	• There are 5 players on a team.
• Each team tries to throw the ball into the basket.	• How many points are given for a basket?	• A basket can count as 1, 2, or 3 points.
• The team that makes the most baskets wins.	• How long does the game last?	• A game is 32 minutes long.
		• The game is played in two parts. Each part takes 16 minutes.
		• Basketball began in the U.S. in 1891.

Flow Chart

A **flow chart** shows the steps in a process.
Arrows show the order of the steps.

How Jeans Are Made

Draw a picture of the jeans. → Use the picture to make a pattern.

Use the pattern to cut the denim fabric.

Sew the pieces of denim together.

Add buttons, rivets, zippers, and labels.

Wash the jeans to make the fabric feel softer or look worn.

Deliver the jeans to the stores for sale.

Time Lines

A **time line** shows a series of important events. It tells about each event and when it happened.

Horizontal Time Line

This time line tells about special events in a person's life. It's called a **horizontal time line** because the line goes from left to right ➡.

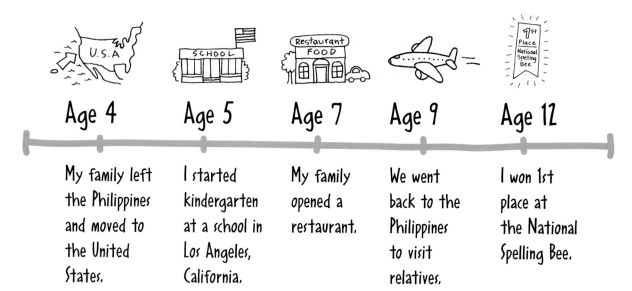

Age 4	Age 5	Age 7	Age 9	Age 12
My family left the Philippines and moved to the United States.	I started kindergarten at a school in Los Angeles, California.	My family opened a restaurant.	We went back to the Philippines to visit relatives.	I won 1st place at the National Spelling Bee.

Vertical Time Line

This time line goes from top to bottom ⬇. That's why it's called a **vertical time line**.

Dr. Franklin Chang-Díaz has spent over 1,033 hours in space.

Dr. Chang-Díaz: Astronaut

1950
Born in San José, Costa Rica

1969
Graduated from Hartford High School in Hartford, Connecticut

1973
Graduated from the University of Connecticut

1977
Graduated from the Massachusetts Institute of Technology

1981
Became an astronaut for the National Aeronautics and Space Administration (NASA)

1986
6-day space shuttle <u>Columbia</u> mission during which he participated in the deployment of the SATCOM KU satellite

1989
5-day space shuttle <u>Atlantis</u> mission during which the crew deployed the Galileo spacecraft on its journey to Jupiter

1992
8-day space shuttle <u>Atlantis</u> mission during which the crew deployed the European Retrievable Carrier satellite

1994
First joint U.S./Russian space shuttle mission

1996
15-day space shuttle mission

Chapter 3
Put It in Writing!

Danny and Aisha love to write! They know that writing is a good way to share ideas with others and to express their own personal thoughts and feelings.

How can you be a spectacular writer? Just look in this chapter and you'll find out! You'll learn how to put your own ideas in writing and how to write everything from letters and reports to stories and even tongue twisters!

The Writing Process

Writing is a great way to express yourself! The five steps in the **Writing Process** will help you plan, create, improve, and publish your work.

STEP
1 Prewriting

Prewriting is what you do before you write. That's when you decide what to write about and organize your ideas.

Brainstorm Ideas and Choose a Topic

An idea is all you need to get started! Try collecting ideas in a writing file. Then, when it's time to write, just find one in your file. You can also brainstorm ideas and jot down those that interest you.

Think about your ideas. Which ideas do you know the most about? Which one means something special to you? Circle one idea. That will be your **topic**.

 The **Good Writer Guide** on pages 148–149 for tips on collecting ideas.

Writing Ideas

facts about Port-au-Prince, Haiti

what I do after school

what my uncle sells in his store

my first day of school in the United States

Plan Your Writing

- **Ask yourself questions about your topic. The answers will help you decide which kinds of details to include.**

Three important questions are:

1. **Why** am I writing? This will be your **purpose** for writing. For example, you might want to describe to your friends where you used to live or go to school.

2. **Who** is going to read my writing? Your **audience**, or readers, can be your family, classmates, or someone you don't know.

3. **What** am I going to write? This will be the **kind of writing** you'll do like a letter, report, or personal narrative.

 The **Good Writer Guide** on pages 150–152 for tips on writing for a specific purpose and audience.

■ Collect the details.

List details about your topic. Talk about your topic with others. They might give you even more details to add. Here are some ways to show your details.

Make a cluster.

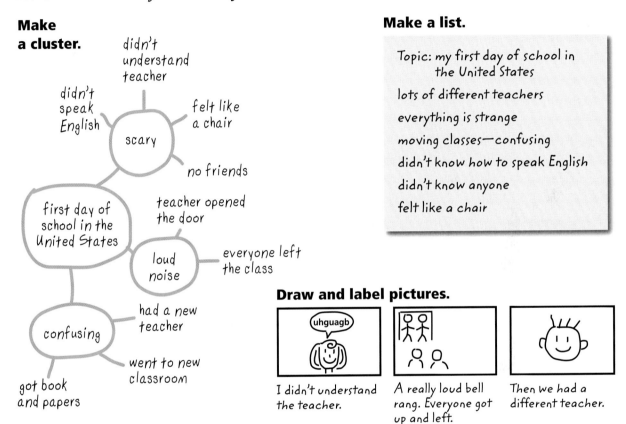

Make a list.

Topic: my first day of school in the United States

lots of different teachers

everything is strange

moving classes—confusing

didn't know how to speak English

didn't know anyone

felt like a chair

Draw and label pictures.

I didn't understand the teacher.

A really loud bell rang. Everyone got up and left.

Then we had a different teacher.

■ Organize the details.

Are the details about your topic in order? Sometimes you can organize the details as you write them down. Other times, you may need to put your details in order. One way to do that is to use numbers to show the order.

 Picture It! on pages 62–83 to find more ways to organize your details.

Topic: my first day of school in the United States

6. lots of different teachers

1. everything is strange

5. moving classes—confusing

2. didn't know how to speak English

3. didn't know anyone

4. felt like a chair

The Writing Process, continued

2 Drafting

Now you're ready to write your **first draft**. That's when you write quickly just to get your ideas down on paper. Turn your details into sentences and paragraphs, but don't worry about making mistakes. Just write!

Details

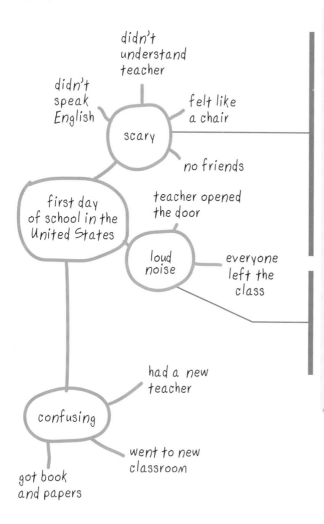

Sentences and Paragraphs

My first day of school in the United States was very scary and I didn't speak English and I didn't know how I was going to talk to people. I didn't have any friends. I felt like a chair. I tried to understand the teacher, but I couldn't.

Suddenly, a very loud bell rang. The teacher opened the door, and all the kids stood up and left the room.

3 Revising

Revise means to make changes. When you revise your writing, you change it to make it clear for your readers. You also make changes to be sure that it says what you want it to say.

Read Your Draft

Ask yourself questions about your writing.

❏ Is my writing interesting?

❏ Did I say what I wanted to say?

❏ Did I include all the details? Should I take any out? Should I add some?

❏ Did I stick to the topic?

❏ Is my writing clear?

❏ Does my writing make sense? Are the sentences, details, and events in the best order?

❏ Are there any words I should change to make my writing clearer?

The Writing Process, continued

Have Someone Else Read Your Draft

Have the person who reads your draft follow these steps to give you ideas for making your writing better. Discussing your writing like this is called a **peer conference**.

The Reader's Role in a Peer Conference

1 **Read the writing at least two times.**

2 **Try summarizing it in one sentence. What is the main idea?**

> This story (report) is all about ____.

3 **Tell which part you liked best. Why?**

> I really liked how you ____. The beginning (ending) is really good because ____.

4 **Tell which part you liked least. Why?**

> The beginning (ending) didn't get my attention because ____. I didn't like ____ because ____.

5 **Tell if any parts confused you.**

> I didn't understand the part where ____.
>
> I was surprised to read that ____.

6 **Tell how to make it better. Be specific.**

> This would be better if ____.
>
> You might try adding (or taking out) ____.

Mark Your Changes

Now **edit**, or mark your changes using the **editing marks**.

Editing Marks	Meaning
∧	Add.
↰	Move to here.
↖	Replace with this.
⤺	Take out.

I used "and" too many times in this sentence.

> My first day of school in the
> United States was very scary
> ∧because ~~and~~ I didn't speak English ~~and~~⊙
> I didn't know how I was going to
> talk to people. I didn't have any
> friends. (I felt like a chair.) I
> tried to understand the teacher,
> but I couldn't. ←
>
> Suddenly, a very loud bell
> rang. The teacher opened the
> door, and all the kids ~~stood~~ jumped up
> and ∧rushed out the door. ~~left the room.~~

Ingrid said it would be better if I put how I felt last.

These changes will give my readers a better picture of what happened.

 The Good Writer Guide on pages 153–156 for tips on improving your writing.

The Writing Process, continued

STEP
4 Proofreading

After revising your draft, **proofread** it. That means to look for mistakes in capitalization, spelling, and punctuation. Use the **proofreading marks** to show what you need to fix.

Proofreading Marks	Meaning
∧	Add.
⋏	Add a comma.
⊙	Add a period.
≡	Capitalize.
◯	Check spelling.
/	Make lowercase.
¶	Start a new paragraph.
⌣	Take out.

Why was everyone leaving? In Haiti⋏ we stayed in the same Classroom all day.
I followed the class⋏ and we went into a new room. A stranger gave me a book and some papers. I was really puzzled. Fortunately, the man spoke some Creole and explained that he was my science teacher.¶ Finally⋏ i understood. In america, there are special teachers for science, music⋏ and gym. Students also move to new classrooms. At first⋏ it was very confusing⋏ but now I like having different
~~diferent~~ teachers for my subjects⊙

Go To ▶ Pages 202-217 for capitalization, punctuation, and spelling tips.

Publishing is the best part of the writing process! Now you can make a clean copy of your writing and share it. Here are some ideas for publishing your writing.

- Send it to a magazine or newspaper.

- E-mail it to your friend in Singapore.

- Put it in a notebook with other students' work and make it a reference book for next year's class.

- Read it out loud to your class.

- Turn it into a book.

- Read it out loud on a stage with music playing in the background.

- Make a home video of you reading it.

- Fax it to your mom at her office.

My First Day in an American School

by Marco Quezada

My first day of school in the United States was very scary because I didn't speak English. I didn't know how I was going to talk to people. I didn't have any friends. I tried to understand the teacher, but I couldn't. I felt like a chair.

Suddenly, a very loud bell rang. The teacher opened the door, and all the kids jumped up and rushed out the door.

Why was everyone leaving? In Haiti, we stayed in the same classroom all day. I followed the class, and we went into a new room. A stranger gave me a book and some papers. I was really puzzled. Fortunately, the man spoke some Creole and explained that he was my science teacher.

Finally, I understood. In America, there are special teachers for science, music, and gym. Students also move to new classrooms. At first, it was very confusing, but now I like having different teachers for my subjects.

Kinds of Writing
Advice Column

Do you have a problem that you can't figure out?
Try writing a letter to an **advice column** in a newspaper,
in a magazine, or on the World Wide Web.

An advice column begins with a description of the **problem**.

The **advice** is a way to solve the problem. It's usually helpful to anyone who reads it.

The person asking for advice often uses a **made-up name**.

AmericanGirl

HELP! FROM you

Dear American Girl

Help! I watch too much TV! I'm hooked on soap operas, and I always go to bed late because I watch the late show. What should I do?
—Couch Potato

We had the same problem. Here's what to do:
1. Put a sign on the TV that says: DO NOT WATCH!
2. Start doing some other fun things like reading and playing sports.
3. Try not to think about TV, and spend more time with your friends.

Try this for a week, and you will soon get into the habit of doing other things. Have fun!
—Anna, age 10, and Jessica, age 9

AG Magazine

Announcements and Advertisements

An **announcement** is a short message that tells about an event.

Advertisements (or ads) tell about services you might need or special products you can buy.

River School's Spring Fair

Saturday, April 15
10–4 at the school
Come for food, games, prizes!

Bicycle Repair
It's Time for Spring Cleaning!

Complete bike repair and cleaning for road and mountain bikes.

Nathan's Bike Shop
756 Mission Fields Center
Alton, IL 60381
555-0099

A company's **name**, **address**, and **telephone number** is given so you can get in touch with them.

Ads often show pictures of what you can buy.

A description tells you more about the item.

Show Your School Spirit!

OAK GROVE SCHOOL

Your school's name and mascot can be on this 100% cotton shirt. Available in an assortment of colors.

Sizes: ☐ S ☐ M ☐ LG ☐ XL
5D143-714 . . . . $15.00

Mail your order to:
School Colors International
P.O. Box 683
New York, NY 11021
or call : 1-800-555-3671

A **code number** identifies the item. You use that code on the order form.

Announcements and Advertisements, continued

Classified ads are short notices that are classified, or put into groups. For example, the "New Today" section groups those items that are appearing for the first time. Look at these ads.

New Today

Help Wanted

DOGGY DAY CARE: Wanted dog lover w/ time to care for energetic puppy 2-3 days per week. 555-1759, lv. msg.

For Sale

UNICYCLE: Brand new! We can't ride it! $80 obo. Call 555-2521.

Wanted to Buy

WANTED: Used longboard, 8 ft. or longer. Call Marc 555-8653 pgr.

People pay for classified ads by the line, so they use **abbreviations**, or shortened words, to keep the ad brief.

w/ = with
lv. msg. = leave message
obo. = or best offer
ft. = feet
pgr. = pager

Autobiography

An **autobiography** is the true story of your life, written by you.

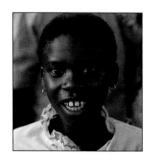

My Haiti

I am from Haiti, a country in the Caribbean Sea. I was born on a hot December day there in 1987. Every day is warm in Haiti. In fact, until I was ten years old and moved to Boston, I had no idea what snow was like...

Biography

A **biography** is the true story of a person's life. When you write a biography, you tell about the most important events and people in another person's life.

Circus Ponies
by María Izquierdo

A biography has **facts** that tell about the person and what he or she did.

It has **dates** and **sequence words** that tell when things happened.

María Izquierdo

María Izquierdo was born in 1902 in San Juan de los Lagos, Mexico. Her mother and father died when she was a child, so María lived with her grandmother and aunt. When she was a teenager, she married and moved to Mexico City.

In Mexico City, María attended art classes at the Academia de San Carlos. It was there that a famous Mexican painter, Diego Rivera, saw and liked her paintings. He helped her show them for the first time.

María became very famous for her paintings of the people and landscapes of Mexico and for her pictures of the circus. In 1929, she showed her paintings in New York City. She was the first Mexican woman to have an exhibit that included only her paintings. María painted for the rest of her life until her death in 1955.

Book Review

Sometimes you read a book that you just have to talk about with someone. You can tell about it by writing a **book review**.

In the first paragraph, tell the **title** of the book and the **author**. Then tell what the book is mostly about, or its **main idea**.

Next, tell how you **feel** about the book and why.

Finally, tell the **most important idea you learned** from the book.

<u>The Lost Lake</u>

   <u>The Lost Lake</u> by Allen Say is about a boy, Luke, who went to live with his father in New York for the summer. Luke was bored there because his dad was always too busy to spend time with him. One Saturday, Dad took Luke on a hiking trip to a secret "lost lake." The lake wasn't really secret, though, because lots of other people were there. So Luke and Dad looked for another lake. They hiked and talked all the next day. Then they found a place to camp and went to sleep. When they woke up, they saw a lake in front of them! No one else was around.

   I like this book because it reminded me of camping trips with my family. I also like that the father and the son talked to each other more when they were out camping.

   This book shows how sometimes adults can get so busy that they forget to spend time with their kids. Maybe people should think about going somewhere else to help them remember what is important.

Cartoons and Comic Strips

Cartoons and **comic strips** are drawings that show funny situations. Which of these makes you laugh the most?

"I'm calling it a surprise cake because I lost my bubble gum in the batter."

Character Sketch

See *Description*.

Description

A **description** uses words to help you picture in your mind what someone or something is like.

Character Sketch

One kind of description is a **character sketch**. It describes a real or an imaginary person.

Name the person in the **topic sentence**.

My Friend Germukh

Germukh is my best friend at school. He has dark brown hair and dark eyes. Germukh is shorter than most of the kids in our class, but that doesn't bother him.

Germukh is a great artist. He can draw creepy outer space creatures with antennae and bug eyes. Actually, his creatures are kind of cute!

Germukh is shy when there are a lot of people around, but he talks a lot when just the two of us work together on a project. Germukh always helps me with my English. Once we had to give an oral report, and Germukh stayed inside during recess to help me practice for it.

Give **examples** of what the person does that makes him or her special.

Use **describing words** and other details that tell what the person looks like and how the person acts.

Description of a Place

When you describe a place, use lots of details
to help your readers imagine that they are there!

Name the subject in the **topic sentence**.	**A Market in Vietnam**
	The outdoor market in Vietnam is jammed full with food and people. Closest to the street, you'll see a row of square wicker or plastic containers filled with parsley, pineapples, apples, taro, and waterlilies as white as clouds. In the next row up are large round bowls of fresh beans, bean sprouts, and a special kind of meat piled high like pyramids. Above the bowls, the seller lies in a hammock to free up space for more things to sell. Just above the seller, plastic bags for carrying the food hang down from the wooden beams of the stall.

Name the subject in the **topic sentence**.

Write the details in **space order**. That means to tell what you see in order from left to right, near to far, or top to bottom.

Use **direction words** and phrases to tell where things are.

Use **sensory words** that tell how things look, sound, feel, smell, or taste.

Use **similes** to help the reader imagine what's being described.

 Go To **Sensory Words** on pages 16 and 17 for more words you can use in a description.

Diary

See *Journal Entry*.

Directions

Directions tell how to play a game, how to get somewhere, or how to make something. When you write directions, the most important thing to do is to put the steps in order.

Game Directions

Tell how many people can play.

Tell how to play the game.

Tell how to win the game.

Rock, Paper, Scissors

Number of Players: 2

How to Play: First make a fist with one hand. Next move your fist up and down three times as you say *rock, scissors, paper.* After you say *paper:*

- keep a fist for rock
- put two fingers out for scissors
- put your palm down for paper.

Finally, look at your hands to see who wins.

Who Wins:

Rock beats scissors, scissors beats paper, and paper beats rock. Play again if both players have the same hand position.

Use **time** and **order words** to show the steps.

Directions to a Place

Use **direction words** to tell people which way to go.

To get to the theater, turn left out of the parking lot. Go four blocks, past the school, to Citrus Street. Turn right. The theater is on the left. It's a yellow building with a big, white sign.

Use **describing words** to help someone find the correct place.

Directions for Making Something

In a **recipe**, tell the name of the food.

First, list the ingredients and the amounts of each thing you need.

What's Cooking?

Chocolate Chip Cookies

You will need:

1 cup butter	3 cups flour
1 1/2 cups sugar	1 teaspoon salt
1 Tablespoon molasses	1 teaspoon baking soda
1 teaspoon vanilla	2 cups chocolate chips
2 eggs	

Write the **steps** in order. Numbers help show the order.

1. Preheat the oven to 375°.
2. Mix the butter, sugar, and molasses together in a bowl.
3. Add the vanilla and eggs. Mix well.
4. Add the flour, salt, and baking soda.
5. Fold in the chocolate chips.
6. Drop the batter—a tablespoon for each cookie—on an ungreased cookie sheet.
7. Bake in the oven for 8–10 minutes.

Begin sentences with **verbs** that tell someone exactly what to do.

Editorial

An **editorial** is a newspaper or magazine article that is written to persuade people to believe the same way you do. When you write an editorial, tell how you feel about something. That's your **opinion**. Give **facts** to support your opinion.

February 6, 2001

Save the Gentle Manatees

Give your **opinion** about the subject in the first paragraph.

Our manatees need protection from speeding boats. If we don't keep boat speeds slow, more and more of these gentle beasts will die.

Next, give **facts** that explain why you feel the way you do.

A few members of the City Council want to pass a law that will increase boat speeds in some waterways where manatees live. When boats go too fast, the manatees can't get out of the way of the dangerous boat propellers in time.

At the end, tell what people can do to help, and state your opinion again.

We need to tell the City Council that saving the manatees is important to us. Increasing boat speeds is not. You can take action no matter where you live. Call, write, fax, or e-mail City Council members. Ask them to support protection for manatees and their home, and to *keep existing slow speed zones in our waters*! Any type of letter or call helps!

Fable

A **fable** is a story written to teach a lesson. It often ends with a moral that states the lesson.

The **beginning** tells what the story is all about.

The **middle** tells about the events and what the characters do.

The **end** tells what finally happens.

The Birds Learn How to Build a Nest

adapted from Tung Chung-ssu

In the ancient forest, the phoenix knew best how to build a nest. Other birds wanted to learn, so they went to see him.

The phoenix said, "To learn this skill, you must listen carefully." The hen fell asleep.

The phoenix said, "If you want to make a good nest, you must first choose three big branches and then stack them on top of each other." The crow said, "Now I know how to do it!" He flew away. But the phoenix continued, "The best nest is under the eaves of someone's house where it is safe from wind and rain." The sparrow thought that was all and flew away. The phoenix said more: "Make the nest with layers of mud mixed with grass." Only the swallow heard these last words.

Today the hen does not know how to make a nest and has to be fed by people. The crow's nest is not very sturdy. The sparrow builds his nest beneath the eaves of people's homes. Only the swallow's nest is sturdy and safe from wind and rain.

Moral: Be like the swallow and listen to everything someone has to say. To learn, we must be patient.

A fable often has **talking animals**.

A fable has a **moral** that tells what you can learn from the story.

Folk Tales and Fairy Tales

Folk Tale

A **folk tale** is a story that people have been telling one another for many years.

The **characters** in a folk tale often have a problem to solve.

The **setting** is often a made-up place, long ago.

The **ending** is usually a happy one.

Stone Soup

ne day, three hungry men walked into a tiny village. Everyone told these travelers that there was no food. Really, the villagers were greedy and didn't want to share with the men.

"Oh well, there is nothing more delicious than a bowl of stone soup," one traveler said.

The villagers thought this was odd, but agreed to lend the men a huge soup pot. The men lit a fire, put three stones in the pot with some water, and waited.

A villager looked at the soup and thought, "Ridiculous! No soup is complete without some carrots." He went home, got a bunch of carrots, and put them in the pot.

Another villager looked at the soup and thought, "What that really needs is onions!" So she took a few onions and added them to the soup.

Soon, lots of people brought beef, cabbage, celery, potatoes— a little of everything that makes a soup good.

When the stone soup was done and everyone tasted it, they all agreed that they hadn't ever had anything so delicious! And imagine, a soup from stones!

Fairy Tale

A **fairy tale** is a special kind of folk tale. It often has royal characters like princes and princesses, and magical creatures like elves and fairies.

Cinderella

Once upon a time, there was a sweet, gentle girl named Cinderella, who wanted to go to the royal ball. Her mean stepmother told her to stay home and scrub the floor while she and her daughters went to the ball. Cinderella wept.

Suddenly, Cinderella's fairy godmother appeared. She waved her magic wand and turned Cinderella's ragged clothes into a sparkling gown and her shoes into glass slippers. She also turned a pumpkin into a coach and mice into horses. Now Cinderella could go to the ball! However, the fairy godmother warned Cinderella that if she wasn't home by midnight, her clothes would change into rags again.

When the prince saw Cinderella, he was overwhelmed by her beauty. All night, he refused to dance with anyone but her. At the stroke of midnight, Cinderella ran away so quickly that she lost a glass slipper, and her clothes turned back into rags. The broken-hearted prince chased her but found only the slipper.

The next day, the prince asked every woman to try on the tiny slipper. No one could squeeze into it except Cinderella. Then the prince knew that he had found the woman of his dreams. Cinderella and the prince were soon married, and they lived happily ever after.

A fairy tale often begins with **Once upon a time.**

It usually has a happy ending.

107

Greetings

Cards

Is your cousin having a birthday? Is your aunt in the hospital? Do you want to send Kwanzaa greetings to your friend? All of these are reasons to send a **greeting card**.

Go To ▶ **Dateline U.S.A.** on pages 264–301 for special days to send greetings.

Postcards

When you go on a trip, you can send greetings to a friend. Just write a postcard!

September 10, 2002

Dear Marc,

Chicago is amazing! O'Hare airport is huge—even bigger than the one in Los Angeles. Can you believe that Sears Tower is 110 stories tall? I walked along Lake Michigan yesterday and found out why Chicago's nickname is "The Windy City."

I'm having a great time. I can't wait to show you my pictures when I get back.

Your friend,
Felipe

Write your **message** here.

Marc Rountree
347 Driscol Street
Los Angeles, CA 90064

Don't forget to add a **stamp**!

Write your friend's **name and address**.

Interview

A good way to find out more about someone is to conduct, or set up, an **interview**. An interview is a meeting where one person asks another person questions to get information.

1 **Prepare for the interview.**

- Read any information you can find about the person you want to interview.

- Call or write the person to plan a time when the two of you can meet.

- Make a list of questions that you want to ask.

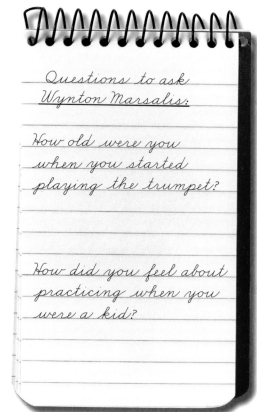

Questions to ask
Wynton Marsalis:

How old were you
when you started
playing the trumpet?

How did you feel about
practicing when you
were a kid?

2 **Conduct the interview.**

- Be sure you have your questions, a pencil, and some paper to make any notes. Try to have a tape recorder with you. You can play the tape later to help you remember what was said.

- Greet the person you are interviewing.

- Ask the questions you planned and others that come up during the interview.

- Thank the person when you are done.

❸ Share the results of the interview.

■ Look over your notes and listen to the tape.

■ Choose the information you want to share.

■ Decide how you want to share it. You might write an editorial, a description, or an article like this one.

Name the person you interviewed in the title.

List the questions (**Q**) you asked and the answers (**A**).

The answers are exact words spoken by the person you interviewed.

Talking Jazz with Wynton Marsalis
by Judy Burke

Q: How old were you when you started playing the trumpet?

A: I was six. Now, I don't want to give you the impression that I could play. I was just holding the horn, basically. My father was known by all the musicians, and they would say, "Let Ellis's son play."

After they heard me play, they would ask me, "Are you sure you're Ellis's son?"

Q: Did your father give you any advice?
A: He said, "The ability to play has a direct relationship to the amount of hours you practice."

Q: How did you feel about practicing when you were a kid?
A: Oh, I hated it. Just like everybody else. Nobody wants to practice.

Invitations

To invite people to come to a party or other special event, send them an **invitation**!

Tell **what** the event is all about.

Tell **when** and **where** the event will take place.

Come to a Party!

Shhhh!
It's a Surprise Birthday Party!

For: Alma

Date: Saturday, March 19

Time: 3 p.m. (Don't be late, please.)

Place: 263 Newland Street

R.S.V.P. 555-8301 (Ask for Casandra, not Alma.)

R.S.V.P. stands for *respondez-vous s'ils vous plâit* in French. That means "Please respond." Write your telephone number if you want people to call you to let you know they are coming.

Journal Entry

A **journal** is a lot like a diary. Begin each **journal entry** with the date. Then tell about your thoughts and feelings, and things that happen to you.

Day _Wednesday, May 3, 2002_

A couple of days ago I was thinking, I really hope to go into one of the Chinese classes during my years in college. I believe that since that's my original background and that's the language of my ancestors and also my parents and relatives — most of my relatives do not speak English at all — I think it's really important to keep the communication going. Also, when we travel, I think it would be hard to communicate if I didn't know any Chinese. I am an American citizen now, but I still have that feeling, that strong feeling, that I want to know about my background.

Letters

Friendly Letters

You can write a **friendly letter** to tell a friend what's going on in your life. A friendly letter has five parts.

Heading

29583 Wayfarer Lane
Albany, NY 12258
January 17, 2000

In the **heading**, write your address and today's date.

Greeting

Dear Anders,

Body

You'll never guess what happened today! After months of wishing, my dream finally came true. Grandpa got John and me a new dog! I've been so lonely since Shadow died last year. Anyway, we got a black Labrador and named her Midnight. She is so friendly—she just keeps wagging her tail and following us around. I can't wait for you to see her when you come in March.

How are you doing? Did you learn how to ski yet? Please write soon.

In the **body**, write your news like you're talking to your friend. Ask what your friend is doing.

Closing
Your Signature

Your friend,

Laura

Here are other **closings** you can use in a friendly letter:
Sincerely,
Love,
Yours truly,
Always,

Electronic Mail

You can use e-mail to send a letter to a friend. E-mail is short for **electronic mail** that is sent by a computer. You can send letters to or receive messages from anyone in the world who has an e-mail address. Here's one kind of computer "mailbox" you might use.

Click here to send a computer file with your letter. A disk icon appears next to the Files folder.

Type your friend's e-mail address here.

Tell what your letter is mostly about.

Choose one of these to send your letter. Most of the time you'll choose **Send Now**.

Click on this to change the style of type.

Choose this to check your spelling.

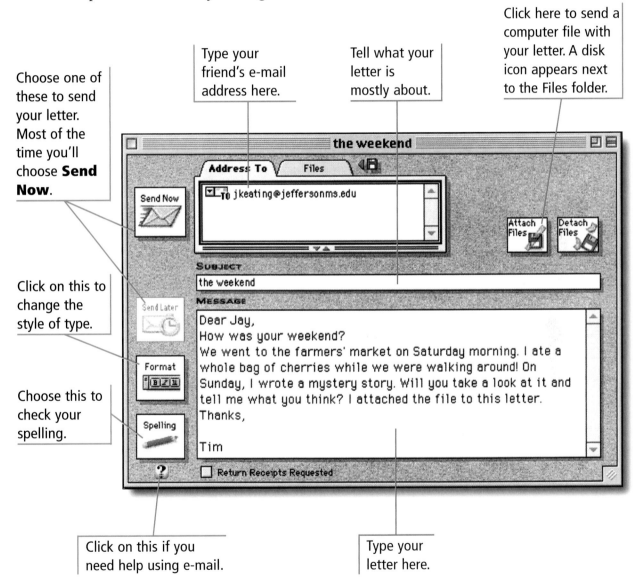

Click on this if you need help using e-mail.

Type your letter here.

Business Letters

A **business letter** is written to someone you don't know in a company or an organization. A business letter is more formal than a friendly letter and its parts are a little different.

Letter of Request

Heading	2397 Casanova Street Neptune Shores, FL 34744 February 6, 2001
Inside Address	Electronic Games, Inc. 57821 Sutter Blvd. New York, NY 10017
Greeting	Dear Sir or Madam:
Body	Please send me your latest catalogue of electronic games. I am especially interested in your latest version of electronic hockey. Thank you for your prompt attention.
Closing	Respectfully,
Your Signature	*Ann Gardner*
Your Name	Ann Gardner

In the **body**, tell what you want. Thank the person for paying attention to your request.

Here are more **closings** you can use in a business letter:

Sincerely,

Respectfully yours,

Very truly yours,

With best regards,

Sometimes you'll write a business letter to complain about something.

Letter of Complaint

2397 Casanova Street
Neptune Shores, FL 34744
June 30, 2001

Electronic Games, Inc.
57821 Sutter Blvd.
New York, NY 10017

Dear Sir or Madam:

I purchased your electronic game, "Invaders from the Purple Planet," on May 30, 2001, at the store Games, Games, Games in Neptune Shores. After playing with it for just three weeks, the button that you press to move the spaceship to the right stopped working. Since your product is warrantied for one year, I am requesting a replacement game. Enclosed is the broken one.

Respectfully,

Ann Gardner

Ann Gardner

Tell why you aren't happy with the product. Tell what you want the company to do about the problem.

Letters, continued

Sometimes you'll write a business letter to persuade someone to do something.

Persuasive Letter

349 Olympic Blvd.
Los Angeles, CA 90064
May 10, 2002

Parent and Teacher Association (PTA)
Valley School
562 North Cañon Drive
Los Angeles, CA 90064

Give your opinion in the first paragraph.

Dear PTA Members:

I think that the PTA should vote to keep a gym teacher for our school. I know that it costs more money to have a teacher who teaches only physical education, but I think it's worth it.

Use opinion words to tell how you feel. Other ways to begin an opinion are:

I feel that
I believe
My opinion is

Next, give reasons for your opinion.

Most of the kids in my class love gym, and our teacher, Mrs. Richards, is really great. If Mrs. Richards doesn't teach us physical education, our homeroom teacher will have to, and he already has too much to do. Also, Mrs. Richards helps us learn how to work in a team and be good sports. Isn't that an important part of our education?

Finally, tell what action you want people to take.

We must have a gym teacher in our school. Please vote "yes" when you meet with the Valley School Board.

Use persuasive words to get people to think the way you do.

Sincerely,

Andy Brown

Andy Brown

Envelope

To send a letter, put it in an **envelope**.

Use **abbreviations** for the names of states. See page 205 for a complete list.

Write the **return address** at the top. That's your address.

Ann Gardner
2397 Casanova Street
Neptune Shores, FL 34744

Write the **mailing address** in the middle. That's the address of the person you are writing to.

Electronic Games, Inc.
57821 Sutter Blvd.
New York, NY 10017

Include the **ZIP code**. This number helps the post office deliver your letter quickly.

List

What foods does your family need at the store? What chores do you need to do today? You can write a quick **list** to help you remember things.

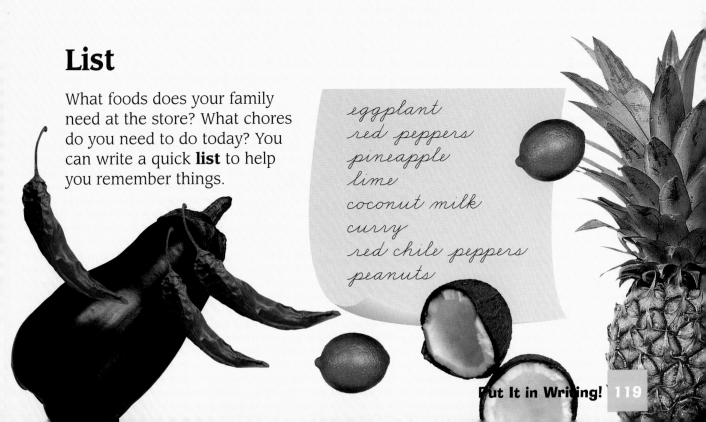

eggplant
red peppers
pineapple
lime
coconut milk
curry
red chile peppers
peanuts

Menu

A **menu** lists the food that a restaurant serves and tells its price. It usually gives a description of the meals.

World Café
DINNER MENU

MAIN DISHES

Shrimp Rice Bowl
Shrimp, red chiles and garden-fresh vegetables, served over rice . . . **$6.50**

Risotto Italian rice dish with chicken and cheese . . . **$7.95**

Southwestern-Style Burrito
Refried beans, beef, and cheddar cheese wrapped in a flour tortilla . . . **$5.75**

Tafelspitz Beef cooked in its own broth with horseradish . . . **$7.25**

Hawaiian Pizza
Thin slices of ham, pineapple, and extra mozzarella cheese . . . **$6.75**

SALADS

Caesar Salad Romaine lettuce with home-made croutons and our own Caesar dressing . . . **$3.95**

Oriental Chicken Salad
All breast meat, spices, almonds, celery, fried wontons, lettuce, and soy sauce dressing . . . **$5.95**

Garden Salad
Lettuce, tomatoes, cucumbers, mushrooms, carrots, onions, and your choice of dressing . . . **$2.50**

DRINKS

Soft Drinks . . . **$1.50**
Iced Tea . . . **$1.00**
Coffee . . . **$1.00**

Messages

See *Notes.*

News Story

A **news story** tells about an event that really happened. It includes only **facts**.

The **headline** uses important words from the story to give a quick idea of what the story is about.

The **lead paragraph** answers the questions *who, what, when, where, why,* and sometimes *how* something happened.

The **body** gives more facts about the event.

Kids Rescue Puffins–Again

BY EVELYN DAVIS
Banner News Service

VESTMANNAEYJAR, Iceland— Last night many of the children of Vestmannaeyjar were out rescuing birds. Pufflings, or young puffins, have wandered into the towns again this year. The children stayed awake to capture them and take them back to the ocean where they belong.

Pufflings were everywhere under bushes and cars, in the streets, on the grass. The six-week-old birds aren't old enough to fly well and are a bit disoriented. The birds went looking for open water but ended up in the city, far from the ocean.

In preparation, the children gathered cardboard boxes all last week. Then, this week, they stayed up and walked around the city with their boxes and flashlights to look for stray birds. The children say that they listen for the sound of flapping wings to lead them to the little birds.

In the early hours this morning, the kids took their boxes of birds to the ocean and let the birds go. The puffins, and the kids, should be back again next year.

Notes

A **note** is a short written message.

Telephone Message

When someone calls your mom and she isn't home, what can you do? Write a note, of course. This kind of note is called a **telephone message**.

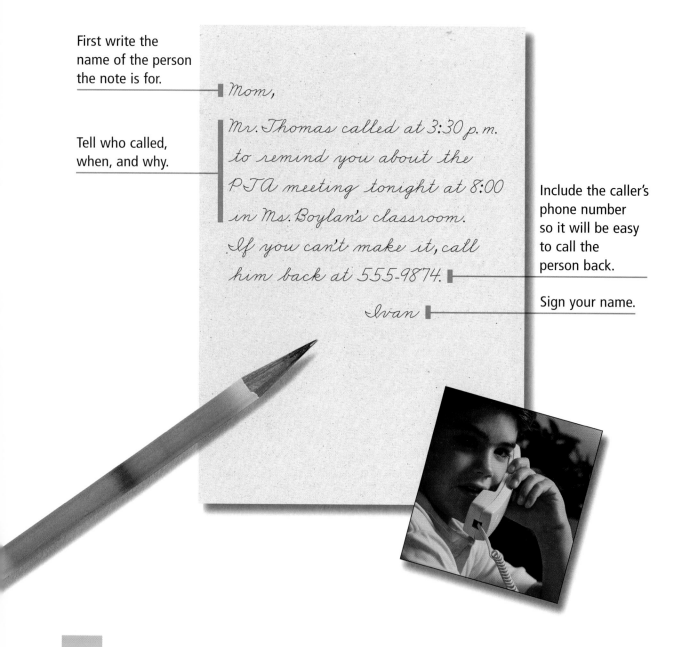

First write the name of the person the note is for.

Tell who called, when, and why.

Mom,

Mr. Thomas called at 3:30 p.m. to remind you about the PTA meeting tonight at 8:00 in Ms. Boylan's classroom. If you can't make it, call him back at 555-9874.

Ivan

Include the caller's phone number so it will be easy to call the person back.

Sign your name.

Thank-you Note

A **thank-you note** thanks someone for doing something or for giving you a gift. It's a lot like a friendly letter.

Write the **date**.

October 31, 2002

Write a **greeting**.

Dear Grandma and Grandpa,

    Thank you so much for the game. It is so fun that my friend Sonia and I play every afternoon after school. Sometimes I win and sometimes she wins. I am so glad that you showed me how to play when I was at your house last summer. I hope that we can play again together soon—this time I might beat Grandpa!

In the **body**, say "thank you" and name the gift. Tell why you like it or how you are using it.

Love,
Liz

Write a **closing** and sign your name.

Here are some other ways to say *thank you*:

Many thanks...
I really appreciate...
Thanks a million...

You are so thoughtful...
I'm so grateful...

Observation Log

An **observation log** is a written record of things you see, or observe. It's a good idea to show dates for your notes to help you remember and carefully study what you saw.

Observations: Growing a Plant
Week 1: Brown dirt, no plant
Week 2: See a tiny, green shoot
Week 3: Shoot is now about
1/2 inch tall
Leaf starting to grow
Week 4: Plant taller
See two leaves
Week 5: Plant bigger
Leaves are reaching
for the sun

Heat and Water

	Temperature	Water Level
Monday	70°	5 inches
Tuesday	95°	4 inches
Wednesday	90°	3 inches
Thursday	77°	2 1/2 inches
Friday	73°	2 inches

Conclusion: Water evaporates faster in hot temperatures.

Order Form

To order something from a catalog or a magazine, you can use an **order form**. Be sure to include all the information about the item and where to send it.

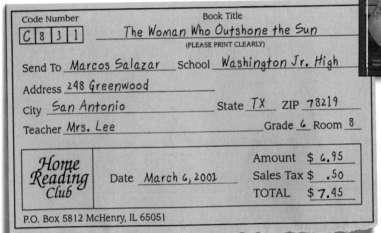

Code Number: C 8 3 1
Book Title: The Woman Who Outshone the Sun
(PLEASE PRINT CLEARLY)
Send To Marcos Salazar School Washington Jr. High
Address 248 Greenwood
City San Antonio   State TX ZIP 78219
Teacher Mrs. Lee   Grade 6 Room 8

Home Reading Club
Date March 6, 2001
Amount $ 6.95
Sales Tax $ .50
TOTAL $ 7.45

P.O. Box 5812 McHenry, IL 65051

Paragraphs

A **paragraph** is a group of sentences that all tell about the same idea. One sentence gives the main idea of the paragraph. The other sentences give details that support the main idea.

Sometimes the paragraph begins with the main idea.

The **topic sentence** tells the main idea of the paragraph.

The **details** in these sentences tell more about the main idea.

> There are so many treasures to see at the beach! Tiny shells, shaped like fans, are everywhere. Colorful rocks sparkle on the soft, warm sand. A little, pink crab shell sits in the middle of a log that has washed up on the sandy shore.

Indent the first sentence of a paragraph. *Indent* means to leave a space before you start to write.

Sometimes the main idea comes at the end of a paragraph.

These sentences give the **details**.

> Tiny shells, shaped like fans, are everywhere. Colorful rocks sparkle on the soft, warm sand. A little, pink crab shell sits in the middle of a log that has washed up on the sandy shore. There are so many treasures to see at the beach!

The **topic sentence** that tells the main idea is last.

 Main Idea Diagram on page 67. It shows how to make a picture of your main idea and details before you write a paragraph.

Paragraphs with Examples

In some paragraphs, the detail sentences give **examples** that go with the main idea.

The **topic sentence** tells the main idea.

Stamps are little works of art that show something about a country. Some stamps from Australia show the country's shape. Others show native Australian animals like a fish and a wombat. In Brazil, there are stamps of Brazilian festivals, like Carnival. Stamps from Botswana or Senegal may have pictures of birds. There are lots of colorful birds in both countries. People in colorful traditional clothing are on some stamps from Ecuador.

Each detail sentence gives an **example** of one type of stamp.

Cause-and-Effect Paragraphs

In a cause-and-effect paragraph, you tell what happens and why. An **effect** is what happens. The **cause** is why it happened.

The topic sentence tells the **cause**.

Last week, my father started giving me a weekly allowance. Now, when I go to the store or the movies with my friends, I have my own money. Also, I can save some of my allowance every week to buy something nice for my sister's birthday. My allowance isn't a lot of money, but it is special to me.

The detail sentences tell what happened after the girl got an allowance. These are the **effects**.

Paragraphs That Compare

Some paragraphs tell how two people, places, things, or ideas are alike. This paragraph compares alligators and crocodiles.

The **topic sentence** names the two things you are comparing.

The **detail sentences** tell how the things are the same.

It's easy to confuse an alligator with a crocodile because these two very large reptiles are a lot alike. Both live in marshes and swamps. They look similar, too. Both have tough skin, short legs, and long tails. Their large jaws have many sharp teeth. Alligators and crocodiles have the same kind of large eyes that stick up above their heads. When they swim, their eyes stay above the water so they always know where they're going!

Special words help you signal that the two things are alike.

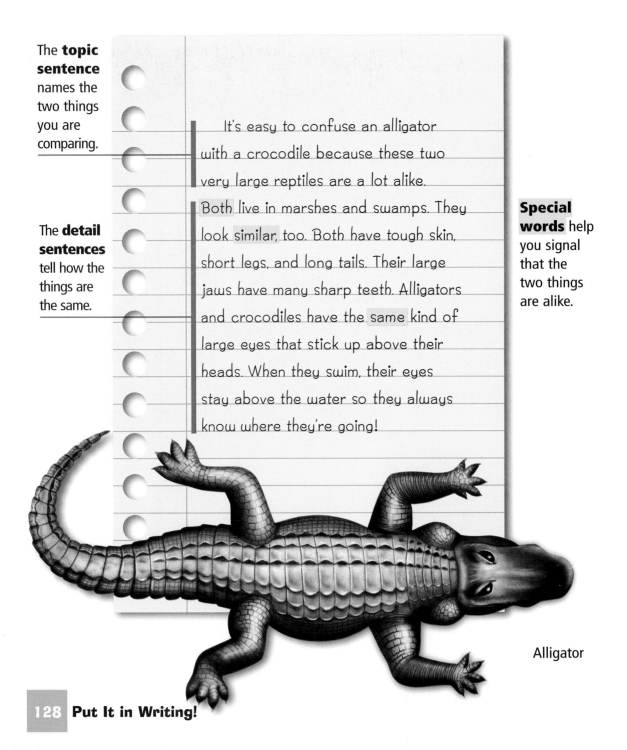

Alligator

Paragraphs That Contrast

Some paragraphs tell how two people, places, things, or ideas are different. This paragraph contrasts alligators and crocodiles.

The **topic sentence** names the two things you are contrasting.

The **detail sentences** tell how the things are different.

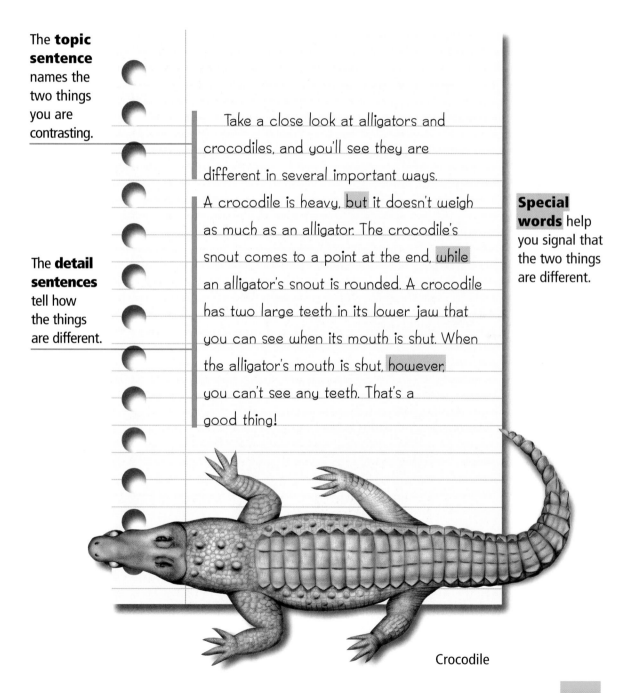

Take a close look at alligators and crocodiles, and you'll see they are different in several important ways. A crocodile is heavy, but it doesn't weigh as much as an alligator. The crocodile's snout comes to a point at the end, while an alligator's snout is rounded. A crocodile has two large teeth in its lower jaw that you can see when its mouth is shut. When the alligator's mouth is shut, however, you can't see any teeth. That's a good thing!

Special words help you signal that the two things are different.

Crocodile

Persuasive Paragraphs

When you write a **persuasive paragraph**, you tell your opinion about something. You try to persuade your readers. That means you try to get them to agree with you.

Give your opinion in the **topic sentence**.

When you change the motor oil in your car, you should recycle the used oil. If you pour the used oil onto the ground, it harms the soil where plants are trying to grow. If you dump the used oil down a storm drain, it will end up in the ocean where it could kill a lot of fish. If you recycle used oil, however, it can be cleaned and reused. Please, you must help our planet! Just take your used oil to a gas station or other place where it can be recycled.

Give the reasons for your opinion in the **detail sentences**.

Use **persuasive words** to get your readers to take action.

Personal Narrative

When you write a **personal narrative**, you tell a story about something that happened to you. Because the story is about you, you'll write it in the first person. That means you'll use the words *I*, *me*, and *my* a lot.

The **beginning** tells what the event is all about.

The **middle** tells more about the event.

The **end** tells what finally happened.

A Good Luck Valentine

I'll never forget my first Valentine's Day. When I got to school, I was surprised to find some bright red envelopes on my desk.

At first, I thought they were gifts for Chinese New Year. Each new year my family gives me money in red envelopes to wish me good luck. But when I opened the little envelopes, I only found some paper hearts.

Then my teacher explained what happens on Valentine's Day. The notes in the envelopes were valentines. Now when I look at my valentines, I feel just as wonderful as when I get gifts for the new year!

A personal narrative has **order words** that tell when something happened.

It has **describing words** that tell what things were like and how you felt.

 Go To Dateline U.S.A. on pages 264–301 for more information about Valentine's Day and other special days and holidays.

Play

A **play** is a story that is acted out on a stage. Every play has characters—the people or animals that tell the story. When you write a play, you decide what the characters will do and say.

1 **Start with a story. Make one up or choose one from a book.**

The Legend of the Chinese Zodiac

In ancient times, the Jade Emperor wanted to name each of the years in the twelve-year cycle after an animal. He couldn't decide which animals to honor, however. He invited all the animals on earth to participate in a race. The first twelve to finish the race would each have a year named for them. The rat won the race; the ox was second. The tiger, rabbit, dragon, snake, horse, sheep, monkey, rooster, dog, and boar were the next ten animals to cross the finish line. The Jade Emperor named a year for the animals in the order they finished the race, starting with the rat and ending with the boar.

2 **Turn the story into a script.**

The script names the characters. It tells the setting, or when and where the story takes place, and it describes what the characters say and do.

Here is how you can make a script.

Write a **title** and **act number**. An **act** in a play is just like a chapter in a book.

List all the **characters**.

Tell about the **setting**.

The Legend of the Chinese Zodiac
Act 2
The Race

Characters: the Jade Emperor, rat, ox, tiger, rabbit, dragon, snake, horse, sheep, monkey, rooster, dog, boar

Setting: Long ago, in front of the Jade Emperor's palace. There is a starting line on the ground. The Jade Emperor is telling all the animals the rules of the race.

Jade Emperor *(loudly, to get everyone's attention)*: Listen! Listen! We are going to start the race in a few minutes. First, I want to explain the course and the rules.

Boar *(raising his hand)*: Will we be allowed to stop for water along the way?

Jade Emperor: Please let me tell you the rules of the whole race before you ask questions. *(pointing at the line on the ground)* This is the starting line. You must have all of your toes behind this line.

Snake *(raising his tail)*: What if you don't have toes?

Jade Emperor *(surprised)*: Good point. You must have your whole body behind this line before I give the signal to start. Are you ready?

Name each character and write the **dialogue**, or the words the characters say.

Use **stage directions** to tell how the characters should say the lines or move around on the stage.

3 **Perform the play.**

Choose people to play the characters. Have them use the script to practice. Then put on the play.

Poem

A **poem** looks and sounds different from other kinds of writing. Poems use rhyme, rhythm, and colorful language to give the reader a special feeling.

Cinquain

There are five lines in a **cinquain**. One kind of cinquain has a certain number of syllables in each line.

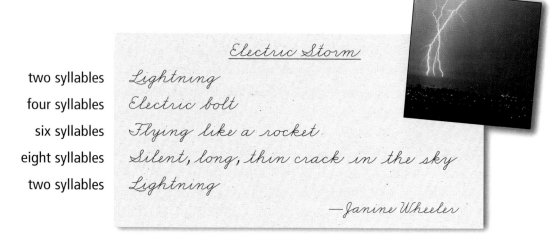

	Electric Storm
two syllables	Lightning
four syllables	Electric bolt
six syllables	Flying like a rocket
eight syllables	Silent, long, thin crack in the sky
two syllables	Lightning

—Janine Wheeler

Diamante

A **diamante** is seven lines long. When you write it, it looks like a diamond.

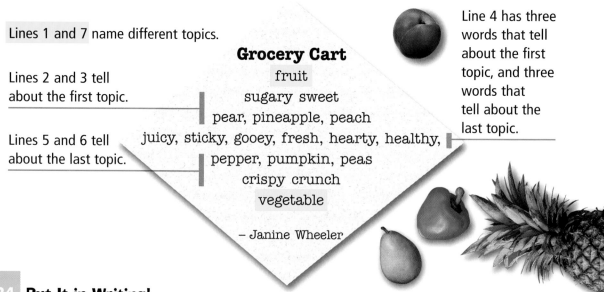

Lines 1 and 7 name different topics.

Lines 2 and 3 tell about the first topic.

Lines 5 and 6 tell about the last topic.

Line 4 has three words that tell about the first topic, and three words that tell about the last topic.

Grocery Cart

fruit
sugary sweet
pear, pineapple, peach
juicy, sticky, gooey, fresh, hearty, healthy,
pepper, pumpkin, peas
crispy crunch
vegetable

– Janine Wheeler

Concrete Poem

A **concrete** poem is written so the words make
a picture of what they are describing.

Oak
(a poem to be read from the bottom up)

this great oak
into the coming night
its capillary ends
its garbled limbs
against the hazy light
now stretches
to stand winter and the wind
from wells far underground

with strength
girthed itself
upon a trunk
upon a branch
upon a sprig
once a leaf
spring by spring
a century ago
from under land
this tree unrolled
Simple as a flower

—Dawn Watkins

A Poem in Free Verse

Free verse is a kind of poetry that doesn't have a regular rhythm. Sometimes a poem written in free verse can have rhyming words, but it doesn't have to.

MATRIARCH

my dark
grandmother

would brush
her long hair

seated out
on her patio

even ferns
would bow

to her splendor
and her power

—Francisco X. Alarcón

Haiku

A **haiku** is three lines long and has a specific number of syllables in each line. A haiku is often about nature.

Dragon Song

five syllables   Upon the blue sky

seven syllables   the dragon kite writes a song.

five syllables   Ah, my heart sings it!

— Shirleyann Costigan

A Rhyming Poem

In a **rhyming poem**, some of the words at the end of the lines rhyme. That means the words have the same ending sounds. The rhyming words help give the poem a special rhythm, or beat.

Today is Very Boring

Today is very boring,
it's a very boring day,
there is nothing much to look at,
there is nothing much to say,
there's a peacock on my sneakers,
there's a penguin on my head,
there's a dormouse on my doorstep,
I am going back to bed.

Today is very boring,
it is boring through and through,
there is absolutely nothing
that I think I want to do,
I see giants riding rhinos,
and an ogre with a sword,
there's a dragon blowing smoke rings,
I am positively bored.

Today is very boring,
I can hardly help but yawn,
there's a flying saucer landing
in the middle of my lawn,
a volcano just erupted
less than half a mile away,
and I think I felt an earthquake,
it's a very boring day.

–Jack Prelutsky

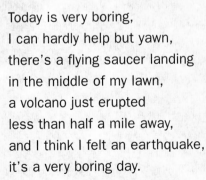

Report

A **report** presents facts about a topic. You can gather facts by reading books, interviewing people, searching for information on the Internet, and doing other kinds of research. Then you can organize the information you find and write the report.

The **title** and **introduction** tell what your report is all about. They get your reader interested.

Each **topic sentence** tells one main idea about your topic.

Types of Fossils

Have you ever wondered about the creatures that roamed the earth thousands of years ago? Take a look at fossils! They can tell us a lot about what those creatures were like.

Long ago, dead plants and animals were buried under the earth or the ocean. For many years, materials like dirt, sand, and oil covered their remains. As the materials hardened, they trapped the remains inside to make fossils. There are many kinds of fossils.

The most common fossils are mold and cast fossils. In a mold fossil, rock hardened around the remains. However, parts of the plant or animal dissolved or disappeared, and left just an outline shape in the rock. In a cast fossil, minerals fill up an empty space left by an animal's body. It looks like a whole animal buried in the rock.

A trace fossil is another type of fossil. It shows the activities of an animal. An example is a dinosaur footprint in mud that later hardened into rock. Other trace fossils show animal trails or burrows.

True form fossils are the actual animals or parts of animals, such as teeth, bones, and shells. An ant caught in tree sap which hardened into amber is a true form fossil. A woolly mammoth frozen in a block of ice and a saber-toothed tiger stuck in a sticky tar pit are also true form fossils.

Fossils come in many forms. They may be in rock, tar, ice, or amber. They are all evidence of animals from long ago.

The **body** of the report has all the facts you found.

The last paragraph is the **conclusion**. It sums up your report.

Go To **The Research Process** on pages 220–233 to find out how to do research.

Story

Writers use their imaginations and make up different kinds of **stories** to entertain their readers. They decide where a story will happen, who will be in it, and what will happen.

Parts of a Story

Every story happens in a place at some time. That place and time are called the **setting**.

Saturday morning in our apartment

The people or animals in a story are called the **characters**. In most stories, the characters speak. Their words are called the **dialogue**.

Come by this afternoon to see if you have won.

woman from the bike store

Anything is possible, but don't count on winning the bike, Alex.

Alex and his mom

The things that happen in a story are the events. The order, or **sequence of events**, is called the **plot**.

1. Mom filled out a form for the bike drawing.

2. We went to the bike store.

3. I saw a huge sign that said that I won!

Realistic Fiction

Some stories have characters that seem like people you know. They happen in a place that seems real. These stories are called **realistic fiction** because they tell about something that could happen in real life.

Another Saturday Morning

The **characters** are like people you know.

Mom and I were eating breakfast Saturday morning when a woman knocked on the door to our apartment.

The **setting** is in a place and a time you know.

"Hello," she said. "I'm from Bikes and Stuff and we're having a drawing for a mountain bike. Would you be interested in signing up?" Mom agreed and filled out a form for me.

The events in the **plot** could really happen.

"Come by this afternoon to see if you have won," the woman said.

"Anything is possible, but don't count on winning the bike, Alex," Mom said when the woman left.

The **dialogue** sounds real.

So I forgot all about the bike and started playing video games. Before I knew it, mom came in the room and said it was time to go to the bike store.

When I walked in, the first thing I saw was a huge sign that said: *Mountain bike winner: Alex Sanchez!* I couldn't believe it!

They put my name and photograph in the newspaper in an ad for Bikes and Stuff. That was the day I learned anything is possible on a Saturday morning.

Historical Fiction

Historical fiction is a story that takes place in the past during a certain time in history. Some of the characters may be real people and some of the events really happened. Even so, the story is fiction because the writer made it up.

January 13, 1778

The characters dress, act, and talk like the people in that time did.

Today when we returned the laundry to the army headquarters, I was astounded to see only General Washington in the parlour, no other officers. I know not where Billy Lee was. The General was sharpening his quill with his penknife. He looked up at us and smiled.

"Thank you, Abigail. Thank you, Elisabeth," he said.

I curtsied, unable to speak. How did he know our names?

He looked at us with kind eyes—they're gray-blue—then he returned to his pen and paper. Mrs. Hewes says Mr. Washington writes at least fifteen letters a day, mostly to Congress. He is pleading for food, clothing, and other supplies for the soldiers, she told us.

It can have **real people** and **made-up characters** who lived during that time.

Fantasy

A **fantasy** is a story that tells about events that couldn't possibly happen in real life. Here is part of a fantasy about some children playing a very unusual board game.

from *Jumanji* by Chris Van Allsburg

The **characters** can be like real people.

At home, the children spread the game out on a card table. It looked very much like the games they already had.

"Here," said Judy, handing her brother the dice, "you go first."

Peter casually dropped the dice from his hand.

"Seven," said Judy.

Peter moved his piece to the seventh square.

"'Lion attacks, move back two spaces,'" read Judy.

"Gosh, how exciting," said Peter, in a very unexcited voice. As he reached for his piece he looked up at his sister. She had a look of absolute horror on her face.

"Peter," she whispered, "turn around very, very slowly."

Some of the **events** could never happen in real life.

The boy turned in his chair. He couldn't believe his eyes. Lying on the piano was a lion, staring at Peter and licking his lips. The lion roared so loud it knocked Peter right off his chair. The big cat jumped to the floor. Peter was up on his feet, running through the house with the lion a whisker's length behind. He ran upstairs and dove under a bed. The lion tried to squeeze under, but got his head stuck. Peter scrambled out, ran from the bedroom, and slammed the door behind him. He stood in the hall with Judy, gasping for breath.

"I don't think," said Peter in between gasps of air, "that I want...to play...this game... anymore."

"But we have to," said Judy as she helped Peter back downstairs. "I'm sure that's what the instructions mean. That lion won't go away until one of us wins the game."

Summary

In a **summary**, you write the most important ideas in something you have read or seen. Read this magazine article. Then follow the steps to see how to write a summary for it.

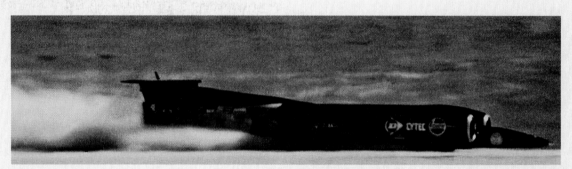

The first supersonic car, Thrust SSC, set a record at 763 miles per hour in Nevada's Black Rock Desert last week.

The World's Fastest Car
Thrust SSC zips through the sound barrier

WHOOSH! KABOOM! For Andy Green, a Royal Air Force pilot, that was the sound of success. Last Wednesday, Green rocketed into the history books by becoming the first person to drive a car faster than the speed of sound. His average speed: **763 miles per hour**!

Green was not driving an ordinary car. He was driving the Thrust SSC (for **S**uper **S**onic **C**ar), which has twin jet engines like those used on Phantom fighter planes. The car packs as much power as 1,000 Ford Escorts. It needs parachutes to help it stop.

Green had been building up speed for more than a month out in Nevada's Black Rock Desert. He had competition from American driver Craig Breedlove. But Breedlove's car couldn't keep up. On September 25, Green blasted away the old land-speed record of 633 miles per hour. His new record: 714 miles per hour.

Richard Noble, Green's fellow Englishman who set the old record in 1983, didn't mind seeing it bite the dust. Noble owns the Thrust SSC, so he was rooting for Green.

The ultimate dream for Noble and Green was to see their car travel faster than sound. The speed of sound varies, depending on weather conditions and altitude. In the Black Rock Desert, it is around 750 m.p.h.

Noble and Green finally saw their dream come true on October 15. When a plane or car reaches the speed of sound, people for miles around hear an explosive noise called a sonic boom. Each time the car broke through the sound barrier, a sonic boom thundered across the Black Rock Desert, announcing Green's amazing feat.

"We have achieved what we set out to do," he said. "We are finished." ∎

REUTERS

1 **Make a list of the most important ideas in the article.**

Look for the important ideas in the title or at the beginning of the paragraphs. In some articles, you can find important details in **bold** letters or *italics*.

2 **Read through your list and cross out details that are not important.**

A detail is important if it answers one of these questions: Who? What? When? Where? Why? How?

3 **Use your own words to turn your notes into sentences.**

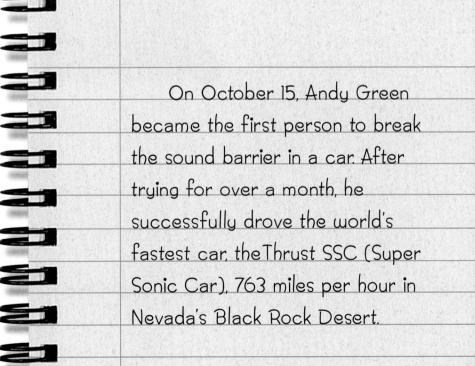

world's fastest car
~~Whoosh! Kaboom!~~
Andy Green
first person to drive a car faster than the speed of sound
763 miles per hour
Thrust SSC (Super Sonic Car)
~~1000 Ford Escorts~~
Nevada's Black Rock Desert
October 15— had been trying for more than a month
~~speed of sound in desert: about 750 m.p.h.~~

On October 15, Andy Green became the first person to break the sound barrier in a car. After trying for over a month, he successfully drove the world's fastest car, the Thrust SSC (Super Sonic Car), 763 miles per hour in Nevada's Black Rock Desert.

Tall Tale

A **tall tale** is a story told just for fun. It has lots of exaggerated details. When details are exaggerated, they make the story impossible to believe.

from *Paul Bunyan* by Steven Kellogg

The **main character** has special powers or great strength and solves a problem in an unusual or exaggerated way.

Paul's next job was to clear the heavily forested midwest. He hired armies of extra woodsmen and built enormous new bunkhouses. The men sailed up to bed in balloons and parachuted down to breakfast in the morning.

Unfortunately the cooks couldn't flip flapjacks fast enough to satisfy all the newcomers.

To solve the muddle, Paul built a colossal flapjack griddle.

The surface was greased by kitchen helpers with slabs of bacon laced to their feet.

Everytime the hot griddle was flooded with batter, it blasted a delicious flapjack high about the clouds. Usually the flapjacks landed neatly beside the griddle, but sometimes they were a bit off target.

Paul took a few days off to dig the St. Lawrence River and the Great Lakes so that barges of Vermont maple syrup could be brought to camp.

Fueled by the powerful mixture of flapjacks and syrup, the men leveled the Great Plains and shaved the slopes of the Rocky Mountains.

Telephone Message

See **Notes**.

Thank-you Note

See **Notes**.

Tongue Twister

A tongue twister is a phrase that is so difficult to say your tongue gets all twisted! Tongue twisters usually don't make much sense—they're just for fun.

Don't light a night-light on a light night like tonight.

Surely Shawn should show Sherry Shawna's shoes.

Chuck chews cherries by the cheekful.

What noise annoys an oyster most? A noisy noise annoys an oyster most.

The Good Writer Guide

A skater can't skate without skates, and a writer can't write without ideas. To be a good writer, first you need to collect ideas. Then, put them to use! Just like skaters, writers get better and better with practice.

How to Collect Ideas

First, set up a file to store your ideas. Choose the kind of file that works best for you.

- You might want to keep a notebook or a journal close by so you can write down ideas as you think of them.

- Maybe you want to save ticket stubs, special photos, cards from your friends, or other things that remind you of people and events. You'll need a box or folder that is big enough for all these things plus your lists and notes, too.

- A great place to keep a list of ideas is in a file on the computer. Your file can get as big as your ideas!

Then gather the ideas that interest you. Here are some tips.

1 Look and listen.

Keep your eyes and ears open. You'll be surprised at how many ideas you'll get!

- What are your friends talking about?

- Did you see something funny or amazing on TV?

- Did you find something interesting on the Internet? Do you want to know more about the topic?

- Is the weather really hot or really cold?

- Is it quiet outside or is it noisy? What do you see? What do you hear?

2 Read a lot!

When you read something you like, draw pictures or
list details to tell about:

■ your favorite characters

■ interesting or unusual facts

■ words and phrases that sound good

■ topics that interest you

> roller hockey—
> "Dribble, pass, shoot, and score."

3 Make charts and lists.

List these headings in your file. Add examples to
them throughout the year.

■ Things I Wonder About

■ What I'll Never Forget

■ Things I Like to Do

■ Funny Things That Have
Happened to Me

■ Places I'd Like to Go

■ My Favorites

■ When I Felt Proud

■ The Most Beautiful
Things I've Seen

> Things I Wonder About
>
> How our team will do in
> the roller hockey league
>
> If I'll get to play goalie
> this year
>
> How many teams will be
> in the league

4 Draw pictures.

Draw pictures to show what you are thinking. Sometimes
the lines and shapes you draw can remind you of people,
places, or things to write about. Try drawing a time line to
show the events in your life. Look at your time line when
you need a writing idea.

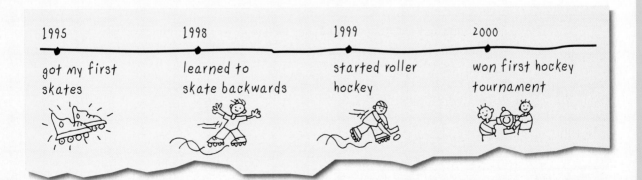

1995	1998	1999	2000
got my first skates	learned to skate backwards	started roller hockey	won first hockey tournament

How to Write for a Specific Purpose

Why are you writing? That's your **purpose**. Good writers change how and what they write to fit their purpose.

Purpose	Writing Examples	
To inform or to explain	You might give directions to explain how to do something. *If you want to stop on your in-line skates, have your brake foot in front. Then, bend your knees. Finally, put your brake down. If this doesn't work, hop onto some nearby grass!*	Or, you could write a paragraph that gives your readers important facts about a topic. Safety equipment protects you when you skate. A hard helmet protects the head in case of a fall. Plastic knee and elbow pads keep knees and elbows from getting scraped.
To describe	You could write a description that has lots of descriptive details to help your reader "see" what you are describing. *My new in-line skates are fantastic! They are a shiny blue with bright red trim.*	For a poem, use many colorful verbs to describe how something moves. *Clicking and Clacking* *Clicking and clacking over the concrete cracks, skates swish and slip by.*
To entertain	You could use a cartoon with a funny picture and words to make your readers laugh. "They call this IN-LINE skating?"	

Purpose	Writing Examples
To persuade	In an advertisement, you can use persuasive words and phrases to convince someone to buy something. **SKATE SALE!** **Check out the HOTTEST new colors of in-line skates.** *They're guaranteed to help you skate better!* In an editorial, give your opinion and use persuasive words to change the way things are. Kids need a place to skate. We think that there should be special times for skaters to use the parking lot behind the school. Sign this paper to vote for an afternoon skating time.
To express	Write a journal entry to tell about your own personal thoughts and feelings. Day ___ June 30, 2001 I'm so excited about our club's in-line skating exhibit during the school fair tomorrow. Dennis, Ahn, and I are going to skate for the exhibition. I just hope that I don't fall because that would be so embarrassing!
To learn	It helps to write things down when you are learning about a topic. That way you can see what you already know—and what you don't know. In-line skating is good exercise. Now I want to know why and if it's good for everyone.

How to Write for a Specific Audience

Who will read what you write? Your **audience**. Knowing who your audience is will help you decide what words to use and what kinds of details to include.

Audience	Writing Examples
Adults and people you don't know	Use formal language and details to help them understand what they might not know. My skating lesson was great. I learned how to cross my right foot over my left foot while making a turn. That's called a crossover.
Your friends	Use informal language because they'll probably understand exactly what you mean. My blading lesson was awesome! Now I can do crossovers like a pro.
Someone younger than you	Use simple language so they'll understand. My skating lesson was fun. Now I can make turns on my skates without stopping.

How to Make Your Writing Better

Good writers work on their writing until it's the best it can be. Here are four important ways to make your writing spectacular!

1 Choose the right words.

Help your reader see what you are writing about by using just the right words.

Marcy got her things.

Use **specific nouns** to tell exactly what you mean.

Marcy got her skates and helmet.

Use **colorful verbs** to give the best picture of the action.

Marcy grabbed her skates and helmet.

Add **describing words** to tell what things are like.

Marcy grabbed her new skates and the blue helmet with the silver spots.

Sometimes you can find the right words to use in a **thesaurus**. A thesaurus is a book of words and their synonyms. Use alphabetical order to look up the entry word. Next to the entry word, you'll find a list of synonyms for it.

get *verb* **1.** ✦ acquire, catch, grab, grasp, pick up, obtain, take

2 Improve your sentences.

Combine Short Sentences

Whenever you have a lot of short sentences, try combining some of them.

Just OK

Marcy loves to skate.
Her friends love to skate.
Marcy skates at the park.

Much Better

Marcy and her friends
love to skate at the park.

Break up Run-on Sentences

Sometimes a long sentence uses *and* too many times.
Break a sentence like this into two sentences.

Not OK

Felicia loves to play roller hockey, and she practices every Tuesday after school, and she has a game every Saturday.

OK

Felicia loves to play roller hockey. She practices every Tuesday after school, and she has a game every Saturday.

Start Sentences in Different Ways

If all your sentences start in the same way, your readers might get bored. Try changing the way some of your sentences begin.

Just OK

Matt went skating for the first time yesterday. Matt fell forward on his knees as he was trying to stand up on his skates. Matt tried to stand up again and fell backward. Matt tried a third time. Matt finally rolled forward!

Much Better

Yesterday, Matt went skating for the first time. As he tried to stand on his skates, Matt fell forward on his knees. When he tried to stand up again, Matt fell backward. He tried a third time. Finally, Matt rolled forward!

Start Off with a Great Sentence

A good beginning sentence will get your readers' attention. They'll want to read everything you have to say and to read it right away!

Just OK

> This article is about Josie Rodríguez.

Much Better

> "On your left," yelled Josie Rodríguez as she zipped by another skater on the bike path.

3 Add details.

Details make writing interesting to read.

Just OK

> This article is about Josie Rodríguez. She has been skating for a long time. She really likes it. I talked to her for a long time.

Much Better

> "On your left," yelled Josie Rodríguez as she zipped by another skater on the bike path. Josie arrived in front of her apartment just in time for our interview last week.
>
> It was a thrill to meet Josie Rodríguez. She is a professional in-line skater who always has her skates on.
>
> "I feel strange without them," she said. "I've been skating since I was two. I had to do something to keep up with my four older brothers."
>
> For four hours Ms. Rodríguez shared her in-line skating experiences, including that she owns fifteen pairs of skates! This is a person who really loves what she does!

Add **specific details** that tell how, when, or where.

Include **dialogue**.

Add **examples**.

Include **your own thoughts**.

4 Show, don't tell.

You can just *tell* your readers about an event or a person. To give your readers the best picture, though, *show* them exactly what you mean!

- Use details to show what something looks, sounds, tastes, smells, or feels like.

- Use dialogue to show what a person is like.

This tells:

> Kristen likes in-line skating because it's great exercise. She skates for a long time after school.

This shows:

Kristen's words show that she thinks skating is good exercise.

> "If I didn't do in-line skating, I would probably be a couch potato," says Kristen, a very athletic fifth grader. As soon as Kristen gets home, she puts her books down, grabs her skates, and doesn't come back in the door until dinner.

Kristen's actions show how much she likes to skate.

How to Evaluate Your Writing

Save everything you write! A collection of your writing is called a **portfolio**. It can be in a large folder or in a notebook. The writing in your portfolio will help you learn how you are doing as a writer.

Organize Your Portfolio

Organize your portfolio so you can find the writing you are looking for. You might want to:

- put all the writing you've done in order by date.

- make special sections in your portfolio to keep pieces you've written for the same purpose or the same audience.

- put all your stories together, all your reports together, and all your poems together. In other words, organize your portfolio by the kinds of writing you've done.

Look Over Your Writing

Look at your writing every now and then to see how you are doing.

- What is your favorite piece of writing?

- How is the first writing you did different from the last?

- What do you need to work on?

- What other kinds of writing do you want to try?

Think About How You Write

As you look over your writing, think about the words you like to use, the kinds of sentences you write, and what you like to write about. All of those things together are your writing **style**. That is what makes you a super writer with a style all your own!

Grammar Made Graphic

it flies really ?

subject predicate

Pedro loves to fly kites. To tell about his kite, he is putting words together to make a sentence. Pedro makes sure to use the correct pronoun, verb, and adverbs so everyone can understand exactly what the kite does.

This chapter will help you make your writing clear, too. Here you'll find all the rules you need to know to write in English.

Sentences

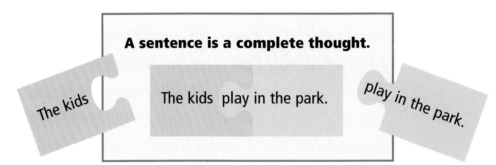

A sentence is a complete thought.

The kids ⊂ The kids play in the park. ⊃ play in the park.

Kinds of Sentences

■ **There are four kinds of sentences.**

A **statement** tells something.

> Danny sees a statue.
> It is big.
> Workers put it up yesterday.

A **question** asks something.

> What does Danny see?
> Is it big?
> Who put it up?

An **exclamation** shows strong feeling.

> Wow!
> It is really big!
> The workers were strong!

A **command** tells someone to do something.

> Don't run into the statue!
> Read me the sign, please.

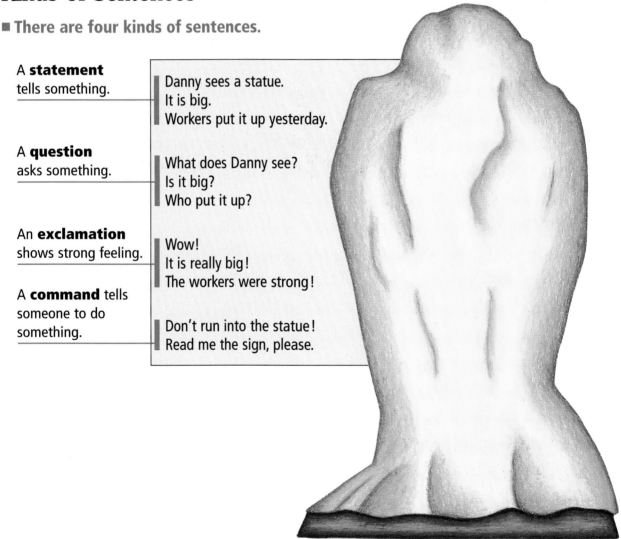

■ **Ask a question to get information.**

Some questions ask for a "yes" or "no" answer.

Question	Answer
1. **Is** the statue ready?	No, it isn't.
2. **Are** the workers finished?	No, they aren't.
3. **Have** you seen the statue?	Yes.
4. **Has** anyone else seen it?	No.
5. **Do** you like the statue?	Yes, I do.
6. **Does** it have a name?	Yes, it does.
7. **Would** you take the cover off?	No.
8. **Could** we peek under the cover?	No.
9. **Should** we come back tomorrow?	Yes.
10. **Will** you show us the statue then?	Sure.

You can also add a question to the end of a statement.

Examples: You are busy.
You are busy, aren't you?   Yes, I am.

You're not busy.
You're not busy, are you?   No, I'm not.

Kinds of Sentences, continued

When you want more information than just "yes" or "no," start your question with one of these words.

Question	Answer
1. **When** did you uncover the statue?	This morning.
2. **How much** does the statue weigh?	I don't know. It's very heavy.
3. **Who** is it?	That's Paul Bunyan.
4. **What** did he do?	He was a lumberjack.
5. **Where** did he live?	He lived in Minnesota.
6. **How** big was he?	He was big enough to pick up railroad tracks.
7. **Why** is he famous?	Some stories say he made all the lakes in Minnesota.
8. **How many** lakes did he make?	More than 10,000!
9. **Which** story about Paul Bunyan is your favorite?	I like the stories about Paul and Babe, his blue ox.
10. **How** can we find out more about Paul Bunyan?	Use the computer at the library.

Go To Practices A and B on page 305.

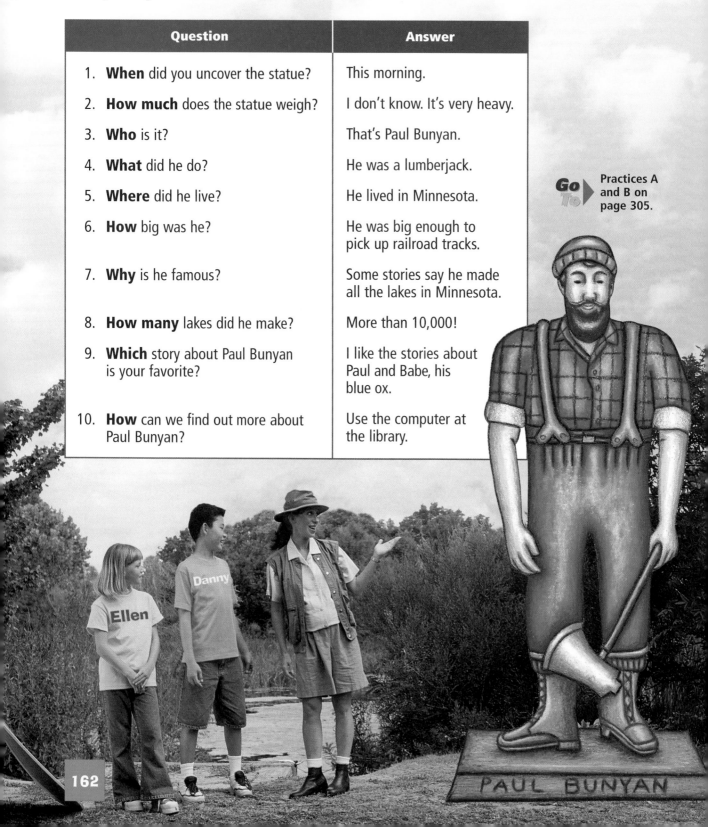

PAUL BUNYAN

■ **Some sentences mean "no."**

Use negative words like these to make a sentence say "no."

Examples:

no	nothing	nobody	never
not	none	no one	nowhere

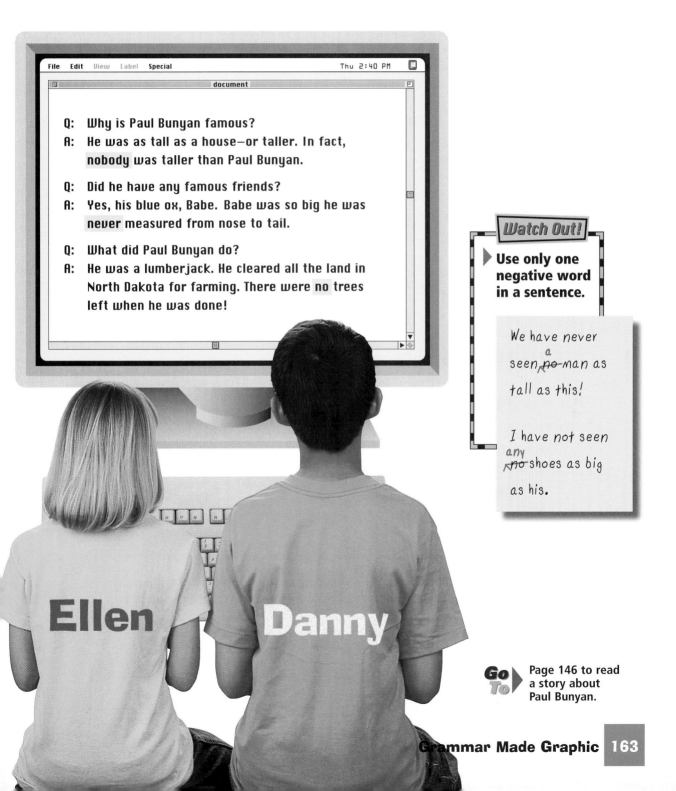

Q: Why is Paul Bunyan famous?
A: He was as tall as a house—or taller. In fact, nobody was taller than Paul Bunyan.

Q: Did he have any famous friends?
A: Yes, his blue ox, Babe. Babe was so big he was never measured from nose to tail.

Q: What did Paul Bunyan do?
A: He was a lumberjack. He cleared all the land in North Dakota for farming. There were no trees left when he was done!

Watch Out!

▶ **Use only one negative word in a sentence.**

We have never
seen ~~no~~ man as
tall as this!
(a inserted above)

I have not seen
~~no~~ shoes as big
as his.
(any inserted above)

Go To Page 146 to read a story about Paul Bunyan.

Subject and Predicate

Every sentence has two main parts.

The friends read some books.

subject   predicate

■ **The subject tells whom or what the sentence is about.**

The subject usually comes at the beginning of the sentence. It can have more than one word.

Paul Bunyan and Babe

10 TALL TALES

The complete subject includes all the words that tell about the subject.

Danny finds a book with tall tales.

It has stories about Paul Bunyan.

One funny **story** is about Babe, his ox.

This big, blue **ox** drank a lake every morning!

Danny and Ellen enjoy the tale.

They laugh and laugh.

The **simple subject** is the most important word in the subject.

A **compound subject** has two or more simple subjects. They are joined by **and** or **or**.

Watch Out!

▶ **Sometimes a subject comes at the end of a sentence.**

Here is my **book**.
There are many **books** to read.

▶ **Sometimes the subject is not named, but you can guess who the subject is!**

Don't talk in the library!
Please return your books here.

■ **The predicate tells what the subject is, does, or has.**

The predicate usually comes at the end of a sentence.

The complete predicate includes all the words in the predicate part of the sentence.

Danny **finds** a book with tall tales.

It **has** stories about Paul Bunyan.

One funny story **is** about Babe, his ox.

This big, blue ox **drank** a lake every morning!

Danny and Ellen **enjoy** the tale.

They **laugh and laugh**.

The **simple predicate** is the most important word in the predicate. It is the **verb**.

A **compound predicate** has two or more verbs that tell about the same subject.

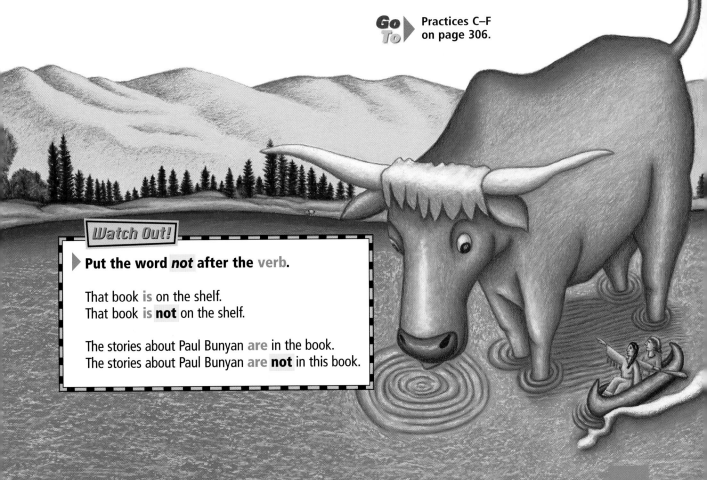

Go To ▶ **Practices C–F on page 306.**

Watch Out!

▶ **Put the word *not* after the verb.**

That book **is** on the shelf.
That book **is** **not** on the shelf.

The stories about Paul Bunyan **are** in the book.
The stories about Paul Bunyan **are** **not** in this book.

Compound Sentences

> **You can put two sentences together to make a compound sentence. Just use a comma in front of:**
>
> **and   but   or**

When you put two ideas that are alike together, use **and**.

Example:
Paul cut down many trees.
Babe carried the logs to the river.

Paul cut down many trees, **and** Babe carried the logs to the river.

When you want to show a difference between two ideas, use **but**.

Example:
The farmers could not clear their land.
Paul did it overnight.

The farmers could not clear their land, **but** Paul did it overnight.

When you want to show a choice between two ideas, use **or**.

Example:
You can find books about Paul Bunyan in the library.
You can download stories from the Internet.

You can find books about Paul Bunyan in the library, **or** you can download stories from the Internet.

Watch Out!

▶ If a sentence uses *and* too many times, make two sentences.

We saw the new statue of Paul Bunyan, and we asked a lot of questions and then we went to the library to find some books.

Go To ▶ Practice G on page 307.

Nouns

> **A noun is the name of a person, place, or thing.**
>
> **Example:** Say hello to **Luisa**.
> She lives in **Galveston**.
> She rides a purple **bicycle**.

Common and Proper Nouns

■ **A common noun names any person, place, or thing.**

■ **A proper noun names one particular person, place, or thing.**

All the important words in a proper noun start with a capital letter.

▶ COMMON NOUNS	▶ PROPER NOUNS	
Any Person The **girl** rides her bike. A **runner** jogs by her.	**One Particular Person** **Luisa** rides her bike. **Max Medina** jogs by her.	
Any Place Our **state** has many cities. This **city** is pretty. We ride by the **bay**.	**One Particular Place** **Texas** has many cities. **Galveston** is pretty. We ride by **Galveston Bay**.	 
Any Thing The **building** is historic. That **street** is famous. Luisa sees the **boat**.	**One Particular Thing** **Ashton Villa** is historic. **Hope Boulevard** is famous. Luisa sees **Tall Ship** *Elissa*.	 

Go To Practice A on page 307.

Singular and Plural Nouns

A **singular noun** shows "one."
A **plural noun** shows "more than one."

Examples: He is flying one **kite**.   She is flying two **kites**.

*My **kites** look like **boxes**.*

*My kite has **dots** on it.*

■ **Most nouns can be counted.**
They have a singular and a plural form.

▶ **PLURAL NOUNS**					
To make most nouns plural, add **-s** to the singular noun.	dot dot**s**	kite kite**s**	flower flower**s**		
If the noun ends in **x**, **ch**, **sh**, **s**, or **z**, add **-es**.	box box**es**	lunch lunch**es**	dish dish**es**	glass glass**es**	waltz waltz**es**
For most nouns that end in **y**, change the **y** to **i** and add **-es**.	story stor**ies**	sky sk**ies**			
For nouns that end in a **vowel** plus **y**, just add **-s**.	boy boy**s**	toy toy**s**	day day**s**	monkey monkey**s**	
For most nouns that end in **f** or **fe**, change the **f** to **v** and add **-es**. For some nouns that end in **f**, just add **-s**.	leaf lea**ves**	knife kni**ves**	roof roof**s**	cliff cliff**s**	

A few nouns change in different ways to show "more than one."

One	man	woman	foot	tooth	mouse	goose	child	person
More than One	men	women	feet	teeth	mice	geese	children	people

Go To ▶ Practice B on page 308.

■ **Some nouns cannot be counted. They have only one form for "one" and "more than one."**

NOUNS THAT CANNOT BE COUNTED

Weather Words Many nouns that refer to weather cannot be counted. **Example: Thunder** and **lightning** scare my dog.	hail snow ice temperature lightning thunder rain wind
Food Many food items cannot be counted unless you use a measurement word like **cup**, **slice**, or **head**. Make the measurement word plural to show "more than one." **Examples:** I love **lettuce**! Mom bought **two heads of lettuce**.	bread meat cereal milk cheese rice corn soup flour sugar lettuce tea
Ideas and Feelings **Examples:** I need some **help**. What **information** do you need?	democracy homework fun information health luck help trouble happiness work
Category Nouns These nouns name a group, or category. Some of the items within the category can be counted. **Example:** I have some **money** in my pocket. There are **four dollars** and **two dimes**.	equipment machinery energy mail fruit money furniture time
Materials **Example:** Is the table made of **wood** or **metal**?	metal water paper wood
Activities and Sports **Examples:** My mom and dad love to play **golf**. **Camping** is my favorite thing to do.	baseball golf camping singing dancing soccer football swimming

Watch Out!

▶ Some nouns have more than one meaning. Add **-s** for the plural only if the noun means something you can count.

football
1. **a ball** *We need two **footballs** for the game.*
2. **a sport** *I like to watch **football**.*

Go To ▶ Practice C on page 308.

Words that Signal Nouns

> **Some words help identify a noun:**
>
> a an some the this that these those
>
> **Examples:** I'd like to buy **a** shirt.
> How about **this** nice shirt?
> Do you like **the** collar?

■ **Use *a*, *an*, or *some* to talk about something in general.**

One	More than One
a hat **an umbrella**	**some hats** **some umbrellas**

Examples: I'll buy **a hat** for me and **an umbrella** for you.

Some hats are too fancy.

Some umbrellas are too expensive.

Watch Out!

▶ Use **an** before a noun that begins with a vowel like:

    a in **a**nt, **a**pron, **a**mount
    e in **e**lbow, **e**el, **e**lection
    i in **i**nch, **i**dea
    o in **o**tter, **o**cean, **o**wl
    u in **u**mbrella

Don't forget to use **an** before a word with silent **h**: **an hour**

■ **Use *the* to talk about something specific.**

One	More than One
the pink hat **the large umbrella**	**the blue hats** **the small umbrellas**

Examples: I'll buy **the pink hat** for me and **the large umbrella** for you.

The blue hat is too fancy.

The small umbrellas are too expensive.

Here are some tips to help you use **a** and **the** correctly.

Never use **the** before the name of a:

- city or state
- language
- day, month, or holiday

Galveston is a city in **Texas**.

Many people there speak **English** and **Spanish**.

We visited the city in **September** on **Labor Day**.

If you talk about the same thing a second time, use **the**.

I found a great beach by the seawall.
The beach was nice and big.

- sport or activity

Several of us played **volleyball**.

- business

Then we went to lunch at **Joe's Cafe**.

When you compare three or more things, use **the**.

Joe serves **the** best hamburgers in the city.

■ Use *this, that, these,* and *those* to talk about something specific.

	One	More than One
Close By	**this** T-shirt	**these** T-shirts
Far Away	**that** umbrella	**those** umbrellas

Do you like **these** pink T-shirts or **this** red one?

That purple umbrella is bigger than **those** green ones.

Go To Practices D and E on page 309.

Grammar Made Graphic 171

Possessive Nouns

A **possessive noun** is the name of an owner.
The name always has an apostrophe: ʼ

Example: **Luisa's** T-shirt is from the Galveston Springfest.
The **boys'** T-shirts are from the Flight Museum.

The placement of the apostrophe depends
on whether there is one owner or more
than one owner. Look at these examples.

One Owner	More Than One Owner
Martin's cap	the **boys'** caps
Mom's umbrella	my **parents'** umbrella
the **umbrella's** handle	the **umbrellas'** stripes
the **student's** T-shirt	the **students'** T-shirts

I just love **Galveston's** *shops! This cap will look perfect with my* **brother's** *T-shirt.*

But the **cap's** *bill is torn. Maybe you would like this one.*

 Practice F
on page 310.

Using Nouns in Writing

> **Use specific nouns to help your reader see what you are writing about.**
>
> **Example:** Two **birds** flew around the restaurant.
> Two **parrots** flew around the restaurant.

The writer replaced **restaurant** with **Parrot Cafe** to let readers know exactly which restaurant it is.

Time for Lunch

Parrot Cafe
The ~~restaurant~~ is a busy place. Many people love to eat there. They serve tasty tacos all through the day. The chef's best dish is black beans and rice.

He also serves great pizza. Have you ever tried a tuna pizza? How about a pizza with apples and walnuts? Now there's a taste not to miss!

Don't forget to save room chocolate fudge cake for ~~dessert~~. It's thick and rich. You shouldn't skip this two-napkin treat.

Are you hungry yet? Come right this way. Welcome to the Parrot Cafe, where your table is waiting.

Replacing **dessert** with **chocolate fudge cake** gives a much clearer picture of the treat. You can almost taste it!

Go To Practices G and H on page 310.

Pronouns

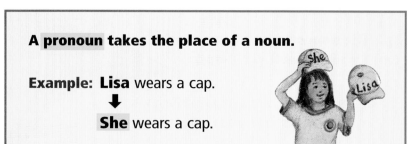

A **pronoun** takes the place of a noun.

Example: **Lisa** wears a cap.

She wears a cap.

Using Different Kinds of Pronouns

■ **When you use a pronoun, be sure you are talking about the right person.**

1. For yourself, use **I**.

Hi! **I** am Mr. Brown.

2. When you speak to another person, use **you**.

Are **you** the coach?

3. For a boy or a man, use **he**.

Yes! **He** is the coach.

Lisa

4. For a girl or a woman, use **she**.

That's Lisa. **She** is on the soccer team.

5. For a thing, use **it**.

Oh, the ball. Where is **it**?

■ **Be sure you are talking about the right number of people or things.**

One	More than One
I	we
you	you
he, she, it	they

1. When you speak to two or more people, use **you**.

2. For yourself and another person use **we**.

Are **you** ready?

Yes! **We** are going to beat the Bobcats.

3. For other people, use **they**.

No, **they** won't! We will win!

Lisa

Tom

Joey

■ **If you talk about a person twice in a sentence, use these pairs of pronouns.**

One		More than One	
I	myself	we	ourselves
you	yourself	you	yourselves
he	himself	they	themselves
she	herself		
it	itself		

Examples:

I hurt **myself**.
She found the ball **herself**.

Using Different Kinds of Pronouns, continued

■ Be sure you use the right pronoun in the right place.

Use these pronouns to tell who or what is doing something.
They take the place of the subject in the sentence.

One	More than One
I	we
you	you
he, she, it	they

Examples:

Juan and Lisa are kicking the ball back and forth.

⬇

They are kicking the ball back and forth.

Juan kicks the ball up in the air.

⬇

He kicks the ball up in the air.

Lisa   Juan

Use these pronouns after a verb or a preposition.

One	More than One
me	us
you	you
him, her, it	them

Examples:

The ball flies past **Jasmine and Tom**.

⬇

The ball flies past **them**.

The goalie reaches for **the ball**.

⬇

The goalie reaches for **it**.

Tom

Jasmine

Go To ▶ Practice A on page 311.

Some pronouns tell who owns something.

Example: This is **Jasmine's** cap.
↓
This is **her** cap.

This is **Jasmine's cap**.
↓
This is **hers**.

These pronouns take the place of a person's name.

One	More than One
my	our
your	your
his, her, its	their

1. Is this **Jasmine's** cap?

Lisa

2. No. I think **her** cap is red.

Joey

These pronouns take the place of a person's name and what the person owns.

One	More than One
mine	ours
yours	yours
his, hers	theirs

Hmm. Is this **my** cap?

Yes. **It's** **mine**.

Watch Out!

▶ **its** = pronoun
it's = it is

Nuff

The dog is wearing **its** cap, too. I like the cap. **It's** cute!

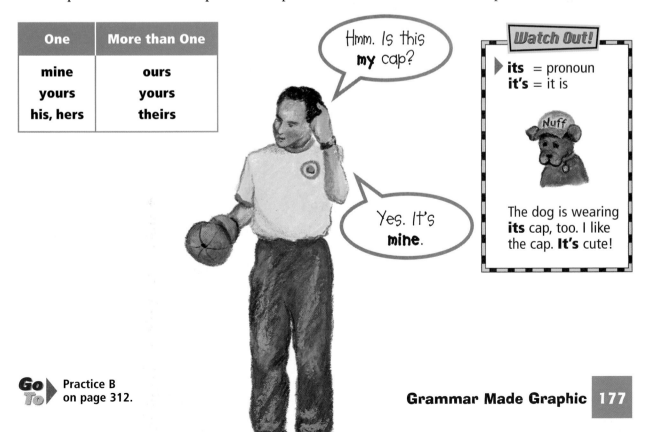

Go To ▶ Practice B on page 312.

When you don't name a specific person or thing, use one of these special **pronouns**.

anyone	someone	everyone
anybody	somebody	everybody
anything	something	everything

Example: Who left a cap on the table?
I don't know, but **someone** did.

178 **Grammar Made Graphic**

Go To Practice C on page 312.

Using Pronouns in Writing

> **In a paragraph, each pronoun must agree with its noun.**
>
> **Example:**
> **Mr. Brown** wears **his** cap at every game. The players say the **cap** is lucky. One day, **it** was missing. Mr. Brown looked everywhere, and finally the **players** found it in his back pocket. He thanked **them** again and again.

By replacing **the Bobcats** ↓ with **they**, the writer makes this paragraph sound better.

Kicking Around!
Soccer Team Wins Again!
by Andy Thomas

Let's hear it for our team! Yesterday the Bobcats won their match. ~~The Bobcats~~ *They* played hard against the Eagles and won by one goal. Lisa Anderson kicked the winning goal. Juan Chávez, her teammate, assisted on the goal.

The team's record is now five wins and one loss—their best record in four years. Juan Silva and Jasmine Cummins also scored one goal each, and Joey Lee, the goalie, had six saves. Congratulations to them, too!

After the game, everyone celebrated at the coach's house. He and his wife thanked all the people who helped organize the celebration.

The players will go to Valley School next Wednesday. We hope they can win again!

The pronoun **them** agrees with ↓ **Juan Silva, Jasmine Cummins,** and **Joey Lee**.

Go To ▶ Practices D and E on page 313.

Adjectives

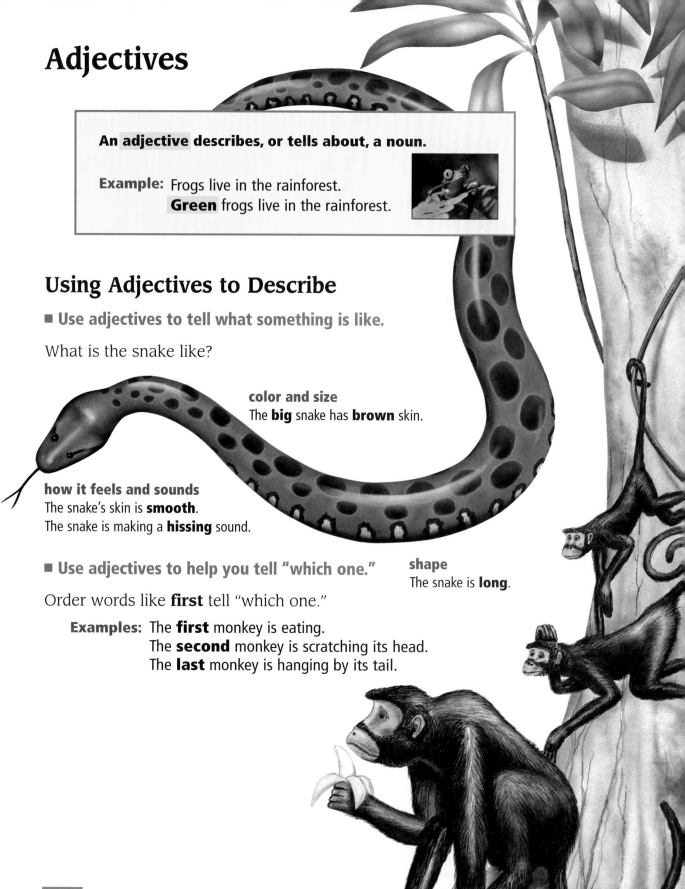

An **adjective** describes, or tells about, a noun.

Example: Frogs live in the rainforest.
Green frogs live in the rainforest.

Using Adjectives to Describe

■ **Use adjectives to tell what something is like.**

What is the snake like?

color and size
The **big** snake has **brown** skin.

how it feels and sounds
The snake's skin is **smooth**.
The snake is making a **hissing** sound.

shape
The snake is **long**.

■ **Use adjectives to help you tell "which one."**

Order words like **first** tell "which one."

Examples: The **first** monkey is eating.
The **second** monkey is scratching its head.
The **last** monkey is hanging by its tail.

■ **Use adjectives to help you tell "how many" or "how much."**

Sometimes you know exactly how many things you see.
Use number words to describe them.

> **Examples:** A sloth has **four** feet.
> It has **three** toes on each foot.
> A **dozen** sloths and **144** toes are in the tree.

If you don't know the exact number, use the words in this chart.

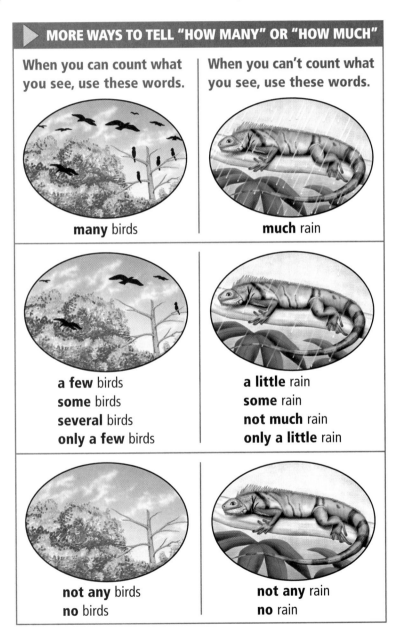

▶ **MORE WAYS TO TELL "HOW MANY" OR "HOW MUCH"**

When you can count what you see, use these words.	When you can't count what you see, use these words.
many birds	**much** rain
a few birds **some** birds **several** birds **only a few** birds	**a little** rain **some** rain **not much** rain **only a little** rain
not any birds **no** birds	**not any** rain **no** rain

Go To ▶ Practices A and B on
pages 313–314.

Using Adjectives to Compare

small

smaller

smallest

Adjectives can help you make a comparison, to show how things are alike or different.

Example: This is a **small** bird.
This bird is **smaller** than that one.
This is the **smallest** bird of all.

■ **When you compare two things, add *-er* to the adjective.**

You'll probably use the word **than** in your sentence, too.

> **Example:** The parrot's beak is **long**.
> The motmot's beak is **longer than** the parrot's beak.

parrot

■ **When you compare three or more things, add *-est* to the adjective.**

Remember to use **the** before the adjective.

> **Example:** The toucan's beak is **the longest** of them all.

You may have to change the spelling of the adjective before you add **-er** or **-est**.

toucan   **motmot**

► SPELLING RULES		
For adjectives that end in a silent **e**, drop the **e** and add **-er** or **-est**.	larg~~e~~ larg**er** larg**est**	nic~~e~~ nic**er** nic**est**
For adjectives that end in **y**, change the **y** to **i** and add **-er** or **-est**.	pretty prett**ier** prett**iest**	sleepy sleep**ier** sleep**iest**
Does the adjective end in one vowel and one consonant? If so, double the final consonant and add **-er** or **-est**.	big big**ger** big**gest**	sad sad**der** sad**dest**

Go To ► Practice C on page 314.

■ **If the adjective is a long word, do not add -er or -est to make a comparison.**

Adjectives with three or more syllables would be too hard to say if you added **-er** or **-est**. To make a comparison with these adjectives, use **more**, **most**, **less**, or **least** instead.

hummingbird   **motmot**   **macaw**

Examples:
The hummingbird is **colorful**.
The motmot is **more colorful** than the hummingbird.
The macaw is **the most colorful** bird of all.

Examples:
The first monkey was **frightened**.
The second monkey was **less frightened**.
The third monkey was the **least frightened** of all.

When you make a comparison, use either **-er** or **more**, but not both.

The hummingbird is ~~more~~ smaller than the monkey.

The macaw is ~~more~~ prettier than the motmot.

Go To ▶ Practice D
on page 315.

Grammar Made Graphic **183**

Watch Out!

▶ Some adjectives have special forms for comparing things.

good	bad
better	worse
best	worst

some	little
more	less
most	least

My photo of the toucan is the **best** picture of all those I took on my trip.

Adding Adjectives to Sentences

> **Adjectives can appear anywhere in a sentence.**
>
> **Examples:** Look at that **big** jaguar.
> Its eyes are **big**, too.
> The **big** jaguar just looks back at me.

Usually, an adjective comes before the noun it tells about.

> **Examples:** An **old** jaguar hides in the **green** leaves.
>
> Its **spotted** coat makes the **big** jaguar hard to see.

Two or more adjectives can also come before a noun.
A comma usually comes between them.

> **Examples:** The **wise, old** jaguar knows where to hide.

An adjective can come after words like **is**, **are**, **look**, **feel**, **smell**, and **taste**. The adjective describes the noun in the subject.

> **Examples:** A rainforest is **beautiful**.
>
> The air smells **clean**.
>
> Each day in the rainforest feels **fresh**.

Using Adjectives in Writing

katydid

> **Use adjectives to help your reader "see" what you are writing about.**
>
> **Example:** The katydid chewed on the leaf.
> The **shiny** katydid chewed on the **green** leaf.

Animal Disguises

These two **adjectives** help you picture the insect.

Some animals in the rainforest are hard to find. That's because their special colors help them hide. For example, a stick insect can look like a ∧*skinny, brown* twig.

Some katydids have bodies that look like green and brown leaves. One kind of katydid has wings with spots that look like big eyes. These ∧*two* spots help them fool the animals that try to eat them.

Now you know how many spots are on the katydid's wings.

The black spots on jaguars make it easy for them to hide in the leaves. Then they can watch for animals on the ground without being seen.

This **adjective** helps you know which disguises.

These disguises protect animals from other animals, but sometimes they can help an animal sneak up on its own food. This is how rainforest creatures survive.

stick insect

katydid

Go To Practices E and F on page 315.

Verbs

Some verbs show action:

Example: The clouds **float** across the sky.

Some verbs link words in a sentence.

Example: The sky **is** blue.

Action and Linking Verbs

■ **An action verb tells what the subject does.**

Most verbs are action verbs.

Some **action verbs** show action that you cannot see.

> The wind **blows** the clouds.
> The clouds **cover** the sun.
> Then the clouds **move** again.
>
> We **learn** about clouds in school.
> The class **enjoys** the lesson.

■ **A linking verb connects, or links, the subject of a sentence to a word in the predicate.**

The word in the predicate can describe the subject.

Examples: Some clouds **look** fluffy on the top.

They **are** flat on the bottom.

Or, the word in the predicate can name the subject in another way.

Example: Those white streaks **are** clouds, too.

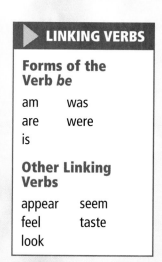

▶ **LINKING VERBS**

Forms of the Verb be

am	was
are	were
is	

Other Linking Verbs

appear	seem
feel	taste
look	

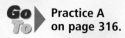

Practice A on page 316.

Helping Verbs

■ **Some verbs are made up of more than one word.**

In these verbs, the last word is called the **main verb**.
The verbs that come before are called **helping verbs**.

The **helping verb** agrees with the subject. The **main verb** shows the action.

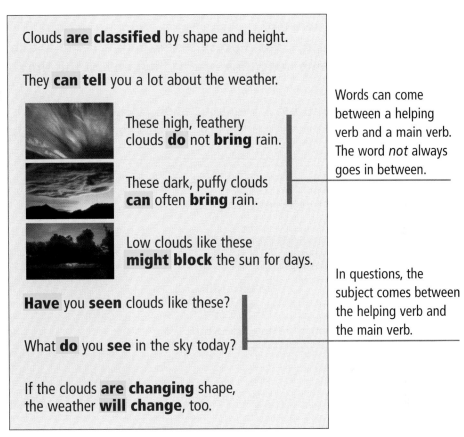

Clouds **are classified** by shape and height.

They **can tell** you a lot about the weather.

These high, feathery clouds **do** not **bring** rain.

These dark, puffy clouds **can** often **bring** rain.

Low clouds like these **might block** the sun for days.

Have you **seen** clouds like these?

What **do** you **see** in the sky today?

If the clouds **are changing** shape, the weather **will change**, too.

Words can come between a helping verb and a main verb. The word *not* always goes in between.

In questions, the subject comes between the helping verb and the main verb.

Here are some useful helping verbs.

▶ HELPING VERBS			
Forms of the Verb *be*	**Forms of the Verb *do***	**Forms of the Verb *have***	**Other Helping Verbs**
am	do	have	can might
are	does	has	could should
is	did	had	may will
was			must would
were			

Go To ▶ Practices B and C on page 316.

Present-Tense Verbs

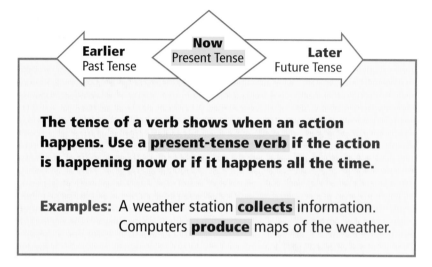

Earlier	Now	Later
Past Tense	Present Tense	Future Tense

The tense of a verb shows when an action happens. Use a present-tense verb if the action is happening now or if it happens all the time.

Examples: A weather station **collects** information.
Computers **produce** maps of the weather.

■ **Some present-tense verbs end in -s, and some do not.**

One	More Than One
I like rain.	We like rain.
You like rain.	You like rain.
He, she, or it **likes** rain.	They like rain.

The use of **-s** depends on who the subject is.

Subjects	Present-Tense Verbs Ending in -s
She	The TV reporter **gives** the weather forecast for the day. She **gives** the weather forecast for the day. Sarita Pérez **gives** the weather forecast for the day.
He	The scientist **gathers** data on big storms. He **gathers** data on big storms. Mr. Taylor **gathers** data on big storms.
It	A newspaper **prints** weather stories. It **prints** weather stories.

Go To Practice D on page 317.

Follow these rules to add -s or -es to a verb.

▶ SPELLING RULES

For most verbs, add **-s**.	**read**	My mother **reads** weather stories.
For verbs that end in **x**, **ch**, **sh**, **s**, or **z**, add **-es**.	**watch**	She **watches** weather reports.
For verbs that end in a consonant and **y**, change the **y** to **i** and add **-es**.	**study**	She **studies** weather patterns.
For verbs that end in a vowel and **y**, just add **-s**.	**say**	She **says** the weather is fascinating!

■ **Some present-tense verbs tell about an action as it is happening.**

These verbs have a helping verb and a main verb. The helping verb is am, is, or are. The main verb ends in -ing.

    Examples: **get**   The clouds **are getting** darker.
              start The rain **is starting**.
              run   I **am running** for cover.

Follow these rules to add -ing to a verb.

▶ SPELLING RULES

For most verbs, add **-ing**.	**fall** **fly** **look**	Big raindrops **are falling**. All the birds **are flying** home. A squirrel **is looking** for its hole.
For verbs that end in silent **e**, drop the **e** and add **-ing**.	**come** **make**	Now the rain **is coming** down harder. It **is making** so much noise!
Does the verb end in one vowel and one consonant? If so, double the final consonant and add **-ing**.	**tap** **clap**	The rain **is tapping** a beat on the roof. The thunder **is clapping** loudly. It likes the rain's music!

 Practices E and F
on pages 317–318.

Past-Tense Verbs

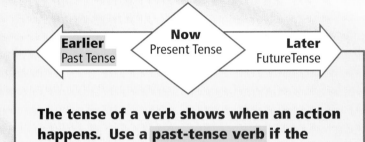

The tense of a verb shows when an action happens. Use a past-tense verb if the action happened earlier, or in the past.

Example: Galileo Galilei **invented** the thermometer around 1600.

■ **Many past-tense verbs end in** *-ed*.

These verbs are called **regular verbs**.

> **Example: measure**   Galileo's thermometer **measured** the air's temperature.

Galileo's thermometer

Follow these rules to add **-ed** to a verb.

▶ SPELLING RULES		
For most verbs, add **-ed**.	**launch**	Scientists **launched** the first weather satellite in 1960.
For verbs that end in silent **e**, drop the **e** and add **-ed**.	**circle**	It **circled** Earth every two hours.
Does the verb end in one vowel and one consonant? If so, double the final consonant and add **-ed**.	**snap**	It **snapped** pictures of the clouds around Earth.
For verbs that end in a consonant and **y**, change the **y** to **i** and add **-ed**.	**study**	Scientists **studied** the pictures to predict a heat wave.
For verbs that end in a vowel and **y**, just add **-ed**.	**stay**	The weather **stayed** hot for a few days, but then it changed!

Go To Practice G on page 318.

■ **Irregular verbs do not add *-ed* to show past tense.**

▶ IRREGULAR VERBS

Verb	Now–In the Present	Earlier–In the Past
be	Our family **is** in Arizona. We **are** excited.	Our family **was** in Arizona. We **were** excited.
begin	Our desert vacation **begins**.	Our desert vacation **began**.
break	The temperature here **breaks** 100°.	The temperature **broke** 100°.
bring	My mom **brings** sunscreen.	My mom **brought** sunscreen.
buy	We **buy** special hats.	We **bought** special hats.
do	We **do** the same things every day.	We **did** the same things every day.
drink	We **drink** a lot of water.	We **drank** a lot of water.
eat	We **eat** very little.	We **ate** very little.
find	My sister and I **find** interesting rocks.	My sister and I **found** interesting rocks.
go	I **go** back to camp at noon.	I **went** back to camp at noon.
get	It **gets** even hotter at that time!	It **got** even hotter at that time!
give	The afternoon **gives** us time to rest.	The afternoon **gave** us time to rest.
hear	We **hear** a sound nearby.	We **heard** a sound nearby.
hide	Something **hides** by our tent.	Something **hid** by our tent.
hold	I **hold** my breath.	I **held** my breath.
keep	I **keep** listening.	I **kept** listening.
know	My dad **knows** it is a lizard.	My dad **knew** it was a lizard.
make	We **make** a drawing of the lizard.	We **made** a drawing of the lizard.
ride	In the evening, we **ride** horses.	In the evening, we **rode** horses.
run	Something **runs** by us.	Something **ran** by us.
say	"Look at that," I **say**.	"Look at that," I **said**.
see	We **see** a big roadrunner.	We **saw** a big roadrunner.
sing	At night, we **sing** together.	At night, we **sang** together.
take	I **take** photos of our family.	I **took** photos of our family.
think	Everyone **thinks** the trip was great.	Everyone **thought** the trip was great.
write	We **write** about our hot vacation in school, and I add my photos.	We **wrote** about our hot vacation in school, and I added my photos.

Go To ▶ Practices H and I on page 319.

Future-Tense Verbs

Earlier	Now	Later
Past Tense	Present Tense	Future Tense

The tense of a verb shows when an action happens. Use a future-tense verb if the action will happen later, or in the future.

Example: **Will** the weather **be** windy next week?
Yes, next week it **will be** windy.

■ **There are two ways to show the future tense.**

1. Use the helping verb **will** along with a main verb.

> Tomorrow I **will build** a weather vane.

2. Use the phrase **going to**.

> Tomorrow I **am going to build** a weather vane, too.

The word **won't** also shows future tense. **Won't** is a contraction, or shortened form, of the words **will** and **not**.

> I bet we **won't** get the same results.

> We will check the wind direction every day.

Go To Practice J on page 320.

Contractions with Verbs

> You can put two words together to make a **contraction**.
> An apostrophe shows where one or more letters have been left out.
>
> **Examples:** **Weather is**   **Weather's** an interesting subject.
>   **I would**   **I'd** like to be a weather reporter.

In many contractions, the verb is shortened.

▶ CONTRACTIONS WITH VERBS

Verb	Phrase	Contraction	Verb	Phrase	Contraction
am	I am	I'm	have	I have	I've
				they have	they've
are	they are	they're			
			will	they will	they'll
is	he is	he's		we will	we'll
	it is	it's			
	where is	where's	would	she would	she'd
	what is	what's		you would	you'd

In contractions with a verb and **not**, the word **not** is shortened to **n't**.

▶ CONTRACTIONS WITH *not*

Verb	Phrase	Contraction	Verb	Phrase	Contraction
do	I do not	I don't	have	I have not	I haven't
does	he does not	he doesn't	could	you could not	you couldn't
did	we did not	we didn't	would	she would not	she wouldn't
are	you are not	you aren't	should	we should not	we shouldn't
is	he is not	he isn't			
was	she was not	she wasn't	**Exception**		
were	they were not	they weren't	can	you cannot	you can't

Go To ▶ Practice K on page 320.

Using Verbs in Writing

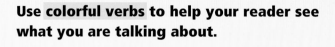

Use **colorful verbs** to help your reader see what you are talking about.

Example: An icicle **fell** to the ground.
An icicle **crashed** to the ground.

Can you see what the skater is doing? The **verbs** tell you.

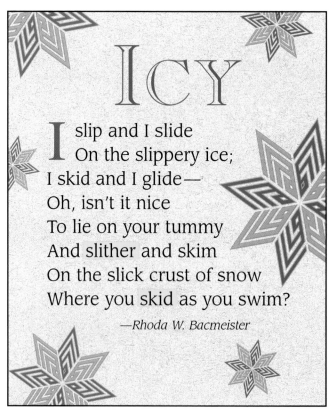

ICY

I slip and I slide
On the slippery ice;
I skid and I glide—
Oh, isn't it nice
To lie on your tummy
And slither and skim
On the slick crust of snow
Where you skid as you swim?

—*Rhoda W. Bacmeister*

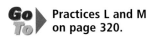

Go To Practices L and M on page 320.

Adverbs

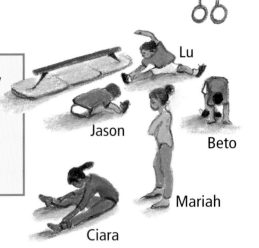

An **adverb** tells "how," "where," or "when."

Examples: Ciara stretches **carefully**.
Mariah stands **nearby**.
She will stretch **later**.

Using Adverbs

■ **Adverbs usually tell more about a verb.**

An **adverb** can come before or after a **verb**.

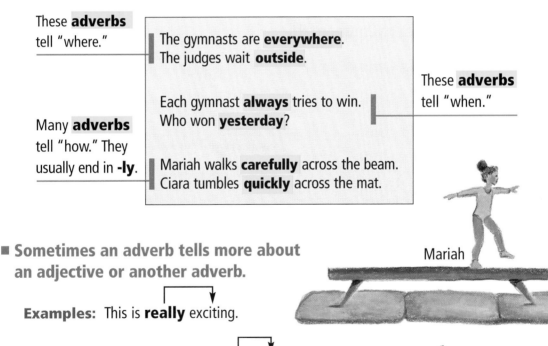

These **adverbs** tell "where."

The gymnasts are **everywhere**.
The judges wait **outside**.

These **adverbs** tell "when."

Each gymnast **always** tries to win.
Who won **yesterday**?

Many **adverbs** tell "how." They usually end in **-ly**.

Mariah walks **carefully** across the beam.
Ciara tumbles **quickly** across the mat.

Mariah

■ **Sometimes an adverb tells more about an adjective or another adverb.**

Examples: This is **really** exciting.

The audience claps **very** loudly.

Ciara

Using Adverbs to Compare

■ **You can use an adverb to compare actions.**

Lu jumps **high**.

Jason jumps **higher** than Lu.

Beto jumps **highest** of all.

1. Add **-er** to an adverb to compare two actions. You'll probably use the word **than** in your sentence, too.

2. Add **-est** to an adverb to compare three or more actions.

Ciara   Mariah

3. If the adverb ends in **-ly**, use **more**, **most**, **less**, or **least** to compare the actions.

Examples: Ciara walks **more quickly** than Mariah.
Both girls fall **less frequently** than other gymnasts.

Watch Out!

▶ **Don't use an adjective when you need an adverb.**

Everyone was sorry that the gymnastics show ended so quick. ^ly

The girls performed good ^well on the balance beam.

Go To Practice A on page 321.

Using Adverbs in Writing

> Use **adverbs** to tell where, when, and how things happen. These important details will make your writing clear.
>
> **Example:** Mariah walked **gracefully** across the balance beam.

1431 Oak Street

Los Angeles, CA 90015

March 4, 2001

Dear Aunt Ann,

   I was in an exciting contest! (yesterday)

I had a great time! I performed on the balance

beam. It was the first time that I walked

on the beam in front of an audience. It

was (very) scary. I had to focus on staying on the beam.

   My friend Ciara was in the show, too. She

can walk on the beam more quickly than anyone.

The audience clapped loudly for her. I wish you

could have seen her. She performed so (well) ~~good~~

that she won.

   Will you come to our next gymnastics show?

I hope so.

            Your niece,

            Mariah

Yesterday is an important detail. It tells Aunt Ann when the contest happened.

Adding **very** shows just how scared Mariah was.

Mariah is telling how Ciara performed, so she changed the adjective **good** to the adverb **well**.

Go To Practice B on page 321.

Prepositions

Prepositions are small words. A prepositional phrase starts with a preposition and ends with a noun or pronoun.

Example: Can you make a fish kite **with** green paper?

Ways to Use Prepositions

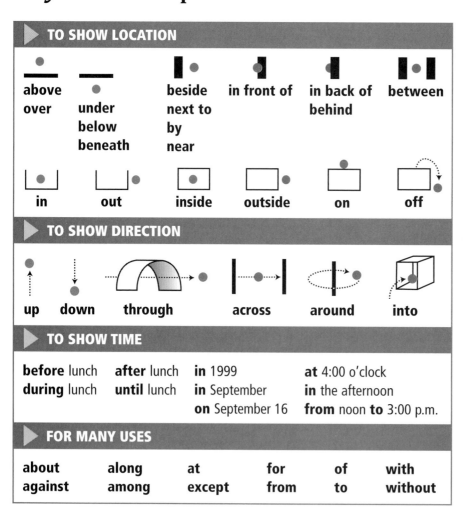

TO SHOW LOCATION

above
over

under
below
beneath

beside
next to
by
near

in front of

in back of
behind

between

in

out

inside

outside

on

off

TO SHOW DIRECTION

up   down   through   across   around   into

TO SHOW TIME

before lunch	**after** lunch	**in** 1999	**at** 4:00 o'clock
during lunch	**until** lunch	**in** September	**in** the afternoon
		on September 16	**from** noon **to** 3:00 p.m.

FOR MANY USES

about	along	at	for	of	with
against	among	except	from	to	without

Go To Practices C, D, and E on pages 321–322.

Using Prepositions in Writing

> **Prepositional phrases** add details to your writing.
>
> **Example:** I will decorate my fish kite.
>
> I will decorate my fish kite **with red dots**.

The information in these **prepositional phrases** helps the reader put the kite together correctly.

How to Make a Fish Kite

1. Fold a piece of tissue like this. Do not press the fold. Then, cut the paper in this shape. Unfold the paper.

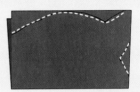

2. Add some glue in a line near the edge of the paper. Put a pipe cleaner by the glue and fold the paper over. Press it down.

3. Turn the paper over and decorate the fish.

4. Bend the pipe cleaner into a circle and twist the ends together.

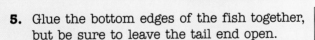

5. Glue the bottom edges of the fish together, but be sure to leave the tail end open.

6. Tie a short string to the mouth like this.

7. Tie the short string to a long string. Tie the long string to a long pole. Then take your fish outside and fly it!

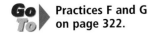 Practices F and G on page 322.

Grammar Made Graphic

Interjections

> Use an **interjection** to show feelings, like surprise.
>
> Example: **Wow!** That was a great catch.

An interjection can be a word or a phrase.

Examples: **Help!**   **Hooray!**   **Oh boy!**   **Wow!**
           Hey!   **Oh!**   **Oops!**   **Yikes!**

A comma follows the interjection if it is part of a sentence.
An exclamation point follows an interjection that stands alone.

Examples: **Hooray,** his catch saved a home run!
           Oh, boy! Now our team can win.

Conjunctions

> To connect words and sentences, use these **conjunctions:**
>
> and   but   or
>
> Example: The Tigers **and** the Eagles are playing today.

▶ HOW TO USE CONJUNCTIONS	
When you want to put two ideas that are alike together, use **and**.	Keith Morrow can hit **and** run well. He hit the ball, **and** then he scored a run.
When you want to show a difference between two ideas, use **but**.	Mom likes the Tigers, **but** I like the Eagles.
When you want to show a choice between two ideas, use **or**.	Either the Tigers **or** the Eagles will be in first place after this game. Mom will be happy, **or** I will be!

Using Conjunctions in Writing

Use conjunctions to avoid short, choppy sentences.

Example:

Should we leave now? Should we stay? It's been raining for twenty minutes. Maybe it will stop soon.

Should we leave now, **or** should we stay? It's been raining for twenty minutes, **but** maybe it will stop soon.

By joining these two sentences with **or**, the choice is easier to see.

Dear Joey,

The baseball game was very close! My mom is a Tigers fan, but my favorite team is the Eagles. In the bottom of the ninth inning, the score was tied 2-2. The Eagles had one man on base, and Keith Morrow hit a fly into left field. Would it be a home run? or Would the Tigers' outfielder catch the ball?

Can you guess? It was a home run and the Eagles won!

Your friend,
Junji

USA
20
1996

Joey Hosaka
998 Sunset Lane, Apt. 3D
San Francisco, CA 94610

Remember to use a comma before a conjunction in a compound sentence.

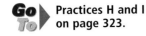 Practices H and I on page 323.

Capital Letters

A word that begins with a **capital letter** is special in some way.

Example: **The** name of this boat is *Lucky Seas*.

Ride on *Lucky Seas!*

Come with us and see big, beautiful whales. The boat leaves every day at 8:00 a.m.

Meet us at pier 9.

■ A capital letter shows where a sentence begins.

■ When you talk about yourself, use the capital letter I.

Oh, *I* see the boat.

Soon, you and *I* will be watching whales!

■ **The name of a person begins with a capital letter.**

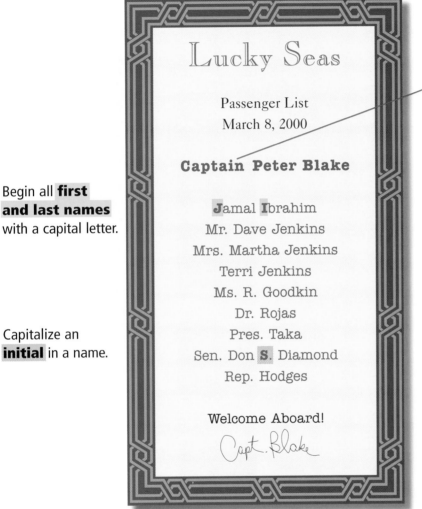

Lucky Seas

Passenger List
March 8, 2000

Captain Peter Blake

Jamal Ibrahim
Mr. Dave Jenkins
Mrs. Martha Jenkins
Terri Jenkins
Ms. R. Goodkin
Dr. Rojas
Pres. Taka
Sen. Don S. Diamond
Rep. Hodges

Welcome Aboard!

Capt. Blake

Begin all **first and last names** with a capital letter.

Capitalize an **initial** in a name.

Capitalize a **title** when it is used with a name.

Sometimes the title is abbreviated, or made shorter. Use these abbreviations:

Mr.   for a man

Mrs.   for a married woman

Ms.   for any woman

Dr.   for a doctor

Pres.   for the president of a country, a company, a club, or an organization

Sen.   for a member of the U.S. Senate

Rep.   for a member of the U.S. House of Representatives

Capt.   for the captain of a boat

Watch Out!

▶ **Do not capitalize a title when it is used without a name.**

I'm Mike Hardin. I work with the **captain.**

▶ **Capitalize words like *Mom* and *Dad* when they are used as names.**

Hey, **Mom**! Come meet Mike. Mike, I'd like you to meet **my mom.**

Go To ▶ Practice A on page 323.

Capital Letters, continued

- **The important words in the name of a special place or thing begin with a capital letter.**

Where do you travel on the <u>L</u>ucky <u>S</u>eas?

We go out of San Francisco Bay to the Pacific Ocean.

▶ NAMES OF SPECIAL PLACES AND THINGS

Streets and Roads
King Boulevard
Avenue M
First Street
Simmons Expressway

Cities

New York City
Houston
Los Angeles

States
New York
Texas
California

Countries
Vietnam
Ecuador
France

Continents
Asia
South America
Australia

Buildings, Monuments, and Ships
Statue of Liberty
Lucky Seas
Three Rivers Stadium
Museum of Natural History

Bodies of Water
Colorado River
Pacific Ocean
Lake Baikal
Mediterranean Sea

Landforms
Rocky Mountains
Sahara Desert
Grand Canyon

Public Spaces
Mesa Verde National Park
Central Park
Arapaho National Forest

Planets and Heavenly Bodies
Earth
Jupiter
Milky Way

Watch Out!

▶ **Capitalize an adjective if it comes from the name of a special place.**

Mike is from **Canada**.
He is a **Canadian** sailor.

Go To ▶ Practice B on page 324.

When you write the abbreviation, or short form, of a place name, use a capital letter.

Dear Kim,

Hello from California. We went whale watching today. Did you know some gray whales are over 40 feet long? I really liked it when they came up for air— I could see their spouts. I'll show you some pictures when I get home.

Your friend,
Jamal

Kim Messina
10250 W. Fourth St.
Las Vegas, NV 89015

▶ ABBREVIATED PLACE NAMES

For State Names on Letters and Cards That Are Mailed

AL	Alabama	**MT**	Montana	
AK	Alaska	**NE**	Nebraska	
AZ	Arizona	**NV**	Nevada	
AR	Arkansas	**NH**	New Hampshire	
CA	California	**NJ**	New Jersey	
CO	Colorado	**NM**	New Mexico	
CT	Connecticut	**NY**	New York	
DE	Delaware	**NC**	North Carolina	
FL	Florida	**ND**	North Dakota	
GA	Georgia	**OH**	Ohio	
HI	Hawaii	**OK**	Oklahoma	
ID	Idaho	**OR**	Oregon	
IL	Illinois	**PA**	Pennsylvania	
IN	Indiana	**RI**	Rhode Island	
IA	Iowa	**SC**	South Carolina	
KS	Kansas	**SD**	South Dakota	
KY	Kentucky	**TN**	Tennessee	
LA	Louisiana	**TX**	Texas	
ME	Maine	**UT**	Utah	
MD	Maryland	**VT**	Vermont	
MA	Massachusetts	**VA**	Virginia	
MI	Michigan	**WA**	Washington	
MN	Minnesota	**WV**	West Virginia	
MS	Mississippi	**WI**	Wisconsin	
MO	Missouri	**WY**	Wyoming	

For Words Used in Addresses

Ave.	Avenue
Blvd.	Boulevard
Ct.	Court
Dr.	Drive
E.	East
Hwy.	Highway
Ln.	Lane
N.	North
Pl.	Place
Rd.	Road
S.	South
Sq.	Square
St.	Street
W.	West

Capital Letters, continued

■ **The first word and all important words in the name of an organization begin with a capital letter.**

© 1993 Sea World, Inc.

▶ NAMES OF ORGANIZATIONS

Clubs
Whale Watcher's Club at Monterey Bay
Girl Scouts of America

World Organizations
International Whaling Commission
United Nations

Sports Teams
Los Angeles Dodgers
Seattle Supersonics

Professional Groups
American Medical Association
Professional Golfers' Association

Political Parties
Democratic Party
Republican Party

Businesses
Sal's Camera Shop
Little Taco House

■ **Names of the months, days of the week, and special days and holidays begin with a capital letter.**

If you abbreviate one of these names, begin the abbreviation with a capital letter and end it with a period.

▶ MONTHS AND DAYS

Months of the Year		Days of the Week		Special Days and Holidays
January	Jan.	**Sunday**	Sun.	April Fool's Day
February	Feb.	**Monday**	Mon.	Christmas
March	Mar.	**Tuesday**	Tues.	Earth Day
April	Apr.	**Wednesday**	Wed.	Graduation Day
May	*These months*	**Thursday**	Thurs.	Hanukkah
June	*are never*	**Friday**	Fri.	Kwanzaa
July	*abbreviated.*	**Saturday**	Sat.	Labor Day
August	Aug.			New Year's Day
September	Sept.			Thanksgiving
October	Oct.			
November	Nov.			
December	Dec.			

Watch Out!

▶ The names of seasons do not start with a capital letter.

In **spring**, the whales go north.

In **fall**, they go south.

Go To ▶ Practice C on page 324.

■ **The important words in a title begin with a capital letter.**

What has a title? Books, magazines, newspapers, and all kinds of written works have titles. So do multimedia works like movies, computer programs, TV shows, and videos. Stories, poems, and songs have titles, too.

Meet a Majestic Sea Mammal

By Sarah O'Neal

Little words like **a**, **an**, **the**, **in**, **at**, **of**, and **for** are not capitalized unless they are the first word in the **title**.

Whales are gigantic animals that live in the oceans and seas of the world. Dr. Gregory Pratt knows. He has just published ***The Largest Mammals on the Planet***. In it, he explains that whales look like fish, but are really mammals. On a recent segment of the television show ***Nature Hour***, Dr. Pratt said, "Like other mammals, whales have well-developed brains. Unlike fish, whales are warm-blooded and their babies are born alive."

According to Dr. Pratt, the respiratory system of whales clearly makes them mammals. He said, "All mammals have lungs. Whales, therefore, must regularly come to the surface of the water to breathe. But, unlike humans, whales can go for 40 minutes or longer without breathing."

■ **When a person's exact words appear in print, the first word begins with a capital letter.**

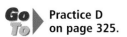 Practice D on page 325.

Punctuation Marks

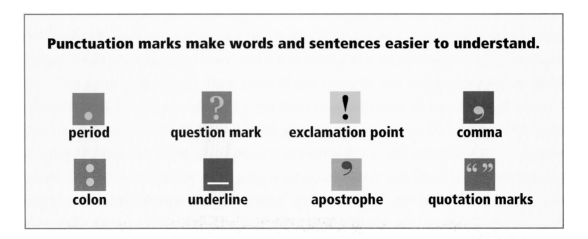

Punctuation marks make words and sentences easier to understand.

period   question mark   exclamation point   comma

colon   underline   apostrophe   quotation marks

Sentence Punctuation

■ **Always use a punctuation mark at the end of a sentence. It gives important information.**

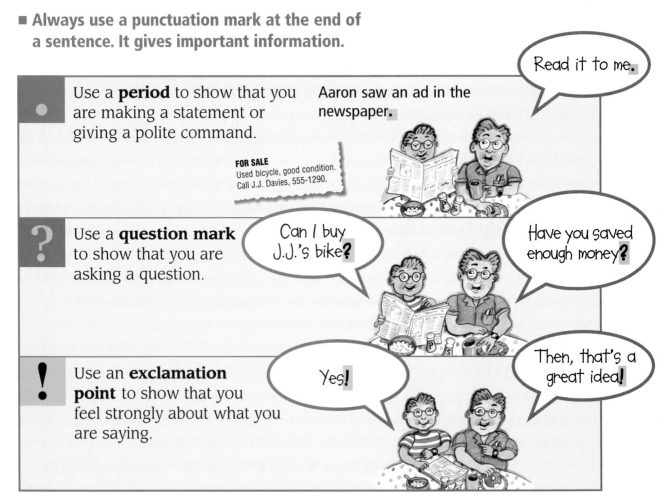

Use a **period** to show that you are making a statement or giving a polite command.

Aaron saw an ad in the newspaper.

FOR SALE
Used bicycle, good condition.
Call J.J. Davies, 555-1290.

Read it to me.

Use a **question mark** to show that you are asking a question.

Can I buy J.J.'s bike?

Have you saved enough money?

Use an **exclamation point** to show that you feel strongly about what you are saying.

Yes!

Then, that's a great idea!

Go To ▶ Practice A on page 325.

More Ways to Use a Period

●	Use a **period** after an initial or an abbreviation.	Aaron called J.J. Mrs. Davies answered the phone.
●	Use a **period** to separate dollars and cents. The period is the decimal point.	Mrs. Davies told Aaron the bike cost $55.00 and no less. Aaron had exactly $50.40 and no more.

The Comma

,	Use **commas** to separate three or more items in a series	Aaron needs 4 dollars, 2 quarters, and one dime after all. He could clean the kitchen, the closet, and the bathroom. He could take out the trash, walk some dogs, or sweep the steps.
,	Use **commas** when you write large numbers.	Aaron has taken out the trash 1,000,000 times, so he decides to walk Mrs. Romero's dog. It weighs 1,200 pounds!
,	**Commas** have important uses in a letter. How many can you find?	

177 North Avenue
New York, NY 10033

October 3, 2000

Dear Mrs. Romero,
    I am saving money to buy a bicycle. Can I walk Brute for you? I know that most people pay $.25 to walk a dog, but Brute is big! Can you pay me $5.00?
    I will take good care of Brute. I like him even though he is bigger than I am!
    Thank you.

            Sincerely,

            Aaron

Use a comma:

- between the city and the state
- between the date and the year
- after the greeting, or "hello" part, of a friendly letter

- after the closing, or "good-bye" part, of the letter

The Comma, continued

Use **commas** to set off certain words in a sentence.

Aaron, it's Mrs. Romero calling.

Set off the name of a person someone is talking to.

Set off a short word or phrase at the beginning of a sentence.

Hello, Mrs. Romero, how are you?

Oh, I'm just fine. I'm calling to see if you'll walk Brute today.

Set off a question that starts at the end of a sentence.

Yes! I'll need a strong leash, won't I?

Set off someone's exact words.

Well, as my husband says, "No leash is strong enough for Brute."

Use a **comma** between two adjectives that tell about the same noun.

Examples:
Brute is a **big, yellow** dog.

His **large, furry** paws are as wide as the door.

Aaron's **small, brown** leash didn't look strong enough.

Go To Practices B and C on page 326.

9 Use a **comma** before **and**, **but**, or **or** in a compound sentence.

Examples:

Brute was big**, and** Aaron could hardly control him.

Aaron tried to stop Brute**, but** he ran right into Mr. Sayeed's deli.

Boxes either flew out**, or** they got crushed.

Apples went everywhere**, and** a newspaper rack fell down.

Mr. Sayeed was calm**, but** he told Brute he was a bad dog.

The Colon

Use a **colon**:

- after the greeting in a business letter

- to separate hours and minutes

- to start a list

179 North Avenue
New York, NY 10033
October 4, 2002

Mr. Omar Sayeed
Sayeed Deli
686 Fifth Street
New York, NY 10033

Dear Mr. Sayeed:

Yesterday, at about 10:30, my neighbor Aaron Jackson took my dog Brute for a walk. Brute is a large dog, and Aaron had some trouble controlling him. Aaron told me that Brute did three bad things:

1. He ate two cartons of apples.
2. He stepped on a customer.
3. He knocked over one newspaper rack.

Aaron said that he apologized to the customer. How much do I owe you for the apples and the rack?

Please accept my apologies. Next time, I will have two boys walk Brute. Or, maybe three!

Sincerely,
Electra Romero
Electra Romero

The Apostrophe

 In a contraction, or shortened form of two words, an **apostrophe** shows that one or more letters have been left out.

	Aaron got $5.00 for walking Brute.
He's = He is	**He's** happy now.
I'll = I will	"**I'll** go over to see J.J.," said Aaron.
hasn't = has not	"I hope he **hasn't** sold the bike."

 An **apostrophe** can also show that someone or something owns something.

Use **'s** when one person owns something.

Aaron and his dad look at each building**'s** number.

Aaron**'s** heart is pounding.

Use **s'** to show that two or more people own something.

Two boys ride by.

The boy**s'** bikes are neat!

If the plural noun does not end in **s**, use **'s**.

A girl rides by.

All the children**'s** bikes are neat!

Go To Practice D on page 327.

212

Underline

Underline the titles of books, magazines, and newspapers.

If J.J. has sold his bike, I'll look in **The Daily News** and find another bike for sale.

Quotation Marks

" " Put **quotation marks** around the title of a:

- song, poem, or short story
- magazine article or newspaper article
- chapter from a book

Aaron sang "Let It Be Mine" as he walked up to J.J.'s apartment building.

" " Use **quotation marks** around words you copy from a book or other printed material.

The words in the ad were "used bicycle, good condition."

" " Use **quotation marks** to show a speaker's exact words.

A new paragraph begins each time the speaker changes.

Aaron knocked on J.J.'s door and said to his dad, "I hope the bike is in really good condition."

"We'll see," said his dad.

Just then a boy opened the door and said, "Hello, I'm J.J. How are you?"

"I'm great," Aaron said. "Can I see your bike? I brought enough money to buy it."

"Sure," J.J. said. "It's a cool bike."

"It sure is," Aaron said happily.

"We'll take it," his dad said. Aaron handed J.J. the money.

"Thank you and enjoy the bike!" J.J. shouted.

"I will! See you later, Dad!" Aaron yelled as he rode off to buy a cookie with the 40¢ he had left.

Go To Practice E on page 327.

Grammar Made Graphic 213

Spelling

Here are some tips to help you spell words correctly.

1.

Look at the new word.

2.

Look again as you **say** the word out loud.

3.

Listen to the word as you say it again.

4.

Make a picture of the word in your head.

5.

a–q–u–a–r–i–u–m

Spell the word out loud several times.

6.

Write the word for practice. Write it five or ten times.

7.

Check the word. You can use a dictionary, a computer spell-check, or a word list.

8.

Hi, Mom. I saw a really neat **aquarium** today.

Make a sentence with the word to be sure that you understand what the word means.

Spelling, continued

Follow these rules and your spelling will get better and better!

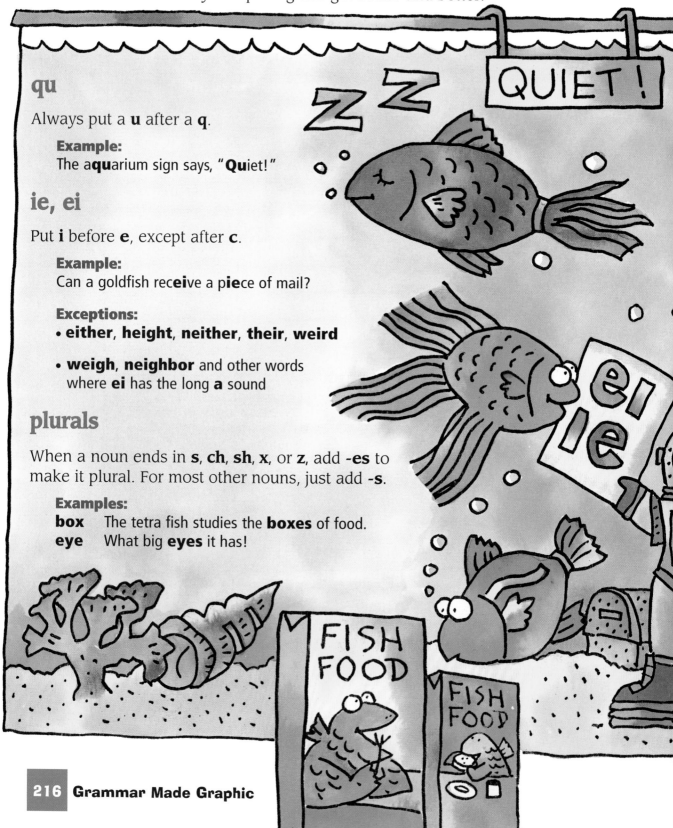

qu

Always put a **u** after a **q**.

Example:
The a**qu**arium sign says, "**Qu**iet!"

ie, ei

Put **i** before **e**, except after **c**.

Example:
Can a goldfish rec**ei**ve a p**ie**ce of mail?

Exceptions:

- **either, height, neither, their, weird**

- **weigh, neighbor** and other words where **ei** has the long **a** sound

plurals

When a noun ends in **s**, **ch**, **sh**, **x**, or **z**, add **-es** to make it plural. For most other nouns, just add **-s**.

Examples:
box   The tetra fish studies the **boxes** of food.
eye   What big **eyes** it has!

y to i

If a word ends in **y**, change the **y** to **i** before you add **-es**, **-ed**, **-er**, or **-est**.

Examples:

baby	Look at the sea horse **babies**.
cry	They **cried** all day yesterday!
happy	Now, they are **happier**.

Exception:

- For **boy**, **monkey**, **play**, and other words with a vowel before the **y**, just add **-s**:

    boys   monkeys   plays

If you add **-ing** to a verb that ends in **-y**, do not change the **y** to **i**.

Example:

study   The two seahorses are **studying** each other.

-ed, -ing, -er, -est

When a word ends in silent **e**, drop the **e** before you add **-ed**, **-ing**, **-er**, or **-est**.

Examples:

taste   Why is that zebra fish **tasting** the plastic plant? He **tasted** it yesterday, too.

Does the word end in one vowel and one consonant? If so, double the final consonant before you add an ending.

Examples:

trip	The starfish **tripped** over the octopus.
mad	The octopus got **madder** and **madder**!

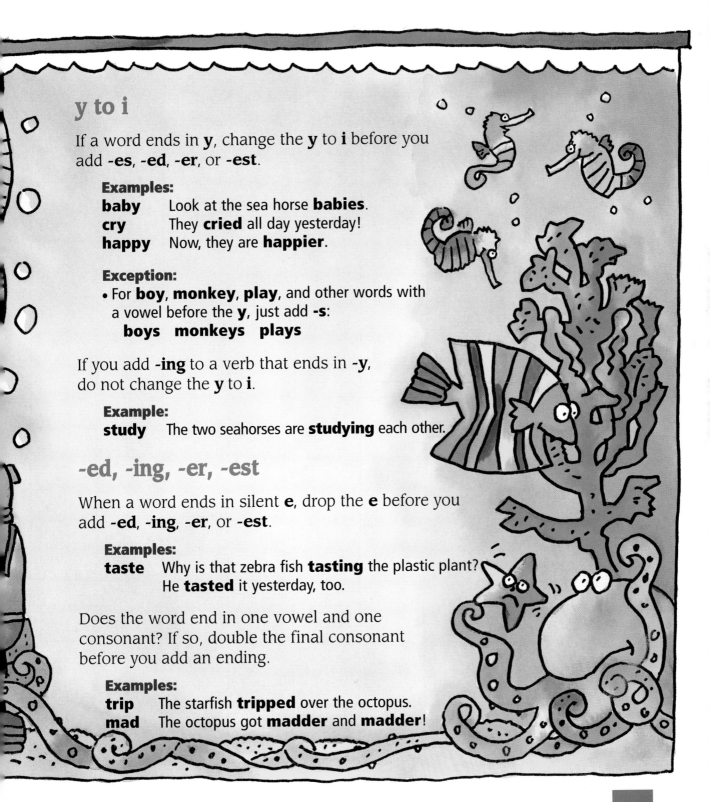

Chapter 5
Look It Up!

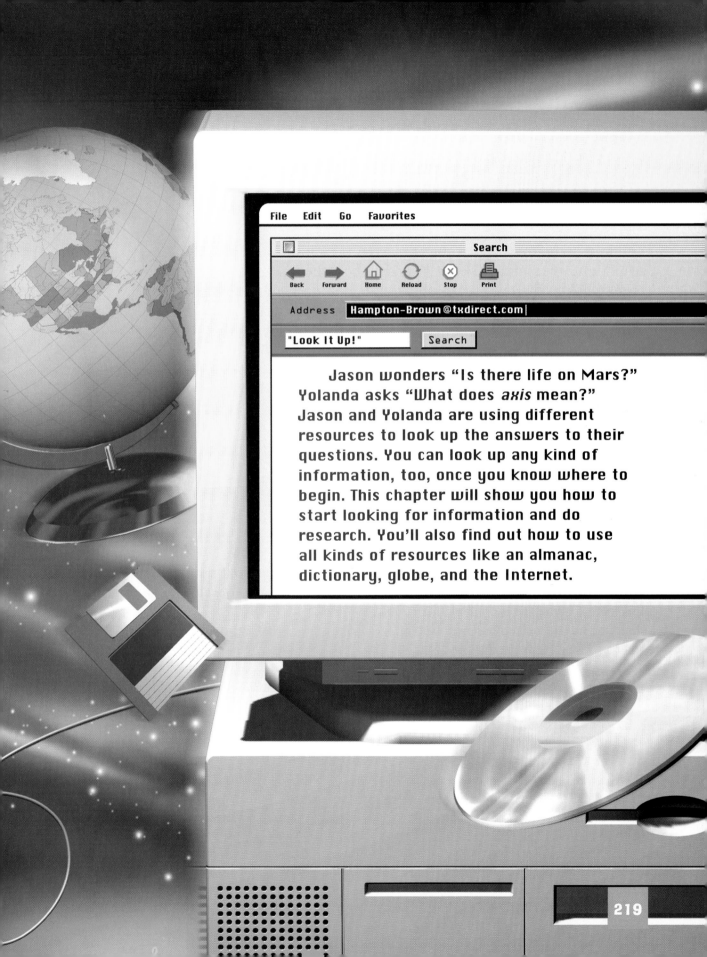

File   Edit   Go   Favorites

Search

Back   Forward   Home   Reload   Stop   Print

Address   Hampton-Brown@txdirect.com

"Look It Up!"   Search

   Jason wonders "Is there life on Mars?" Yolanda asks "What does *axis* mean?" Jason and Yolanda are using different resources to look up the answers to their questions. You can look up any kind of information, too, once you know where to begin. This chapter will show you how to start looking for information and do research. You'll also find out how to use all kinds of resources like an almanac, dictionary, globe, and the Internet.

The Research Process

When you **research**, you look up information about a topic. You can use the information you find to write a story, article, book, or research report.

STEP
1 Choose a Topic

Think of something you want to learn more about and something that interests you. That will be your research **topic**. Make sure you pick a topic that is not too general. A specific, or smaller, topic is easier to research and to write about. It is also more interesting to read about in a report.

Outer Space
This is a big topic! There are a lot of things in outer space: stars, suns, planets, moons, and black holes. That would be too much to research or write about in one report.

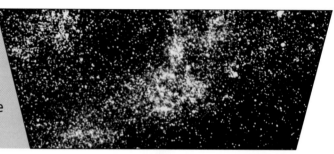

Planets
This topic is better, but it's still too big. There are nine planets in our solar system! You could do a report on the planet Mars. But what is it you want to know about Mars?

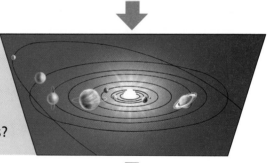

Life on Mars
The topic "Life on Mars" is more specific than "Mars." Finding out if Mars has water, plants, animals, or Martians could be VERY interesting!

STEP
2 Decide What to Look Up

What do you want to know about your topic?
Write down some questions. Look at the most
important words in your questions. Those are
key words you can look up when you start
your research.

STEP
3 Locate Resources

Now that you know what to look up, you can go
to different **resources** to find information about your
topic. Resources can be people, such as librarians,
teachers, and family members. Resources can also be
books, magazines, newspapers, videos, or the Internet.
You can find resources all around you.

Whatever your topic is, try exploring
the library first. There you'll discover
a world of information!

Is there life on Mars?

Is there water or
oxygen on Mars?

Can people, plants,
or animals live on
the surface of Mars?

Have there been any
space missions there?

Did anyone find proof
of Martian life forms?

The Library

A **library** is a place full of books and other kinds of resources like videos, magazines, and newspapers. It's organized in a special way so you can find things easily.

Reference Section
The **reference section** has lots of special resources. You can't check out reference books like these, but you can make copies of pages or articles.

Atlas

Information Desk
If you can't find what you're looking for, you can ask a **librarian**. The librarian will usually be at the **Information Desk**.

Fiction
One section of the library has all of the **fiction** books. These are stories that are not true. If you're looking for facts about life on Mars, you won't find them here!

Nonfiction
In the **nonfiction** section, there are books that have **facts** about all kinds of topics.

Children's Room
The **children's room** is full of books and magazines especially for kids.

Reference Section

Information Desk

Fiction

Nonfiction

Children's Room

Almanac

Encyclopedia

Dictionary

Checkout Desk

Periodicals

Internet

Card Catalog

Checkout Desk

The **checkout desk** is where you check out books. You can get your library card here, too.

Periodicals

Magazines and newspapers are called **periodicals**. To find the most recent, or current, information about a topic, look for articles in periodicals.

Computers for the Internet

Some libraries have **computers** for looking up information on the **Internet**.

Card Catalog

The computer and **card catalogs** list all the books in the library.

Go To ▶ **The Resources** section on pages 234–262 to find out more about the library and special resources.

The Research Process, continued

STEP
4 Gather Information

When you **gather information**, you find the best resources for your topic. You look up your key words to find facts about your topic. Then you take notes.

How to Find Information Quickly

■ **Use alphabetical order to look up words in a list.**

In many resources, the words, titles, and subjects are listed in **alphabetical order**.

Look at these words. They are in order by the **first** letter of each word.

> **a**steroid
> **m**oon
> **p**lanet
> **s**un

If the word you are looking up has the same first letter as other words in the list, look at the **second** letters.

> **Ma**rs
> **Me**rcury
> **mi**ssion
> **mo**on

If the word you are looking up has the same first <u>and</u> second letters as others in the list, look at the **third** letters.

> **mag**netic
> **map**
> **Mar**s
> **mas**s

■ Skim and scan the text to decide if it is useful.

When you **skim** and **scan**, you look at text quickly to see if it has the information you need. If it does, then you can take the time to read it more carefully. If it doesn't, you can go on to another source.

To Skim:

Read the **title** to see if the article is useful for your topic.

Read the **beginning** sentences and **headings** to find out more about an article's topic.

Skim the **ending**. It often sums up all the ideas in the article.

To Scan:

Look for **key words** or **details** in dark type or italics. If you find key words that go with your topic, you'll probably want to read the article.

PLANETS, STARS, AND SPACE TRAVEL

LOOKING FOR LIFE ELSEWHERE IN THE UNIVERSE

For years scientists have been trying to discover if there is life on other planets in our solar system or life elsewhere in the universe. Some scientists have been looking for evidence based on what is necessary for life on Earth—basics like water and proper temperature.

WHAT SCIENTISTS HAVE LEARNED SO FAR

Mars and Jupiter. In 1996, two teams of scientists examined two meteorites that may have come from **Mars** and found evidence that some form of life may have existed on Mars billions of years ago. In 1997, in photographs of Europa, a moon of **Jupiter**, scientists saw areas with icy ridges and areas without ice. It seemed that underneath the ice there might be water—one of the essentials of life.

New Planets. In 1996, astronomers believed they found several new planets traveling around stars very far away (many light-years away) from our sun. Scientists do not think life exists on these planets, because they are so close to their sun that they would be too hot. But scientists are hoping to find other stars with planets around them that might support life.

AND THE SEARCH CONTINUES

NASA (the National Aeronautics and Space Administration) has a program to look for life on Mars. Ten spacecraft are to be sent to Mars over the next ten years. Some will fly around Mars taking pictures, while others will land on Mars to study the soil and rocks and look for living things. The first two, *Mars Pathfinder* and *Mars Global Surveyor*, launched in 1996, were scheduled to reach Mars in 1997.

Another program that searches for life on other worlds is called **SETI**. SETI (an acronym for Search for Extraterrestrial Intelligence) uses powerful radio telescopes to look for life elsewhere in the universe.

■ **Question:** Is there life elsewhere in the universe? **Answer:** No one knows yet.

The Research Process, continued

4 Gather Information, continued

How to Take Notes

Notes are important words, phrases, and ideas that you write while you are reading and researching. Your notes will help you remember **details**. They'll also help you remember the **source**. The source is where you got the information.

■ **Write notes in your own words.**

In this book it says: "Mars may look dry as dust, but water once flowed over the surface."

Okay. I'll write: Mars—dry now, used to have water

Mars—dry

If you copy exactly what you read, put **quotation marks** around the words.

Is there water on Mars?

<u>Mars</u> by Seymour Simon, page 28

— "Mars may look dry as dust, but water once flowed over the surface"

■ **Set up your notecards like these so you can easily put your information in order when you write.**

Notecard for a Book

Include your **research question**.

Write down the **source** so you can remember where you found your facts. List the title, author, and page number.

> Is there life on Mars?
>
> Mars by Seymour Simon, page 27
>
> — Viking spacecraft supposed to find out if
>   there's life
>
> — some think experiments showed there isn't
>
> — others believe experiments were the wrong kind;
>   maybe scientists looked in wrong places

List **details** and **facts** in your own words.

Notecard for a Magazine or Newspaper

List the name, date, volume, and issue number of your **source**. Also write the name of the article in quotation marks.

> Is there life on Mars?
>
> Time for Kids, Sept. 13, 1996   Vol. 2, No. 1
>
> "Next stop: Mars"
>
> — maybe—Mars has some features like Earth.
>   "It has volcanoes and giant canyons."
>
> — hard to prove, but maybe space missions like
>   Pathfinder can find something

Include your **research question**.

Use **quotation marks for exact words** you copy from a source.

5 Organize Information

Make an Outline

Follow these steps to turn your notes into an outline.
Your outline will then help you write your report.

1 **Put all the notecards with the same research question together.**

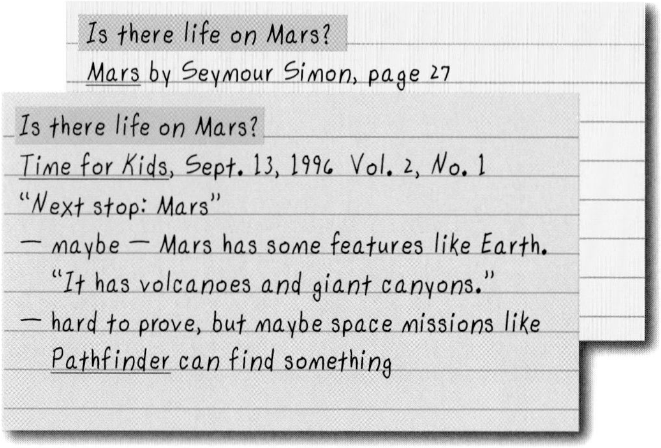

Is there life on Mars?
   Mars by Seymour Simon, page 27

Is there life on Mars?
Time for Kids, Sept. 13, 1996 Vol. 2, No. 1
"Next stop: Mars"
— maybe — Mars has some features like Earth.
   "It has volcanoes and giant canyons."
— hard to prove, but maybe space missions like
   Pathfinder can find something

2 **Turn your notes into an outline.**

First, turn your question
into a main idea.

Next, find details in your notes
that go with the main idea.
Add them to your outline.

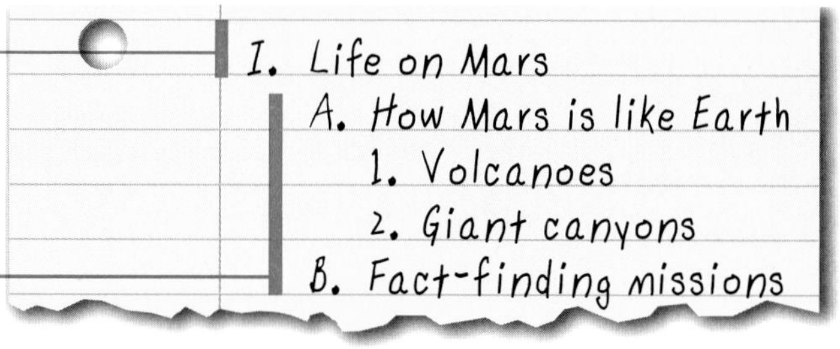

I. Life on Mars
    A. How Mars is like Earth
       1. Volcanoes
       2. Giant canyons
    B. Fact-finding missions

3 **Write a title for your outline.**

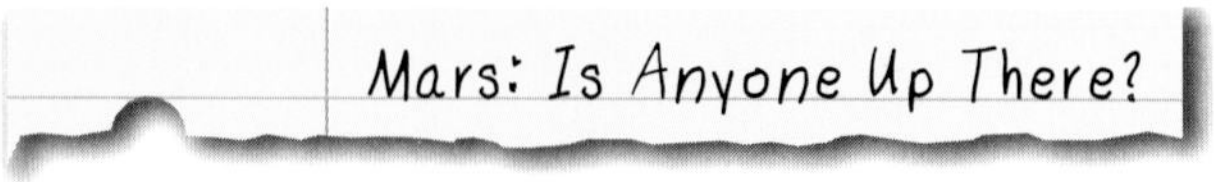

Mars: Is Anyone Up There?

Here's an outline for a research report about life on Mars.

Title
The title tells what your outline is all about. You can use it again when you write your report.

Main Idea
Each main idea follows a Roman numeral.

Details and **related details**.
Each detail follows a capital letter. Each related detail follows a number.

Mars: Is Anyone Up There?
I. Life on Mars
    A. How Mars is like Earth
       1. Volcanoes
       2. Giant canyons
    B. Fact-finding missions
       1. Viking
       2. Pathfinder
II. Signs of life on Mars
    A. Studied by David McKay's team
    B. Meteorite
       1. Contains bacteria fossils
       2. Found in Antarctica
       3. From Mars
III. Continued search for life on Mars
    A. Look underground
    B. More study
       1. Mission planned for 2005
       2. Gases in atmosphere
       3. What rocks are made of

The Research Process, continued

Write a Research Report

Once you've finished your outline, you're ready to write a **research report**. Turn the main ideas and details from your outline into sentences and paragraphs.

1 **Write the title from your outline and an introduction.**

The title and introduction should tell what your report is mostly about and should be interesting to your readers.

Outline

Mars: Is Anyone Up There?

Title and Introduction

Mars: Is Anyone Up There?

You've probably seen some pretty creepy outer space creatures in movies and TV. Do they really look like that? Are there really living beings up there?

2 **Turn your first main idea into a topic sentence for the next paragraph.**

Look at Roman numeral I on your outline. Turn the words into a sentence with a subject and a predicate. That sentence will be the topic sentence for your first paragraph.

Outline

I. Life on Mars

Topic Sentence

People have always wondered if there is life on any other planet, especially Mars.

❸ Turn the details and related details into sentences.

Look at the letters and numbers on your outline. Turn those words into sentences that tell more about the main idea. Add them to your paragraph.

Outline

> I. Life on Mars
>   A. How Mars is like Earth
>   1. Volcanoes
>   2. Giant canyons
>   B. Fact-finding missions
>   1. Viking
>   2. Pathfinder

Topic Sentence and Supporting Details

> People have always wondered if there is life on any other planet, especially Mars. Because Mars is similar to Earth with features like volcanoes and giant canyons, it seems possible that there is life on Mars. There are lots of missions to Mars like the spacecrafts Viking and Pathfinder, so it seems like we might find out soon!

❹ Follow steps 2 and 3 to write the other paragraphs for your report.

❺ Write a conclusion to sum up your report.

Look back at all the main ideas on your outline. Write a sentence for each main idea to include in the last paragraph of your report. The last paragraph is a summary of the most important information about your topic.

Outline

> I. Life on Mars

> II. Signs of life on Mars

> III. Continued search for life on Mars

Conclusion

> Basically, no one knows if there is or isn't life on Mars. It is possible that life does or did exist there. Spacecraft that go to Mars in the future will give us more proof. Hopefully, the mystery will be solved soon for all of us!

6 Write a Research Report, continued

A good **research report** gives facts about a topic in an organized and interesting way.

The **title** and introduction tell what your report is about. They get your reader interested.

The **body** of the report presents the facts you found. Each paragraph goes with one main idea from your outline.

Mars: Is Anyone Up There?

You've probably seen some pretty creepy outer space creatures in movies and TV. Do they really look like that? Are there really living beings up there?

People have always wondered if there is life on any other planet, especially Mars. Because Mars is similar to Earth with features like volcanoes and giant canyons, it seems possible that there is life on Mars. There are lots of missions to Mars like the spacecrafts Viking and Pathfinder, so it seems like we might find out soon!

Recently, David McKay and his team of scientists discovered possible signs of ancient Martian life. They found bacteria fossils in a meteorite that crashed into Antarctica thousands of years ago. They know the meteorite is from Mars because it has the same chemicals in it as the Martian atmosphere. They believe the fossils, which are a lot smaller than the width of a human hair, were alive on Mars from 3 to 4 billion years ago. At that time, there was water on the planet. Since the fossils were deep in the center of the meteorite, McKay's team feels that the fossils were definitely from Mars, and not from Earth.

No one has seen a live Martian, but some scientists feel that we need to keep looking. Since no one has found water on the surface of Mars, maybe Martians live underground where there is water. A mission to look for Martian life and bring soil samples back to Earth is planned for 2005. Until then, scientists will continue to study other aspects of Mars like the gases in its atmosphere and what its rocks are made of.

Basically, no one knows if there is or isn't life on Mars. It is possible that life does or did exist there. Spacecraft that go to Mars in the future will give us more proof. Hopefully, the mystery will be solved soon for all of us!

Each paragraph in the **body** begins with a **topic sentence** that tells a main idea. The other sentences give **details** and **related details**.

The last paragraph is the **conclusion**. It sums up the report.

STEP 6

STEP 5

The Resources

You can find information in books, periodicals, videos, on computers, and in many kinds of special resources.

Finding Information in Books

Card Catalog

Some libraries have a set of drawers called a **card catalog**. In the drawers are cards that tell what books are in the library and where to find them. Each card has:

■ a **book title** and **author**

■ **publishing information**

Here you will find:

- the book's edition number. When books are printed all at the same time, they have the same edition number (**1st ed.** means **first edition**).

- whether the book has a bibliography, or list of other books the author used to write the book (**bibl.** means **bibliography**)

- the city where the publisher is located and the publisher's name

- the copyright date (**c** means **copyright**)

- the number of pages in the book (**p.** means **pages**)

- if the book is illustrated or has photographs (**ill.** means **illustrated**)

- how tall the book is (**cm.** means **centimeters**)

```
              Are we moving to Mars?
J
620.4    Schraff, Anne.
Sch         Are we moving to Mars? / Anne Schraff.--
         1st ed.--Santa Fe: John Muir Publications.
         c1996. 32 p.: ill. (some color); 20 cm.

         ISBN 1-56261-310-3.


         1. Mars (Planet)--Surface--Juvenile literatur
         2. Life on other planets--Juvenile literature
         3. Extraterrestrial (anthropology--Juvenile
         literature). I. Title.
```

■ **cross references** to other related subjects

Each card also has a **call number** that tells you what section of the library the book is in. Call numbers with a **J** mean that the books are in the **J**uvenile, or children's, section of the library.

- **Fiction books** are stories made up by an author. They are arranged on the library shelves in alphabetical order by the author's last name. Their call numbers usually show the first two or three **letters of the author's last name**.

```
J
KIT   Kitamura, Satoshi.
        UFO Diary / Satoshi Kitamura. –
      Farrar, Straus and Giroux, 1991.
      unpaged: color ill. ; 23cm.

        ISBN 0-374-48041-9
```

- **Nonfiction books** contain facts about a subject. They are arranged on the library shelves by **call numbers**. These numbers stand for subject areas from the Dewey Decimal System:

```
        Are we moving to Mars?
J
620.4 Schraff, Anne.
Sch     Are we moving to Mars? / Anne
      1st ed.--Santa Fe: John Muir Pu
      c1996. 32 p.: ill. (some color)

        ISBN 1-56261-310-3.
```

000–099	General Books	500–599	Pure Sciences
100–199	Philosophy	600–699	Technology
200–299	Religion	700–799	The Arts
300–399	Social Sciences	800–899	Literature
400–499	Language	900–999	History and Geography

Biographies are an exception. These nonfiction books give facts about people who really lived. Biographies are grouped on the shelves by the last name of the person the book is about.

Finding Information in Books, continued

The cards in a card catalog are in alphabetical order according to the first word or words on the card. Here are the three kinds of cards you'll find in a card catalog.

Subject Card

The **subject** of a book appears first on a subject card. Only nonfiction books have subject cards.

```
        MARS (PLANET)
J
620.4   Schraff, Anne.
Sch        Are we moving to Mars? / Anne Schraff.--
        1st ed.--Santa Fe: John Muir Publications.
        c1996. 32 p.: ill. (some color); 20 cm.

        ISBN 1-56261-310-3.


        1. Mars (Planet)--Surface--Juvenile literature.
        2. Life on other planets--Juvenile literature.
        3. Extraterrestrial (anthropology--Juvenile
        literature). I. Title.
```

Title Card

The **title** of a book appears first on a title card. If the first word is *A* or *The*, look up the next word in alphabetical order.

```
          Are we moving to Mars?
J
620.4   Schraff, Anne.
Sch        Are we moving to Mars? / Anne Schraff.--
        1st ed.--Santa Fe: John Muir Publications.
        c1996. 32 p.: ill. (some color); 20 cm.

        ISBN 1-56261-310-3.


        1. Mars (Planet)--Surface--Juvenile literature.
        2. Life on other planets--Juvenile literature.
        3. Extraterrestrial (anthropology--Juvenile
        literature). I. Title.
```

Author Card

The **author's name** appears first on an author card. The author's last name appears first. Look it up in alphabetical order.

```
J
620.4   Schraff, Anne.
Sch        Are we moving to Mars? / Anne Schraff.--
        1st ed.--Santa Fe: John Muir Publications.
        c1996. 32 p.: ill. (some color); 20 cm.

        ISBN 1-56261-310-3.


        1. Mars (Planet)--Surface--Juvenile literature.
        2. Life on other planets--Juvenile literature.
        3. Extraterrestrial (anthropology--Juvenile
        literature). I. Title.
```

Computerized Card Catalog

A **computerized card catalog** is a card catalog on the computer. It's a lot like the paper card catalog, but faster to use because the computer looks up a book for you.

Computerized catalogs are not all the same. Here's one example and the steps you might follow to find *Are We Moving to Mars?* by Anne Schraff.

1 **Read the instructions on the computer screen.**

> The **instructions** will help you find the information you're looking for in the computer.

2 **Type a letter to start your search.**

> To search for available information about a **subject**, you would type an **S**.

3 **Type in a word or words that name your subject and press return.**

> For the subject Mars, type in **the planet mars** or just **mars**. It doesn't matter to the computer if you use capital letters or not.

```
Welcome to the library!
       You may search
             A   AUTHOR
             T   TITLE
             Y   AUTHOR/TITLE SEARCH
             S   SUBJECT
             W   WORDS in title
             C   CALL No.
             P   Repeat PREVIOUS Search
Choose one (A, T, Y, S, W, C, P):  S

For assistance, please ask any staff member.
```

```
Subject:   mars
Type as much or as little of the subject as
you want.
        for example    →  gold rush
        or             →  california
        or just        →  calif

If the subject is a person, type LAST NAME,
FIRST NAME.
        for example    →  washington, george
        or             →  washington
              ....then press the Return key.
```

Finding Information in Books, continued

④ Look at the subjects that come up. Choose the ones you want.

For information about the planet Mars, press ④ on your keyboard.

This number shows how many **entries** there are for a subject. An entry can be a book, video, or a cassette tape.

You can press other keys to go to more entries or to start a new search.

```
You searched for the SUBJECT: mars
78 SUBJECTS found, with 144 entries; SUBJECTS 1-8 are:

1 Mars.................................................................1 entry
2 Mars Mines and Mineral Resources Fiction ...............1 entry
3 Mars Planet ➜ See also narrower term SPACE FLIGHT TO ..........1 entry
4 Mars Planet........................................................16 entries
5 Mars Colonization Forecasting...............................1 entry
6 Mars Planet Drama ..............................................1 entry
7 Mars Planet Exploration ➜ See Related Subjects ...................2 entries
8 Mars Planet Exploration .......................................5 entries

Please type the NUMBER of the item you want to see, OR
F>Go FORWARD                    A>ANOTHER search by SUBJECT
W>Same search as WORD search    P>PRINT
N>NEW search                    +>ADDITIONAL options
Choose one [1-8, F, W, N, A, P, +]
```

⑤ Look at the entries that come up. Choose the ones you want.

Read the **titles** and **locations** to see which books are best for you. Press ③ to learn about *Are We Moving to Mars?*

```
You searched for the SUBJECT: mars
16 entries found, entries 1-8 are:

Mars Planet                                        LOCATION
1 Guide to Mars  ...........................ADULT NON-FICTION
2 The hunt for life on Mars ...................ADULT NON-FICTION
3 Are we moving to Mars? ...................YOUTH NON-FICTION
4 The inner planets: new light on the rocky worlds ...ADULT NON-FICTION
5 Mars and the inner planets ...................YOUTH NON-FICTION
6 Mars at last! .............................ADULT NON-FICTION
7 Mars beckons  ...........................ADULT NON-FICTION
8 Mars, the Red Planet ......................YOUTH NON-FICTION

Please type the NUMBER of the item you want to see, OR
F>Go FORWARD                    A>ANOTHER search by SUBJECT
R>RETURN to Browsing            P>PRINT
N>NEW search                    +>ADDITIONAL options
Choose one [1-8, F, R, N, A, P, +]
```

6 **Read the information about the entry you chose.**

Would you like to read this book? If so, use the information on the screen to help you find it in the library.

The **location** tells you if the book is in the Juvenile or Adult part of the library.

The **call number** will help you find the book on the shelves.

The **status** tells you if the book is currently in the library or if someone has checked it out.

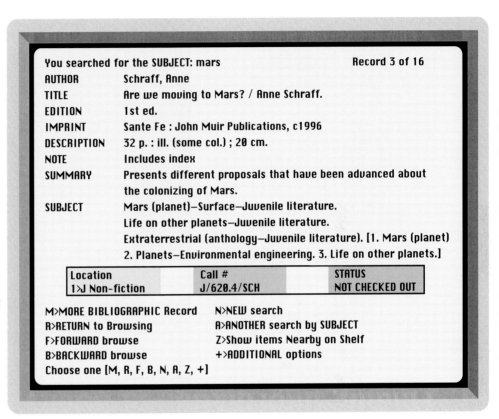

You searched for the SUBJECT: mars   Record 3 of 16
AUTHOR   Schraff, Anne
TITLE   Are we moving to Mars? / Anne Schraff.
EDITION   1st ed.
IMPRINT   Sante Fe : John Muir Publications, c1996
DESCRIPTION   32 p. : ill. (some col.) ; 20 cm.
NOTE   Includes index
SUMMARY   Presents different proposals that have been advanced about
                the colonizing of Mars.
SUBJECT   Mars (planet)–Surface–Juvenile literature.
                Life on other planets–Juvenile literature.
                Extraterrestrial (anthology–Juvenile literature). [1. Mars (planet)
                2. Planets–Environmental engineering. 3. Life on other planets.]

Location	Call #	STATUS
1>J Non-fiction	J/620.4/SCH	NOT CHECKED OUT

M>MORE BIBLIOGRAPHIC Record   N>NEW search
R>RETURN to Browsing   A>ANOTHER search by SUBJECT
F>FORWARD browse   Z>Show items Nearby on Shelf
B>BACKWARD browse   +>ADDITIONAL options
Choose one [M, R, F, B, N, A, Z, +]

7 **Record the call number or press 🅰 to print out the information. Use it to look up your book.**

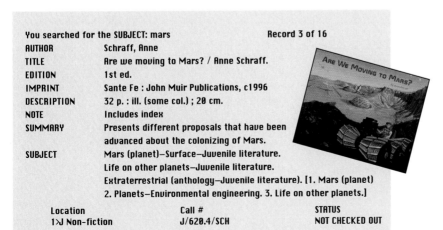

You searched for the SUBJECT: mars   Record 3 of 16
AUTHOR   Schraff, Anne
TITLE   Are we moving to Mars? / Anne Schraff.
EDITION   1st ed.
IMPRINT   Sante Fe : John Muir Publications, c1996
DESCRIPTION   32 p. : ill. (some col.) ; 20 cm.
NOTE   Includes index
SUMMARY   Presents different proposals that have been
                advanced about the colonizing of Mars.
SUBJECT   Mars (planet)–Surface–Juvenile literature.
                Life on other planets–Juvenile literature.
                Extraterrestrial (anthology–Juvenile literature). [1. Mars (planet)
                2. Planets–Environmental engineering. 3. Life on other planets.]

Location	Call #	STATUS
1>J Non-fiction	J/620.4/SCH	NOT CHECKED OUT

Parts of a Book

The pages at the front and back of a book help you know what the book is about and how it's organized. Look at these pages first to find out quickly if the book has the information you need for your research.

Title Page

The **title page** is usually the first page in a book.

It gives the **title** of the book and the **author**.

It tells the **publisher** and often names the cities where the publisher has offices.

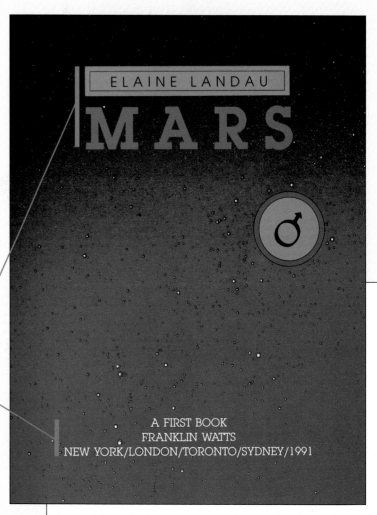

E L A I N E   L A N D A U

MARS

A FIRST BOOK
FRANKLIN WATTS
NEW YORK/LONDON/TORONTO/SYDNEY/1991

Copyright Page

The **copyright** (©) **page** gives the date when the book was published.

Check the **copyright** to see how current the information is.

Landau, Elaine.
 Mars / by Elaine Landau.
 p. cm. — (First book)
 Includes bibliographical references and index.
 Summary: Uses photographs and other recent findings to
describe the atmosphere and geographic features of Mars.
 ISBN 0-531-20012-4 (lib. bdg.)—ISBN 0-531-15773-3 (pbk.)
 1. Mars (Planet)—Juvenile literature. [1. Mars (Planet)]
I. Title. II. Series.
QB641.L36 1991
523.4'3—dc20   90-13097 CIP AC

Table of Contents

The **table of contents** is in the front of a book.
It shows how many chapters, or parts, are in a book.
It tells the page numbers where those chapters begin.

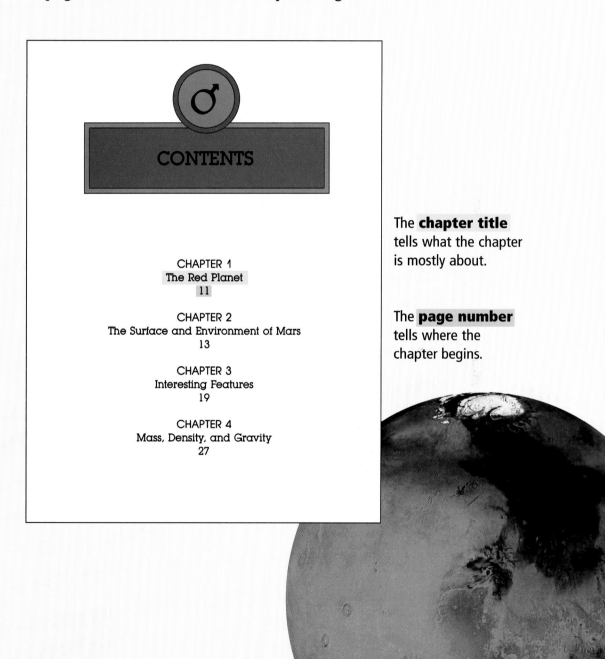

CONTENTS

The **chapter title**
tells what the chapter
is mostly about.

The **page number**
tells where the
chapter begins.

Index

The **index** is usually in the back of a book. It lists all the subjects in the book in alphabetical order. It gives page numbers where you can find information about those subjects.

Names of people are listed in alphabetical order by their last names.

Related details are often listed for a subject.

Sometimes page numbers are in *italics* to show that there is an illustration or photograph on that page.

Some indexes have words in **parentheses** that explain more about the subject. For example, these pages tell about the moons on Mars.

Glossary

A **glossary** is a short dictionary of important words used in the book. It appears at the back of the book. In a glossary, the words are listed in alphabetical order.

GLOSSARY

Astronomer—a scientist who studies the stars, planets, and all of outer space

Atmosphere—the various gases that surround a planet or other body in space

Axis—the invisible line through a planet's center around which it spins, or rotates

Crater—an irregular oval-shaped hole created through a collision with another object

Density—the compactness of materials

Equator—an imaginary circle around the center of the Earth, another planet, or the sun

Erosion—the process of being worn away by the action of wind, water, or other factors

55

Finding Information in Special Resources

Almanac

An **almanac** is a book filled with facts about things like inventions, animals, sports, science, movies, and TV. It's rewritten every year, so all the information is very up-to-date.

How to Use an Almanac

1 Look up your key words in the index.

2 Find those pages. Skim and scan to see if the pages have the information you are looking for.

PLANETS, STARS, AND SPACE TRAVEL

The SOLAR SYSTEM

Nine planets, including Earth, travel around the sun. These planets, together with the sun, form the **solar system**.

Look at the **titles** and **headings** for the main ideas.

THE SUN IS A STAR

Did you know that the sun is a star, like the other stars you see at night? However, astronomers have found that it is hotter, bigger, brighter, and more massive than most other stars. The diameter of the sun is 864,000 miles. The gravity of the sun is nearly 28 times the gravity of Earth.

How Hot Is the Sun? The temperature of the sun's surface is close to 11,000°F, and the inner core may reach temperatures near 35 million degrees! The sun provides enough light and heat energy to support all forms of life on our planet.

THE PLANETS ARE IN MOTION

Look at the **key words** and **details** in dark print.

The planets move around the sun along oval-shaped paths called **orbits.** Each planet travels in its own orbit. One complete path around the sun is called a **revolution.** Earth takes one year, or 365 days, to make one revolution around the sun. Planets that are farther away from the sun take longer. Some planets have one or more **moons.** A moon orbits a planet in much the same way that the planets orbit the sun.

Each planet also spins (or rotates) on its axis. An **axis** is an imaginary line running through the center of a planet. The time it takes for one rotation of the planet Earth on its axis equals one day. Below are some facts about the planets and the symbol for each planet.

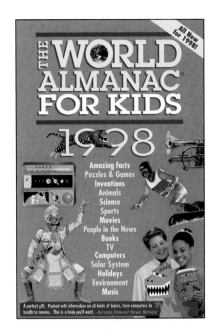

③ If the information seems useful for your research, read the pages carefully and take notes.

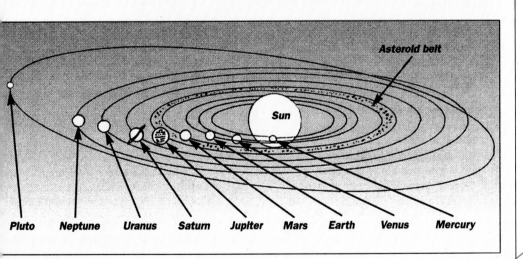

PLANETS, STARS, AND SPACE TRAVEL

Asteroid belt

Sun

Pluto | Neptune | Uranus | Saturn | Jupiter | Mars | Earth | Venus | Mercury

Sometimes **tables**, **lists**, and **diagrams** will give useful information for your report.

3. EARTH
Average distance from the sun:
93 million miles
Diameter: 7,926 miles
Time to revolve around the sun:
365 ¼ days
Time to rotate on its axis:
23 hours, 56 minutes, 4.1 seconds
Number of moons: 1

DID YOU KNOW? Earth's path around the sun is nearly 600 million miles long. To make the trip in one year, Earth travels more than 66,000 miles per hour.

4. MARS
Average distance from the sun:
142 million miles
Diameter: 4,220 miles
Time to revolve around the sun:
687 days
Time to rotate on its axis:
24 hours, 37 minutes, 26 seconds
Number of moons: 2

DID YOU KNOW? Mars is the home of Olympus Mons, the largest volcano found in the solar system. It stands about 17 miles high, with a crater 50 miles wide.

Special features like this one may give interesting facts.

Look It Up! 245

Atlas and Globe

An **atlas** is a book of maps. A **globe** is a round map that shows the curve of the earth.

Physical Map

A **physical map** shows features of a place like rivers, forests, mountains, lowlands, coastlines, or oceans.

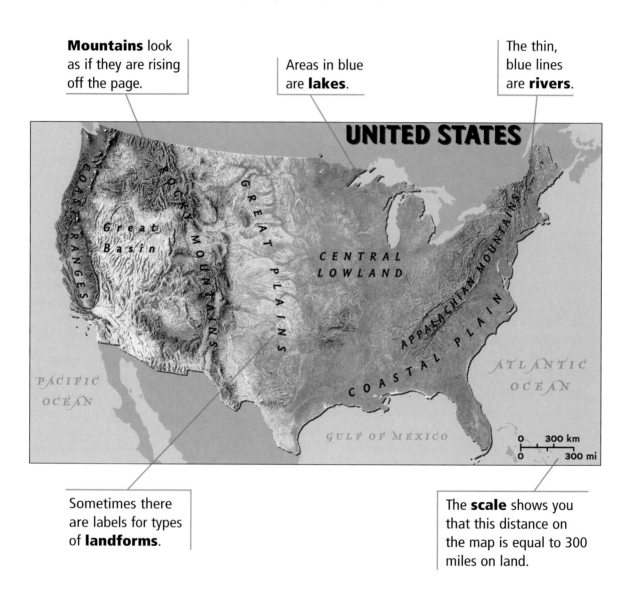

Mountains look as if they are rising off the page.

Areas in blue are **lakes**.

The thin, blue lines are **rivers**.

Sometimes there are labels for types of **landforms**.

The **scale** shows you that this distance on the map is equal to 300 miles on land.

Political Map

A **political map** shows the boundaries between countries and states. It also shows the capitals and other major cities.

How to Find a Place on a Political Map

1 **Use alphabetical order to look up the name of the place in the index.**

In the index, you'll find the **page number** for the map. You might also find a special code, like **L-6** you find the exact **location** of the place on the map.

Index

Bristol	H-5	11
Brunswick	K-6	11
Cape Canaveral	L-6	11
Cape Charles	H-8	11
Cape Fear	J-8	11
Cape Fear R.	I-7	11

2 **Look up the map and locate the place.**

First turn to the page noted in the index. Then use the code **L-6** to find the place:

- Look for **L** on the side of the map.

Each letter is between two lines of **latitude**. Latitude lines are lines that go from east to west ⟷ around the earth.

- Look for **6** along the top or bottom of the map

Each number is between two lines of **longitude**. Longitude lines are lines that go from north to south. ⭥

- Find the section where the lettered and numbered spaces meet. Then look for the name of the place.

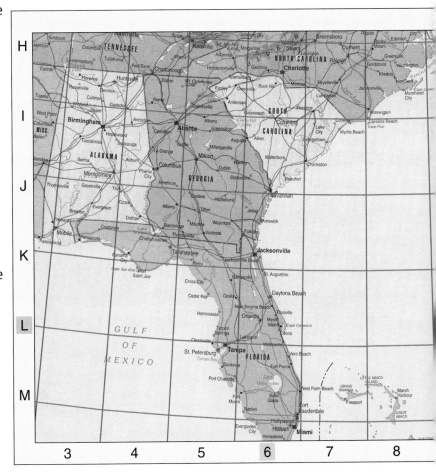

Historical Map

A **historical map** shows when and where certain events happened.

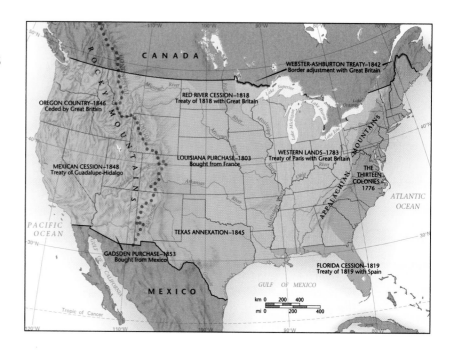

Product Map

A **product map** uses pictures and symbols to show where products come from.

A **compass rose** shows which directions are **north**, **south**, **east**, and **west** on the map.

A **legend** shows what each picture stands for.

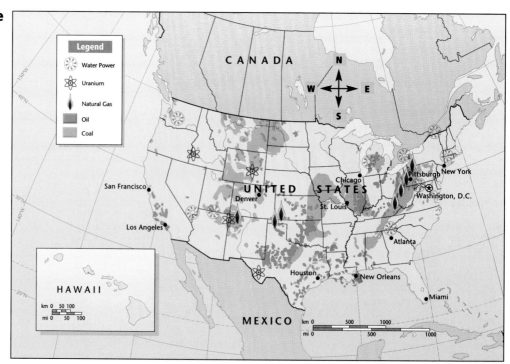

Globe

A **globe** is a small model of the Earth. A globe has a round shape like the Earth does. It gives a better picture of Earth than a flat map does.

This is the **equator**. The equator is an imaginary line around the middle of the Earth. It divides the Earth into two parts, or **hemispheres**.

The **North Pole** is the point on Earth that is the farthest north.

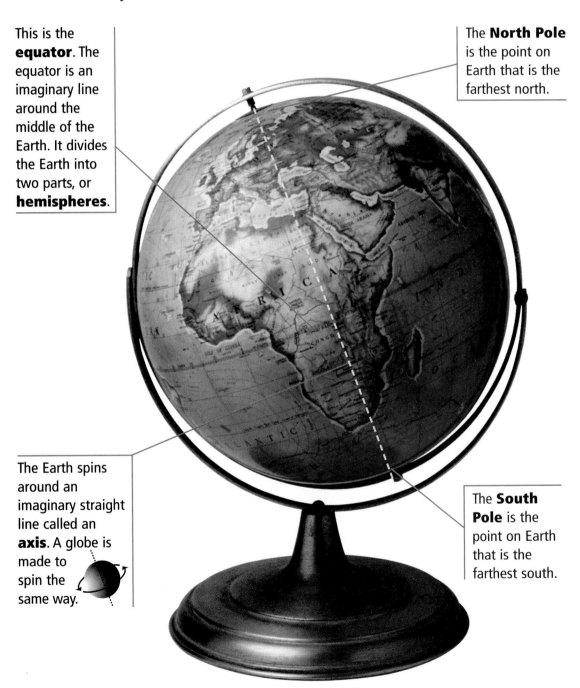

The Earth spins around an imaginary straight line called an **axis**. A globe is made to spin the same way.

The **South Pole** is the point on Earth that is the farthest south.

Dictionary

A **dictionary** is a book filled with all kinds of information about words. It lists the words in alphabetical order from A to Z.

How to Look Up a Word

1 **Look at the beginning letter of your word and turn to the part of the dictionary it would be in.**

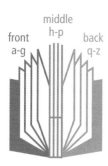

middle
h-p
front
a-g
back
q-z

Suppose you want to look up *spacesuit*. Words that begin with *S* are in the back part of a dictionary.

 southwards ➤ **space shuttle**

ward slope of the mountain. Adjective.
south·ward (south'wərd) *adverb; adjective.*
southwards Another spelling of the adverb southward: *They drove* **southwards.** **south·wards** (south'wərdz) *adverb.*
southwest 1. The direction halfway between south and west. 2. The point of the compass showing this direction. 3. A region or place in this direction. 4. **the Southwest.** The region in the south and west of the United States. *Noun.*
○ 1. Toward or in the southwest: *the southwest corner of the street.* 2. Coming from the southwest: *a southwest wind. Adjective.*
○ Toward the southwest: *The ship sailed southwest. Adverb.*
south·west (south'west') *noun; adjective; adverb.*
souvenir Something kept because it reminds one of a person, place, or event: *I bought a pennant as a souvenir of the baseball game.* **sou·ve·nir** (sü'və nîr' *or* sü'və nîr') *noun, plural* **souvenirs.**
sovereign A king or queen. *Noun.*
○ 1. Having the greatest power or highest rank or authority: *The king and queen were the sovereign rulers of the country.* 2. Not controlled by others; independent: *Mexico is a sovereign nation. Adjective.*
sov·er·eign (sov'ər ən *or* sov'rən) *noun, plural* **sovereigns;** *adjective.*
Soviet Union Formerly, a large country in eastern Europe and northern Asia. It was composed of 15 republics and was also called the U.S.S.R. The

largest and most important of the 15 republics was Russia.
sow[1] 1. To scatter seeds over the ground; plant: *The farmer will sow corn in this field.* 2. To spread or scatter: *The clown sowed happiness among the children.*
Other words that sound like this are **sew** and **so.**
sow (sō) *verb,* **sowed, sown** *or* **sowed, sowing.**
sow[2] An adult female pig. **sow** (sou) *noun, plural* **sows.**
soybean A seed rich in oil and protein and used as food. Soybeans grow in pods on bushy plants. **soy·bean** (soi'bēn') *noun, plural* **soybeans.**
space 1. The area in which the whole universe exists. It has no limits. The planet earth is in space. 2. The region beyond the earth's atmosphere; outer space: *The rocket was launched into space.* 3. A distance or area between things: *There is not much space between our house and theirs.* 4. An area reserved or available for some purpose: *a parking space.* 5. A period of time: *Both jets landed in the space of ten minutes. Noun.*
○ To put space in between: *The architect spaced the houses far apart. Verb.*
space (spās) *noun, plural* **spaces;** *verb,* **spaced, spacing.**
spacecraft A vehicle used for flight in outer space. This is also called a spaceship. **space·craft** (spās'kraft') *noun, plural* **spacecraft.**
space shuttle A spacecraft that carries a crew into space and returns to land on earth. The same

space shuttle

flight deck and crew's quarters — orbiter
— external fuel tank
— tank for liquid oxygen
remote-control arm
container for experiments
— payload bay
— solid-rocket booster
rudder
— cargo bay door
booster nozzle
— satellite inside protective cocoon
— wing

2 **Use the guide words to help you find the page your word is on.**

3 **Look down the columns to find your entry word.**

space shuttle can be used again. A space shuttle is also called a shuttle.

space station A spaceship that orbits around the earth like a satellite and on which a crew can live for long periods of time.

spacesuit Special clothing worn by an astronaut in space. A spacesuit covers an astronaut's entire body and has equipment to help the astronaut breathe. **space·suit** (spās′süt′) *noun, plural* **spacesuits.**

Astronauts take spacewalks to repair satellites and vehicles.

spacewalk A period of activity during which an astronaut in space is outside a spacecraft. **space·walk** (spās′wôk′) *noun, plural* **spacewalks.**

spacious Having a lot of space or room; roomy; large. —**spa·cious** *adjective* —**spaciousness** *noun.*

spade¹ A tool used for digging. It has a long handle and a flat blade that can be pressed into the ground with the foot. *Noun.*
○ To dig with a spade: *We spaded the garden and then raked it. Verb.*
spade (spād) *noun, plural* **spades;** *verb,* **spaded, spading.**

spade² 1. A playing card marked with one or more figures shaped like this. 2. **spades.** The suit of cards marked with this figure. **spade** (spād) *noun, plural* **spades.**

spaghetti A kind of pasta that looks like long,

thin strings. It is made of a mixture of flour and water. **spa·ghet·ti** (spə get′ē) *noun.*

> ### WORD HISTORY
> The word spaghetti comes from an Italian word meaning "strings" or "little cords." Spaghetti looks a bit like strings.

Spain A country in southwest Europe. **Spain** (spān) *noun.*

spamming The sending of the same message to large numbers of e-mail addresses or to many newsgroups at the same time. Spamming is often thought of as impolite behavior on the Internet. **spam·ming** (spa′ming) *noun.*

span 1. The distance or part between two supports: *The span of that bridge is very long.* 2. The full reach or length of anything: *Some people accomplish a great deal in the span of their lives. Noun.*
○ To extend over or across. *Verb.*
span (span) *noun, plural* **spans;** *verb,* **spanned, spanning.**

This bridge spans a wide river.

spaniel Any of various dogs of small to medium size with long, drooping ears, a silky, wavy coat, and short legs. The larger types are used in hunting. **span·iel** (span′yəl) *noun, plural* **spaniels.**

Spanish 1. The people of Spain. The word *Spanish* in this sense is used with a plural verb. 2. The language spoken in Spain. It is also spoken in many countries south of the United States as well as in parts of the U.S. *Noun.*
○ Of or having to do with Spain, its people, or the Spanish language. *Adjective.*
Span·ish (span′ish) *noun; adjective.*

The first **guide word** is *space station* because that word comes first on the page. The second guide word is *Spanish* because that word comes last. Your word will be on the page if it comes between the two guide words in alphabetical order.

Look at the **entry word** *spacesuit.* It's in alphabetical order on the page.

Look It Up! 251

Dictionary, continued

Each **entry** gives you important information about the word.

The **definition** tells you what the word means. If a word has more than one meaning, the definitions are numbered.

An entry may also give the **plural form** or **verb forms** of the word and how to spell them.

...ch in oil... ...and used as food. Soybeans grow in pods on bushy plants.
soy·bean (soi′bēn′) *noun, plural* **soybeans**.

space 1. The area in which the whole universe exists. It has no limits. The planet earth is in space. 2. The region beyond the earth's atmosphere; outer space: *The rocket was launched into space.* 3. A distance or area between things: *There is not much* **space** *between our house and theirs.*
4. An area reserved or available for some purpose: *a parking* **space**. 5. A period of time: *Both jets landed in the* **space** *of ten minutes.* Noun.
○ To put space in between: *The architect spaced the houses far apart.* Verb.
space (spās) *noun, plural* **spaces**; *verb,* **spaced, spacing**.

spacecraft A vehicle used for flight in outer space. This is also called a spaceship.
space·craft (spās′kraft′) *noun, plural* **spacecraft**.

space shuttle A spacecraft that carries a crew ...space and...rns to land on earth. The sa...

Some entries have a **sample sentence** to help you know how to use the word.

This information tells you **how to pronounce** the word. You can look up the marks in the **pronunciation key**. The mark **ā** tells you to say the **a** the same way you would say the **a** in **āpe**. The mark **′** tells you to emphasize the first part of the word, **space**.

Pronunciation Key

PRONUNCIATION KEY:													
at	āpe	fär	câre	end	mē	it	īce	pierce	hot	ōld	sông	fôrk
oil	out	up	ūse	rüle	pull	tûrn	chin	sing	shop	thin	this	

hw in white; zh in treasure. The symbol ə stands for the unstressed vowel sound in about, taken, pencil, lemon, and circus.

All entries include words like *noun*, or its abbreviation *n*, that tell the word's **part of speech**. A word's part of speech shows how the word can be used in a sentence.

Abbreviations for the parts of speech are:

adj   adjective
adv   adverb
conj   conjunction
interj   interjection
n   noun
prep   preposition
pron   pronoun
v   verb

for long periods of time.

spacesuit Special clothing worn by an astronaut in space. A spacesuit covers an astronaut's entire body and has equipment to help the astronaut breathe. **space·suit** (spās′süt′) *noun, plural* **spacesuits.**

Astronauts take spacewalks to repair satellites and vehicles.

spacewalk A period of activity during which an astronaut in space is outside a spacecraft. **space·walk** (spās′wôk′) *noun, plural* **spacewalks.**

spacious Having a lot of space or room; roomy; large. —**spa·cious** *adjective* —**spaciousness**

Some entries have a **picture** and a **caption**. They give you more information about a word and its meaning.

Encyclopedia

An **encyclopedia** is a set of books. Each book is called a **volume**. Each volume has articles that give facts about many different topics. The volumes and articles in an encyclopedia are arranged in alphabetical order.

How to Find Information in an Encyclopedia

1 **Find the correct volume.**

What is the first letter of the word you plan to look up? Find the volume that has articles beginning with that letter.

An article about **M**ars would be in this volume.

This is where you would find information about **sp**ace travel.

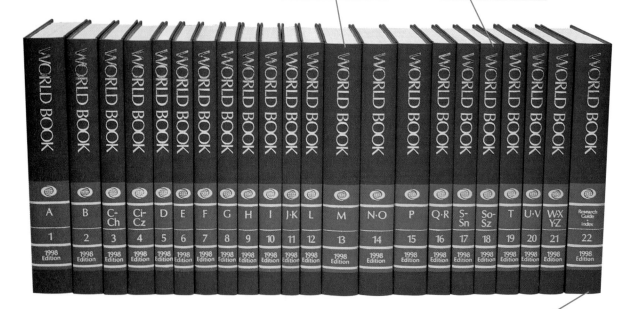

Most encyclopedias have a volume called an **Index**. The index lists other related subjects to look up.

2 Use alphabetical order to find the article.

Flip through the pages looking just at the **guide words** to get to the page where the article appears. Then find the article on the page.

3 Skim and scan the article to see if it has the information you need.

Mars's surface features are visible in a photograph taken from the earth, *left.* The earth's atmosphere makes the picture blurry. A series of canyons called the Valles Marineris (Mariner Valleys) make up the diagonal landform in the photo at the right, taken by the U.S. Viking 1 space probe. This landform is more than 2,500 miles (4,000 kilometers) long.

This is an **entry word**. It is the title of the article.

Mars is the only planet whose surface can be seen in detail from the earth. It is reddish in color, and was named Mars after the bloody-red god of war of the ancient Romans. Mars is the only planet other than the earth to produce evidence suggesting that it was once the home of living creatures. However, there is no evidence that life now exists on Mars.

Mars is the fourth closest planet to the sun, and the next planet beyond the earth. Its mean distance from the sun is 141,600,000 miles (227,900,000 kilometers), compared with about 93,000,000 miles (150,000,000 kilometers) for the earth. At its closest approach to the earth, Mars is 34,600,000 miles (55,700,000 kilometers) away. Venus is the only planet in the solar system that comes closer to the earth.

The diameter of Mars is 4,223 miles (6,796 kilometers), a little over half that of the earth. Pluto and Mercury are the only planets smaller than Mars.

Headings tell what each section in the article is about.

Orbit and rotation

Mars travels around the sun in an *elliptical* (oval-shaped) orbit. Its distance from the sun varies from about 154,800,000 miles (249,200,000 kilometers) at its farthest point, to about 128,400,000 miles (206,600,000 kilometers) at its closest point. Mars takes about 687 earth-days to go around the sun.

As Mars orbits the sun, it spins on its *axis,* an imaginary line through its center. Mars's axis is not *perpendicular* (at an angle of 90°) to its path around the sun. The axis tilts at an angle of about 24° from the perpendicular position. For an illustration of the tilt of an axis, see **Planet** (The axes of the planets). Mars rotates once every 24 hours and 37 minutes. The earth rotates once every 23 hours and 56 minutes.

The contributor of this article is Hyron Spinrad, Professor of Astronomy at the University of California, Berkeley.

Mars at a glance

Mars, shown in blue in the diagram, is the next planet beyond the earth. The ancient symbol for Mars, *right,* is still used today.

Distance from the sun: *Shortest*—128,600,000 miles (206,600,000 kilometers); *Greatest*—154,800,000 miles (249,200,000 kilometers); *Mean*—141,600,000 miles (227,900,000 kilometers).

Distance from the earth: *Shortest*—34,600,000 miles (55,700,000 kilometers); *Greatest*—248,000,000 miles (399,000,000 kilometers).

Diameter: 4,223 miles (6,796 kilometers).

Length of year: About 1 earth-year and $10\frac{1}{2}$ months.

Rotation period: 24 hours and 37 minutes.

Temperature: −225 to 63 °F (−143 to 17 °C).

Atmosphere: Carbon dioxide, nitrogen, argon, oxygen, carbon monoxide, neon, krypton, xenon, and water vapor.

Number of satellites: 2.

4 If the article has the information you need, read it and take notes.

Telephone Directory

Sometimes you need to make a phone call to set up an interview or to get information for a report. You can find the phone numbers you need in the **telephone directory**, or phone book.

White Pages

In the **white pages** you'll find telephone numbers for people and businesses. Names for people are listed in alphabetical order by their last names. Businesses are listed in alphabetical order by the first important word in their name.

Guide words show the first name and last name included on the page.

Some businesses will pay to have their names printed in **larger type**. The larger type makes the name stand out from the rest.

SANTOS–SETA

Santos Sally	555-1273
Santoso Rini	555-8924
Sarma Karan	555-5639
Sarma Sanjay	555-0956
Search for Extraterrestrial Intelligence (SETI)	
75 Atlantic	555-4563
Seguin G	555-5629
Serrano Aaron	555-1870
Serrano Anthony 51 Porter	555-0446
Serrano E 62 Falconcrest	555-0830
Serrano Nera 160 Devon	555-4974
Serrano Q	555-0223
Serre A	555-3856
Serre Francis	555-3847

SERVICE CENTER

199 Townsend	555-5833
Service Deli 111 East St	555-2446
Seta Elizabeth 1462 Zamora	555-9877

Sometimes people or businesses list their **addresses** as well as their telephone number.

Yellow Pages

The **yellow pages** have names and telephone numbers for companies or businesses in your area.

The **guide words** name the kinds of businesses listed on the page in alphabetical order.

Most yellow pages have **guide letters** to help you find a section easily.

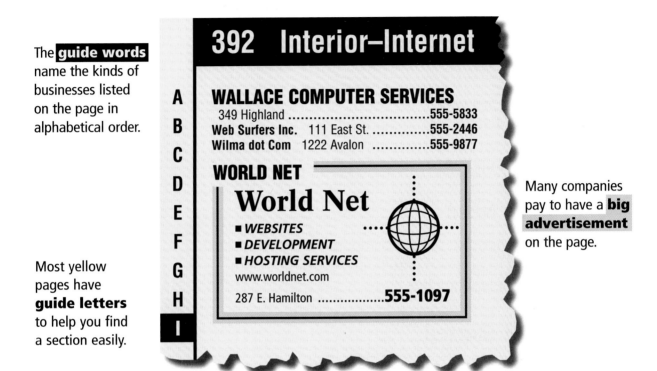

392 Interior–Internet

A
B
C
D
E
F
G
H
I

WALLACE COMPUTER SERVICES
349 Highland **555-5833**
Web Surfers Inc.   111 East St. **555-2446**
Wilma dot Com   1222 Avalon **555-9877**

WORLD NET

World Net
■ *WEBSITES*
■ *DEVELOPMENT*
■ *HOSTING SERVICES*
www.worldnet.com
287 E. Hamilton **555-1097**

Many companies pay to have a **big advertisement** on the page.

Special Sections

Many telephone directories also have special sections that give information such as

- emergency telephone numbers for the fire and police department

- guidelines for first aid

- names and telephone numbers for government officials

- museums, parks, and other places to visit.

Look in the front pages of the directory to find out more about these special sections.

3. Customer Guide

Emergency Telephone Numbers ....**Section A**
Calling and Service Information ....**Section B**
First Aid and Survival Guide ....**Section C**
Páginas en Español ....**Section D**
Government Offices (Federal and State) ..**Section D**
Downtown Attractions ....**Section E**
Turn to the first page in each section for a complete table of contents.

Finding Information on the Internet

The **Internet** is an international network, or connection, of computers that share information with one another. The **World Wide Web** allows you to find, read, go through, and organize information. The Internet is like a giant library, and the World Wide Web is everything in the library including the books, the librarian, and the computer catalog.

The Internet is a *fast* way to get the most current information about your topic! You'll find resources like encyclopedias and dictionaries on the Internet and amazing pictures, movies, and sounds.

What You'll Need

To use the Internet, you need a computer with software that allows you to access it. You'll also need a modem connected to a telephone line.

How to Get Started

You can search on the Internet in many different ways. In fact, you'll probably find something new whenever you search on it. Don't be afraid to try something—you never know what you'll find!

Check with your teacher for how to access the Internet from your school. Usually you can just double click on the **icon**, or picture, to get access to the Internet and you're on your way!

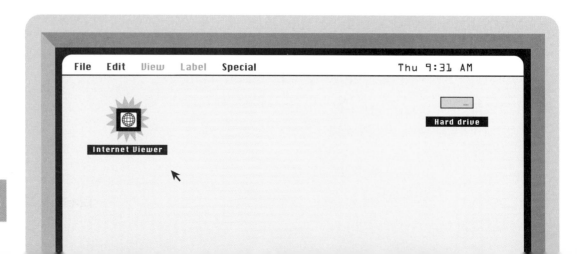

Doing the Research

Once the search page comes up, you can begin the research process. Just follow these steps.

1 **Type your subject in the search box and then click on the Search button.**

You'll always see a **toolbar** like this one at the top of the screen. Click on the pictures to do things like print the page.

This is where you type in your **subject**.

Try different ways to type in your subject. You'll get different results!

■ If you type in **Mars**, you'll see all the sites that have the word *Mars* in them. This may give you too many categories and sites to look through!

■ If you type in **"life on Mars"** you'll see all the sites with the exact phrase, or group of words, *life on Mars*.

■ If you type in **+Mars +life** you'll see all the sites with the words *Mars* and *life* in them.

Finding Information on the Internet, continued

② **Read the search results.**

All underlined, colored words are **links**, or connections, to other sites. They help you get from page to page quickly.

If you want to go directly to a **web page**, click on a **site**.

Click on a **category** to see more options for information related to your topic.

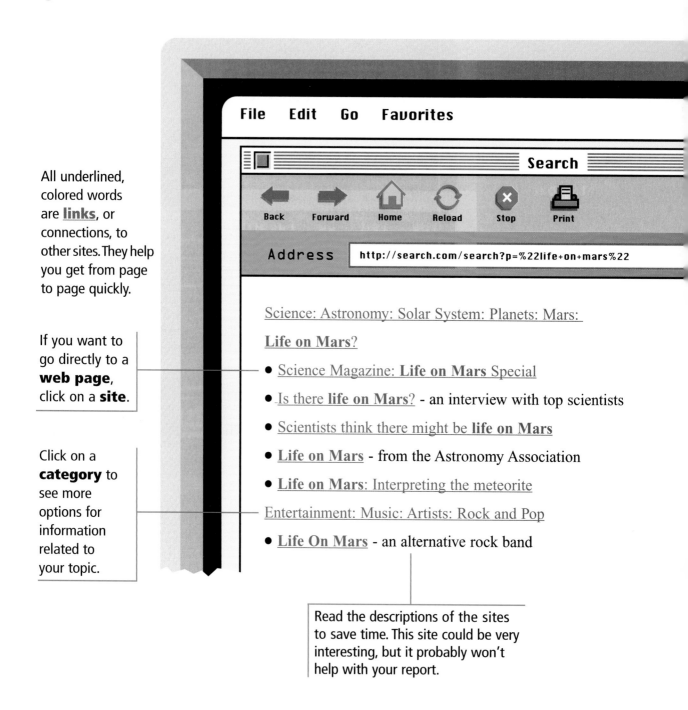

File   Edit   Go   Favorites

Search

Back   Forward   Home   Reload   Stop   Print

Address   http://search.com/search?p=%22life+on+mars%22

Science: Astronomy: Solar System: Planets: Mars:

Life on Mars?

● Science Magazine: **Life on Mars** Special

● Is there **life on Mars**? - an interview with top scientists

● Scientists think there might be **life on Mars**

● **Life on Mars** - from the Astronomy Association

● **Life on Mars**: Interpreting the meteorite

Entertainment: Music: Artists: Rock and Pop

● **Life On Mars** - an alternative rock band

Read the descriptions of the sites to save time. This site could be very interesting, but it probably won't help with your report.

③ Select a site, and read the article.

You might want to pick a new site or start a new search. If so, click on the **Back** arrow to go back a page to the search results.

If you want to go to another web page, click on a **link**.

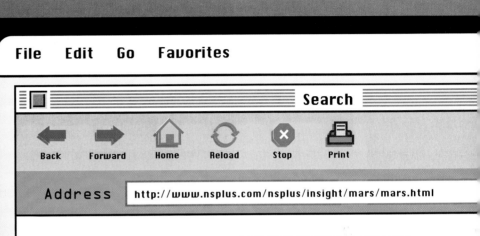

File   Edit   Go   Favorites

Search

Back   Forward   Home   Reload   Stop   Print

Address   http://www.nsplus.com/nsplus/insight/mars/mars.html

Mars

In this special section we bring you all the stories on the Mars probe landing, from New Scientist's award-winning team of reporters. We also offer an extensive archive of articles on NASA's earlier claim that Mars once supported life and a look at the search for life in space, as well as numerous web links. From the August 1996 heady excitement of that announcement--"life on Mars"--to the disappointing revelation-- "no, probably not", Planet Science was there.

MORE ON MARS:

● **Mission to Mars makes do with robots**
THE US has formally abandoned its goal of landing astronauts on Mars by 2019. Instead, the new national space policy unveiled last week commits the nation to a permanent robot presence on the Red Planet starting no later than 2000. Human exploration might come later, depending on what the robots find.

MARS LATEST:

13 DEC 97: Hop, skip and jump
A little robot in a lab in Arizona is preparing to take several giant leaps for robotkind. If it reaches Mars in the next century, as its developers hope, it will produce its own fuel and be able to fly, hop and hover over the surface of the Red Planet.

12 NOV 97: In the dark
If life developed on ancient Mars, it got going in almost complete darkness, say scientists in the US and France. The newborn planet was shrouded in dense clouds of frozen carbon dioxide which acted like a mirror, they say, reflecting up to 95 percent of incident lighting. "In its early days, Mars was the white planet rather than the Red Planet".

④ Print the article if it is helpful for your research.
Later on, you can use the article to take notes.

Locating More Resources

If you already know the **URL** (Uniform Resource Locator), or address, of a Web site, you can type it in the address box at the top of the screen.

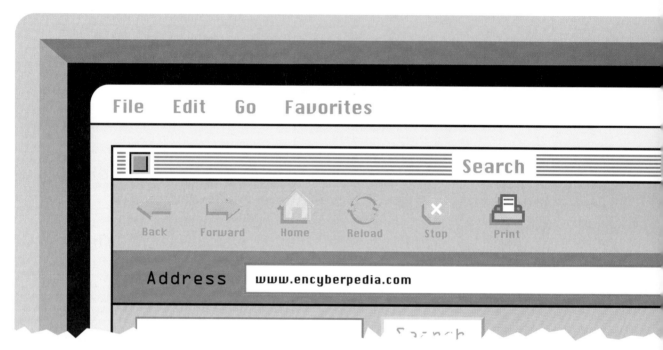

Here are a few good references to try. Because the Internet is always changing, these addresses might change. If you can't find a site, try searching by using its name.

Encyberpedia (Encyclopedia)
www.encyberpedia.com

Encyclopedia Britannica
www.eb.com

Grolier Encyclopedia
www.grolier.com

Kids Web Digital Library
www.npac.syr.edu/textbook/kidsweb/

Merriam Webster Dictionary
www.m-w.com

Old Farmer's Almanac
www.almanac.com

One Look Dictionary
www.onelook.com

The Virtual Reference Desk
thorplus.lib.purdue.edu/reference/

Dateline U.S.A.™

January

New Year's Day

On the Roman calendar, January 1 is the first day of the calendar year.

■ At the beginning of the new year, people often make **resolutions**, or promises to themselves, to stop bad habits like eating too much and to start good habits like exercising. On New Year's Day, people start trying to make their resolutions come true.

■ Many people watch parades like the Tournament of Roses Parade in Pasadena, California, or football games like the Cotton Bowl in Texas.

Martin Luther King, Jr., Day

The third Monday in January honors Martin Luther King, Jr., a courageous American. People celebrate by remembering his message of peace and what he did for our country.

■ Martin Luther King, Jr., was a minister who helped the sick and needy. He was a leader promoting **nonviolence** during the Civil Rights movement. He and many others helped end laws that were **discriminatory**, or unfair, because they treated different groups of people in different ways.

■ In the summer of 1963, Martin Luther King, Jr., gave a famous speech called "I Have a Dream." He said that his dream was for people to judge each other by the "content of their character." He thought people should see each other as individuals and not as groups separated by the color of their skin.

Inauguration Day

Every four years a president is elected to be the leader of the United States. The president's term officially begins on January 20. On that day, people across the nation listen to speeches by the president and invited guests. This ceremony is called an **inauguration**.

The president of the United States lives in the White House.

Who has been president of the United States?

President		Term
1	George Washington	1789–1797
2	John Adams	1797–1801
3	Thomas Jefferson	1801–1809
4	James Madison	1809–1817
5	James Monroe	1817–1825
6	John Quincy Adams	1825–1829
7	Andrew Jackson	1829–1837
8	Martin Van Buren	1837–1841
9	William H. Harrison	1841
10	John Tyler	1841–1845
11	James Knox Polk	1845–1849
12	Zachary Taylor	1849–1850
13	Millard Fillmore	1850–1853
14	Franklin Pierce	1853–1857
15	James Buchanan	1857–1861
16	Abraham Lincoln	1861–1865
17	Andrew Johnson	1865–1869
18	Ulysses S. Grant	1869–1877
19	Rutherford B. Hayes	1877–1881
20	James A. Garfield	1881
21	Chester A. Arthur	1881–1885
22	Grover Cleveland	1885–1889
23	Benjamin Harrison	1889–1893

President		Term
24	Grover Cleveland	1893–1897
25	William McKinley	1897–1901
26	Theodore Roosevelt	1901–1909
27	William Howard Taft	1909–1913
28	Woodrow Wilson	1913–1921
29	Warren G. Harding	1921–1923
30	Calvin Coolidge	1923–1929
31	Herbert Hoover	1929–1933
32	Franklin D. Roosevelt	1933–1945
33	Harry S. Truman	1945–1953
34	Dwight D. Eisenhower	1953–1961
35	John F. Kennedy	1961–1963
36	Lyndon B. Johnson	1963–1969
37	Richard M. Nixon	1969–1974
38	Gerald R. Ford	1974–1977
39	Jimmy Carter	1977–1981
40	Ronald Reagan	1981–1989
41	George Bush	1989–1993
42	William Jefferson Clinton	1993–

Chinese New Year

Many Americans celebrate the Chinese New Year, which begins in late January or early February.

- For about two weeks, families wish each other luck, health, happiness, and wealth for the coming year.

- During the celebrations, people set off fireworks and have feasts. They march in big parades, sometimes under a lion's head or a long, colorful dragon. It takes a lot of people to move a dragon down the street!

- The new year is a time of gift-giving, too. Adults give children red envelopes with money inside for good luck.

Where is one of the biggest
Chinese New Year parades in the U.S.?

San Francisco

This is Chinatown in San Francisco, California. It has the largest Chinese community in the United States. Thousands of people go to see the Chinese New Year parade every year.

Tet

Tet is another new year's celebration. It occurs on the first three days of the Vietnamese calendar, usually in late January or early February.

- The first visitor to a home on the first morning of Tet is important. If the visitor is kind and honest, the family will have good fortune for the rest of the year.

- Red is considered to be a lucky color, so people eat red food, like dyed watermelon seeds which stain their hands and mouth.

- People also hang banners on their doors that have greetings like "compliments of the season."

Groundhog Day

An old legend says that a groundhog comes up from its winter nest on February 2.

- If the groundhog sees its own shadow, it means that there will be six more weeks of winter.

- If the groundhog does not see its shadow, it means that spring is about to begin.

Valentine's Day

- On February 14, people exchange cards, or valentines, to show they care about each other.

- Many valentines are decorated with red hearts and have messages written on them. Some show Cupid, a boy with wings, whose arrows make people fall in love.

Be My Valentine

Black History Month

African Americans have made significant contributions in many areas from science and mathematics to literature and the fine arts. In the month of February, we recognize their contributions and learn more about the experiences of African Americans throughout the history of the United States.

Who are some courageous African Americans who fought for freedom and civil rights in the U.S.?

1841

Frederick Douglass spoke out against slavery.

Until the 1860s, African Americans were slaves, forced to work without pay. Frederick Douglass was born a slave but escaped to New England when he was 21. There Douglass began writing and speaking against slavery. He fought long and hard to stop slavery and to change the way African Americans were treated. ★

1850

Harriet Tubman helped slaves become free.

Harriet Tubman helped over 300 slaves leave the South for freedom in the North. She was a leader for the "Underground Railroad," a group of people who helped slaves by hiding them and moving them north in farm wagons. ★

1861–1865

African Americans fought in the Civil War.

During the Civil War, the Union army fought for the North who wanted to end slavery. About 180,000 African Americans fought with the Union army even though it did not treat them as equals and forced them to serve in all-black regiments. These regiments fought bravely and were important to winning the war and ending slavery. ★

★ **1840s**   ★ **1850s**   ★ **1860s**

My People

The night is beautiful,
So the faces of my people.

The stars are beautiful,
So the eyes of my people.

Beautiful, also, is the sun.
Beautiful, also, are the souls of my people.

— *Langston Hughes*

1947
Jackie Robinson joined the Brooklyn Dodgers.

Although many African Americans were playing baseball in the 1940s, they had to play in leagues that were separate from the major leagues. In 1947, Jackie Robinson became the first African American to play on a modern American major league team, the Brooklyn Dodgers. From then on, blacks and whites were able to play baseball in the same leagues. ★

1955
Rosa Parks inspired the Civil Rights movement.

Rosa Parks refused to give up her seat on a bus to a white person. Her protest inspired others to act against unfair laws. This was one event that helped get the Civil Rights movement started. **Civil rights** means that all people should be treated equally under the law. ★

1967
Thurgood Marshall joined the Supreme Court.

Thurgood Marshall presented the argument for **desegregation** of the public schools. Desegregation meant that African American students could go to the same schools as white children. Later, Marshall became the first African American Supreme Court justice. ★

★**1940s**   ★**1950s**   ★**1960s**

Presidents' Day

On the third Monday in February, Americans honor two great American presidents.

■ **George Washington** became the first president of the United States in 1789. He is called the "Father of Our Country."

■ **Abraham Lincoln,** the sixteenth president, was a great leader during difficult times. He helped to end the Civil War and slavery.

Both presidents were important leaders in the government of the United States.

How does the United States government work?

The Constitution of the United States of America

After the Revolutionary War, the American people needed a plan to help them organize the new government.

In 1787 several important leaders approved the United States **Constitution**. The Constitution is a written document that tells what the main laws of the country are and the powers and duties of each part of the government. It includes the **Bill of Rights** which protects the rights and freedoms of every citizen, such as freedom of religion, freedom of speech, and freedom of the press.

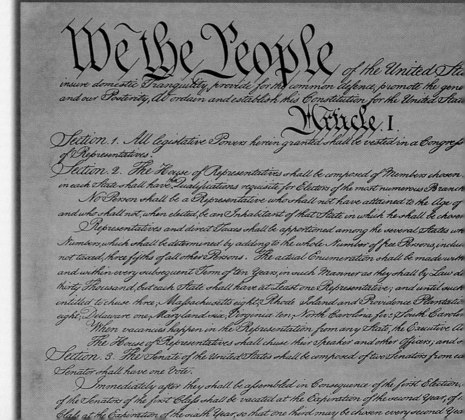

The Three Branches of Our Government

Executive Branch

People who work in the executive branch make sure that the laws of the country are obeyed. The president, the vice president, and other advisors to the president are the leaders in this branch of the government.

Legislative Branch

People who work in this branch write and pass new laws. This branch, also known as Congress, is made up of two parts: the House of Representatives and the Senate. Each state elects Representatives and Senators to work in Congress.

Judicial Branch

In the judicial branch, judges and justices listen to cases in court. They decide what the laws mean and if the laws are in agreement with the Constitution. The most important court is the United States Supreme Court.

U.S. Government

Saint Patrick's Day

On March 17, be sure to wear green or you might get pinched! Wearing green is a tradition on Saint Patrick's Day. You might also see lots of green decorations like three-leaf clovers called shamrocks and tiny elves called leprechauns.

This holiday began as a Catholic holiday in Ireland, a country with lots of green hills and valleys. It was a special day to honor the good works of a man named Saint Patrick. When Irish immigrants came to live in the United States in the 1700s, they brought this tradition with them and it has been celebrated here ever since.

What other groups of people have immigrated to the United States?

When	Who	About How Many
1840–1860	Irish	1,500,000
1840–1890	Germans	4,000,000
1870–1910	Danes, Norwegians, and Swedes	1,500,000
1880–1930	Eastern Europeans	3,500,000
	Austrians, Czechs, Hungarians, and Slovaks	4,000,000
	Italians	4,500,000
1910–1930	Mexicans	700,000
1950–1990	Mexicans	5,000,000
1960–1990	Cubans	700,000
1970–1990	Dominicans, Haitians, and Jamaicans	900,000
1970–1990	Vietnamese	500,000
1981–1996	Chinese	500,000
1981–1996	Filipinos	800,000

Statue of Liberty

When many immigrants came to the United States they arrived in New York. In New York Harbor, they were welcomed by this statue which stands for freedom and opportunity. The Statue of Liberty is still an important symbol today for all Americans.

Easter

Easter is a Christian holiday that occurs between March 22 and April 25. It is also a time when people celebrate new life and the coming of spring.

- Some people wear new suits, dresses, and hats to church on Easter Sunday.

- Children decorate hard-boiled eggs for an imaginary "Easter bunny" to hide, but it is really the parents who hide the eggs for children to find.

Passover

Jewish families celebrate Passover for eight days between March 27 and April 24. Passover is a time to celebrate freedom for all Jews and people everywhere.

- During Passover, families clean house very carefully. This is a time when everything must be orderly and clean.

- On the first night, families talk about their history. They also eat a traditional meal called a *Seder* that includes *matzo*, a flat bread, and other special foods.

Ramadan

Ramadan is a Muslim celebration in the ninth month of the Islamic calendar. It lasts almost thirty days.

- At this time, Muslims follow directions from the *Koran*, a holy book, and eat only before sunrise and after sunset.

- Ramadan ends with a festival called *Ed al-Fitr* which means "a festival of happiness and a time of great joy." That's when families exchange gifts and have a large meal, or **feast**.

National Library Week

You can find out anything you want to know in a library. During April, people honor all that libraries have to offer. They might celebrate by going to the library to read books or to listen to favorite stories.

American literature has lots of characters and heroes. Some of the characters are real, while others are made-up. Many of the heroes have become so popular that they are featured in movies and television shows.

Who are some of the well-known characters and people in American literature?

From Cartoon Strips:

Superman

Superman is a comic book super hero who was created by Jerry Siegel and Joe Shuster. Superman is "more powerful than a locomotive" and "able to leap tall buildings in a single bound." When he isn't rescuing someone, he disguises himself as Clark Kent, a reporter for the *Daily Planet* newspaper.

Charlie Brown and Snoopy

Charlie Brown and his dog, Snoopy, are characters in the comic strip "Peanuts" by Charles M. Schulz. Some of their friends are Linus, Lucy, and Peppermint Patty. They all enjoy things like baseball and going to summer camp.

Wonder Woman

William Moulton Marston created Wonder Woman, a quick and strong super hero who had been an Amazonian princess before coming to the United States. She helps others with her magic lasso and can dodge bullets with her magic bracelet. When not fighting off evil, she teaches a message of peace and equality.

From Tall Tales:

John Henry

John Henry built railroad tracks. He was so strong that he could pound steel faster and longer than a steam drill.

Pecos Bill

Pecos Bill was a cowboy who wasn't afraid to do anything. Stories about him tell how he rode a hurricane to shake the rain out of it and rounded up every steer in Texas for his ranch.

From the Wild West:

Annie Oakley

Annie Oakley was so good with a rifle that she could shoot a dime out of her husband's hand.

From Literature:

Dorothy

Dorothy is a girl in the series of books about the magical land of Oz by Frank L. Baum. There she meets creatures like a scarecrow, a tin man, and a lion.

Tom Sawyer and Huckleberry Finn

Tom Sawyer and Huckleberry Finn are two characters in books by Mark Twain. Tom and Huck often get into trouble but always have amazing adventures in their hometown near the Mississippi River.

Laura Ingalls

Laura Ingalls Wilder was a real woman who wrote about growing up in the Midwest. She tells about traveling in a covered wagon and living in a log cabin. Her books are called the *Little House* books.

April

April Fools' Day

On April 1, don't believe everything you see and hear! On this day, many people play tricks on each other. For example, a friend might tell you that your shoes are untied. When you look down and see that nothing's wrong, your friend will say "April Fools!"

Earth Day

Earth Day is a day to think about and appreciate the Earth. On April 22, people talk about ways to protect our resources and environment. It's important to care about the Earth because people need clean air, water, and land to live a healthy life.

What are some of the special environments to protect in the United States?

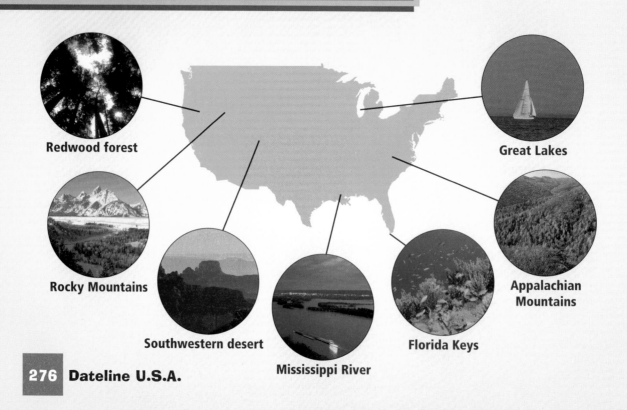

Redwood forest

Great Lakes

Rocky Mountains

Southwestern desert

Mississippi River

Florida Keys

Appalachian Mountains

May

Cinco de Mayo

On May 5th, 1862, the Mexican and French armies fought near Puebla, Mexico. The small Mexican army won the battle that day. Every year on May 5th, or *cinco de mayo* in Spanish, the people of Mexico celebrate this victory. Mexican immigrants brought this celebration with them when they came to the United States.

Today, people in many U.S. towns also celebrate *cinco de mayo*. Some people go to carnivals. Others enjoy watching parades and traditional Mexican dancing and listening to Mexican music.

Mother's Day

On the second Sunday in May, sons and daughters remind their mothers how much they love them.

- Many people give their moms cards, flowers, or chocolates, and an extra big hug!

- Some people also send greetings to other special women like their grandmothers, aunts, or close female friends.

Memorial Day

Memorial Day began as a way of honoring soldiers who died in the Civil War. Since then, the last Monday in May has become a day to remember all soldiers who have died fighting for the United States.

- On this day, people place flowers or flags on soldiers' graves.

- Some cities have military parades and other special programs.

- Because summer vacation begins on this day in many places, families often celebrate by having outdoor picnics and barbecues.

Flag Day

The United States flag is the most important symbol of our nation. On June 14, Americans pay respect to the flag and all it stands for by displaying it at their homes, schools, and businesses.

- The first flag had thirteen stars and thirteen stripes that stood for the number of original colonies.

- As the United States grew and more territories became states, the flag changed. Today there are still thirteen stripes, but there are fifty stars. Each star stands for a state.

The Flag of 1777

The United States Flag Today

How did the United States grow?

1803

The United States made the Louisiana Purchase.

In the 1700s, the western border of the United States was the Mississippi River. In 1803 the United States bought, or **purchased**, the land on the other side of the Mississippi from the French. This purchase made the United States twice as big! ★

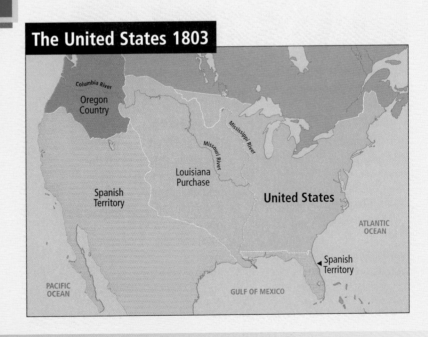

The United States 1803

- Columbia River
- Oregon Country
- Missouri River
- Mississippi River
- Louisiana Purchase
- Spanish Territory
- United States
- ATLANTIC OCEAN
- Spanish Territory
- PACIFIC OCEAN
- GULF OF MEXICO

★**1800s**

The United States 1804–1836

Columbia River

Oregon Country

Mississippi River

The Lewis and Clark expedition route ▶

Missouri River

This territory belonged to Spain until 1821, and then to Mexico after it won its independence from Spain.

United States

ATLANTIC OCEAN

PACIFIC OCEAN

GULF OF MEXICO

Spain gave Florida to ◀ the U.S. in 1819.

1804–1806
Lewis and Clark explored the West.

In 1804, two explorers, Meriwether Lewis and William Clark, journeyed through Louisiana and Oregon to the Pacific coast. They traveled along the Missouri and Columbia Rivers. As they explored, they created maps and took notes. It took them a year and a half to reach the Pacific. ★

Sacagawea

Lewis and Clark may not have been able to reach the Pacific Ocean without the help of Sacagawea, their translator and guide. She was a member of the Shoshone tribe. Sacagawea asked her relatives to help the explorers cross the Rocky Mountains before the winter snows. ★

1819
Florida became part of the United States.

Beginning in 1814, General Andrew Jackson lead American troops through Florida. They fought the Spanish until 1819 when the Spanish agreed to give Florida to the United States. ★

★1800s

★1820s

The United States 1845–1846

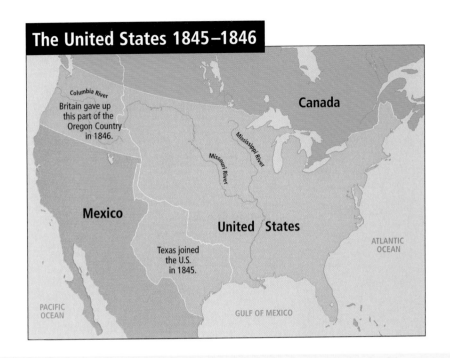

Columbia River

Britain gave up this part of the Oregon Country in 1846.

Canada

Missouri River

Mississippi River

Mexico

United States

ATLANTIC OCEAN

Texas joined the U.S. in 1845.

PACIFIC OCEAN

GULF OF MEXICO

1845
Texas became part of the United States.

So many Americans had moved to Texas that there were more American than Mexican citizens. People started fighting because of this. Sam Houston led a Texan army to victory in the Battle of San Jacinto. Mexico signed the Treaty of Velasco, which made Texas free from Mexico. Almost ten years later, the U.S. Congress offered to **annex**, or unite, Texas with the U.S. ★

1846
Britain gave up this part of the Oregon Country.

Many people had traveled by covered wagon across the U.S. to settle in the British-controlled Oregon Country. The settlers wanted the country to be a part of the United States. Because Great Britain did not want to go to war, they agreed to give up all the land south of the 49th parallel, which is now the Canadian border. ★

★1840s

The United States 1846–1848

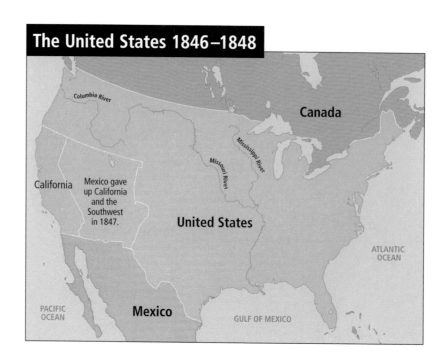

Columbia River

Canada

Mississippi River

Missouri River

California

Mexico gave up California and the Southwest in 1847.

United States

ATLANTIC OCEAN

PACIFIC OCEAN

Mexico

GULF OF MEXICO

CALIFORNIA REPUBLIC

Today's flag is based on the original flag.

1847
Mexico gave California and the Southwest to the U.S.

American settlers in the Mexican territory of California wanted to be free and become the Bear Flag Republic, named after the flag they designed. The United States sent armies and ships to help them. Mexico surrendered and signed the Treaty of Guadalupe Hidalgo, which gave the United States all of California and the Southwest. ★

1848
The California Gold Rush began.

Gold was discovered in California in 1848. As news spread about the discovery, thousands of Americans moved west to pan for gold. They were hoping to get rich. Very few people became rich, but many of them settled in California. ★

★1840s

★1850s

The United States 1862–1912

Alaska

Alaska became a U.S. territory in 1912.

Hawaii

Hawaii became a U.S. territory in 1900.

Columbia River

Canada

Transcontinental Railroad

Mississippi River

Missouri River

GREAT PLAINS

United States

Mexico

PACIFIC OCEAN

ATLANTIC OCEAN

GULF OF MEXICO

1862
Congress gave away free farmland with the Homestead Act.

By the mid-1800s, every part of the United States was settled except the Great Plains. The Homestead Act of 1862 was a law that said anyone who farmed on the Great Plains for five years could keep the land for free. Eventually, hard-working farmers turned the area into "America's breadbasket" and grew most of the food for the rest of the U.S. ★

1869
The first transcontinental railroad was finished.

In 1863, two companies began building railroads. One set of tracks went west from Nebraska; the other went east from California. In 1869, the two tracks joined in Promontory, Utah, to form a transcontinental railroad. This railroad made it possible for millions of people to travel west to establish farms and raise cattle. ★

★**1860s**

★**1870s**

June

Puerto Rican Day

Several cities in the United States celebrate Puerto Rican culture with a big parade. One of the biggest is in New York City where lots of Puerto Ricans live. Millions of people gather for this parade, which is held every year on the second Sunday in June.

- Floats, marching bands, folk musicians, and people waving Puerto Rican flags march up Fifth Avenue.

- Lots of people do traditional dances like the rhumba.

- People wear traditional Puerto Rican clothing like an embroidered *guayabera*, a long shirt for a man.

Father's Day

The third Sunday in June is a special day for fathers. That's when sons and daughters give their fathers gifts and cards to show their love.

- Father's Day is also a great time for children to go on a picnic, to a baseball game, or any place where they can be with their fathers.

- Often people send "Happy Father's Day" greetings to other men they respect like their uncles or grandfathers.

Dragon Boat Festival

In late June, on the fifth day of the fifth month of the Chinese lunar calendar, there are dragon boat races all over the world. These races are part of the Dragon Boat Festival, held in memory of an ancient Chinese poet named Qu Yuan.

When Qu Yuan was punished for saying bad things about his government, he jumped into a river and drowned. Today boat races are held in cities like Boston, New York City, and Honolulu to act out what his friends did to try to save Qu Yuan.

- Teams use boats that look like dragons. Since dragons are symbols of good luck, the boats are said to spread good luck as they race across the water.

- The teams race each other to a finish line. The team that wins shares the prize money.

July

Independence Day

Independence Day is the fourth of July. On this day, many Americans march in parades, wave the American flag, and watch fireworks at night. They are celebrating the time when America fought for and won its **independence**, or freedom, from Britain.

What events led to America's independence?

1773

The colonists took part in the Boston Tea Party.

In the 1700s, America belonged to Britain. The **colonists**, or the people living in colonial America, got tired of paying unfair British taxes on tea. They dressed as Mohawk Indians and protested by throwing the tea into the ocean. This was one of the events that led to the Revolutionary War. ★

1775

The Revolutionary War began.

On April 19, American soldiers fought against the British at Lexington and Concord in the first battle of the Revolutionary War. The soldiers were called "minutemen" because they were ready to fight "at a minute's notice." ★

★**1770s**

1781
The British surrended at Yorktown.

The last major battle of the Revolutionary War was fought in Yorktown, Virginia, in 1781. That's when the British surrendered to American General George Washington. ★

1776
The Declaration of Independence was signed.

On July 4, 1776, the American colonists signed the Declaration of Independence. This important paper stated that the thirteen American colonies were free from Britain. This meant that the colonies would no longer obey the laws of Great Britain or pay taxes to the British government. ★

1783
The Revolutionary War ended.

Benjamin Franklin, John Adams, John Jay, and Henry Laurens went to Paris to sign a peace treaty with the British. ★

★**1780s**

Dateline U.S.A.　287

July

Anniversary of the First Moon Walk

On July 20, 1969, the world watched as two American astronauts became the first human beings to walk on the moon.

- As astronaut Neil Armstrong stepped from the landing craft *Eagle*, he said, "That's one small step for a man, one giant leap for mankind."

- Armstrong and his partner, Edwin Aldrin, gathered samples of rocks and soil for over two and a half hours. Before they climbed back into the *Eagle*, they put an American flag in the ground.

Who are some other American astronauts? What did they do?

1961
Alan Shepard became the first American in space.

Alan Shepard traveled in space in *Freedom 7* for fifteen minutes. ★

1962
John Glenn, Jr., orbited the Earth.

John Glenn, Jr., was the first American to **orbit**, or go around, the Earth. His spacecraft, *Mercury 6*, flew around the Earth three times in a little over four and a half hours. ★

1965
Edward H. White II walked in space.

The first American to go outside the spacecraft while in space was Edward H. White II. He was on this spacewalk outside of *Gemini 4* for 21 minutes. ★

1983
Sally Ride became the first American woman in space.

Sally Ride and four other astronauts went on a six-day flight in the space shuttle, *Challenger*. ★

★**1960s**   ★**1970s**   ★**1980s**

Traditional dancing

Native American Powwows

From August 12–17 Native Americans get together for the Inter-Tribal Indian Ceremonial at Red Rock State Park in Gallup, New Mexico. This is just one of many powwows held by Native Americans across the United States throughout the year.

A powwow is a gathering of Native Americans to celebrate their culture and heritage.

- Families and friends meet every year for reunions.

- Some groups of people play drums and sing while others tape-record the traditional music. Later, people will use the tapes to practice singing and dancing.

- Family members of all ages compete in dance contests. They can win prizes for traditional, fancy, grass, or jingle-dress dancing.

Jingle dress

- There are also special ceremonies. During an **introduction ceremony**, a family dances to introduce their child as a powwow dancer.

Playing the drums

Labor Day

Americans honor working people on the first Monday in September. Many workers get this day off so they can rest and enjoy the holiday. Labor Day is usually the last day of summer vacation for many students, too! People arrange special events like parades, picnics, and concerts to celebrate the occasion.

Labor Day began during a period of time called the Industrial Revolution. That was a time when people invented many new products, businesses got bigger, more machines made more products, and more people moved to the cities to work in factories.

How did life change during the Industrial Revolution?

1882
Jan Matzeliger invented a shoe machine.

Jan Matzeliger invented the shoe-lasting machine to shape and then attach the top of a shoe to its sole. Shoes cost a lot less because this machine could do what had been done before by hand. ★

1876
Alexander Graham Bell invented the telephone.

Alexander Bell's first telephone was one-way, which meant that only one person could talk while the other listened. Within a year, Bell made a two-way telephone. As people started using this invention, communication became faster and easier for everyone around the world. ★

1879
Thomas Edison invented the electric light bulb.

Thomas Edison was one of America's greatest inventors. He is best known for inventing a practical light bulb, but he also invented many other things including the phonograph which recorded and replayed sounds. Edison's inventions were so useful that soon everyone had them in their homes. ★

★1870s

★1880s

Expanding Factories and New Inventions

From the mid-1800s to the early 1900s, many people started working in factories. At that time, they had to work twelve to sixteen hours a day for very little money. To improve the unfair working conditions, many workers formed groups called unions. The unions asked factory owners for better pay and safer workplaces.

This was also a time when many Americans thought of new things to make and new ways to do things. From those ideas and inventions, people began to make more and more products and new companies and businesses were formed.

1886
Samuel Gompers became a labor leader.

Samuel Gompers became an important leader of a large labor union. He worked hard to establish labor laws for all workers, including women and children. These laws led to improvements in working conditions and limited the number of hours people had to work. ★

1889
Jane Addams opened Hull House for workers.

During the late 1800s, many immigrants came to the city of Chicago to work. Jane Addams and another social worker created a special center called Hull House to help immigrants learn English and train for new jobs. With Addams's help, immigrants were able to demand fair working conditions. ★

1913
Henry Ford started the first modern assembly line.

Henry Ford created the modern assembly line, which made it faster and less expensive to build cars. Workers would do only one job such as tightening bolts as the cars moved past them on a conveyor belt. Because of the assembly line process, Ford was able to build the first car that many people could afford, the Model T. ★

★ **1890s**   ★ **1900s**   ★ **1910s**

September

Rosh Hashanah and Yom Kippur

In September in the Hebrew month *Tishri*, people celebrate the Jewish New Year.

Rosh Hashanah begins on the first day of *Tishri* and usually lasts for two days. *Rosh Hashanah* means "beginning (or head) of the year."

- Some people give each other cards, greetings, and good wishes.

- People fix a special treat made of apple slices dipped in honey. The honey stands for hope for a sweet new year!

Yom Kippur is from sunset on the ninth day of *Tishri* until three stars appear in the sky after the tenth day.

- People do not work but go to their synagogue or temple to ask forgiveness and promise to make the new year a good one.

- In order to concentrate on their religion, people do not eat or drink anything for twenty-four hours. Then they have a festive meal.

Citizenship Day

September 17 is Citizenship Day. It begins a week-long celebration called Constitution Week. People give speeches and display the American flag to show that they are proud to be American citizens.

In 1952, President Harry S. Truman established Citizenship Day to honor the date the United States Constitution was signed in 1787. Then in 1956, Congress established Constitution Week which lasts from September 17 through September 23. Congress did this because the Constitution is such an important document and symbol of freedom for all Americans.

What are some other symbols of the United States?

The Capitol

This building is located in Washington, D.C., the capital of the United States. It is where people in Congress work together to make laws. The Capitol stands for democracy. That's the kind of government that gives people the right to govern themselves.

The Great Seal of the United States

This **emblem**, or picture, is printed on official documents and on the one dollar bill. It shows an American bald eagle holding an olive branch and arrows. The olive branch is a symbol of peace. The arrows stand for strength. The paper, or scroll, in the eagle's beak says, *E pluribus unum.* That's Latin for "one (nation) out of many (states)."

Uncle Sam

Uncle Sam is a made-up man who stands for the United States. His name probably came from the initials U.S., the abbreviation for **U**nited **S**tates. You'll see Uncle Sam on posters and cartoons. You might also see him marching in a parade! He'll always be dressed in America's colors: red, white, and blue.

Columbus Day

On the second Monday in October, people remember Christopher Columbus's trip to the Americas in 1492. Columbus was an Italian sea captain who had been looking for a way to sail from Europe to China and India. He landed on an island in the Bahamas on October 12, 1492.

■ After Columbus, explorers from other countries sailed to the Americas. They were looking for gold, silver, spices, and other valuable things. They also wanted to conquer new lands for their countries.

■ Columbus and the other explorers called the land the "New World" because it was new to them. Native Americans had lived in the Americas for thousands of years before the explorers arrived.

Who were some of the explorers?

1492
Christopher Columbus landed in the Bahamas.

Christopher Columbus made four trips to the "New World." He explored the Bahamas, Puerto Rico, Cuba, the Dominican Republic, Jamaica, Trinidad, Venezuela, and Central America. ★

1497
John Cabot explored the northeastern American coast.

John Cabot, an Italian sea captain, made two trips to the northeastern American coast. His journeys began the exploration and settlement of North America. ★

1513
Juan Ponce de León landed in Florida.

Juan Ponce de León came from Spain. He was the first explorer to land in Florida. Some people say he was seeking the Fountain of Youth, a magical water that would keep him young forever. ★

★ **1490s**   ★ **1500s**   ★ **1510s**

Native North America

There were many different Native American tribes living in North America when the explorers arrived. Each tribe had its own language, culture, and way of life.

Some Native Americans were farmers who stayed in one place. Others were hunters who moved all year long, following the migrations of animals. One thing the tribes had in common was their deep respect for the land and close relationship with nature.

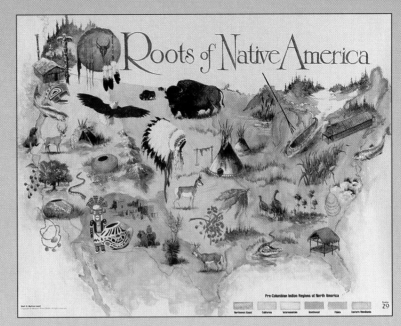

Native Americans taught explorers how to grow and prepare vegetables like tomatoes and corn. Europeans brought horses which the Native Americans used to follow and hunt migrating animals.

Sadly, Europeans brought diseases, and many Native Americans died. The explorers also thought they had the right to take whatever land they wanted. Many Native Americans died fighting for their homes.

1540–1542
Francisco de Coronado explored the Southwest.

Francisco Vázquez de Coronado of Spain traveled through much of the Southwest, including the villages of the Zuni tribes.★

1565
Don Pedro Menéndez de Avilés established a fort in Florida.

Don Pedro Menéndez de Avilés also came from Spain. He established a settlement at St. Augustine, Florida, which is now the oldest city in the United States.★

★ **1540s**   ★ **1550s**   ★ **1560s**

Halloween

On October 31, children and adults celebrate Halloween. It is a time to have fun and be creative.

- People put jack-o'-lanterns on their porches. A jack-o'-lantern is made from a hollow pumpkin with a face carved in it.

- Lots of children dress in costumes and masks and go to different houses in their neighborhoods. The children knock on the door and, when someone opens it, they say, "Trick or treat!" Then they get candy or other treats.

- Some families have Halloween parties instead of going out. One popular game at this kind of party is "bobbing for apples." A large tub is filled with water, and then apples are put in the water. Two players kneel next to the tub. Each player tries to bite an apple and take it out of the water. The first one to do this wins!

Day of the Dead

On November 1 and 2, for the Day of the Dead, people remember friends and relatives who have died.

- Families create an **altar**, or a memorial table, at home. These altars are decorated with candles, flowers, fruits, chocolate, and photographs of people who have died.

- People make skeleton figures and papier-mâché masks that look like skulls. They wear the masks as they walk to a cemetery to honor those who have died.

Veterans Day

On November 11, Americans honor veterans who have fought in wars for the United States. All over the country there are parades and speeches to thank veterans for their service to the United States and its people.

At the end of World War I, President Woodrow Wilson named November 11 Armistice Day. An **armistice** is an agreement between countries to stop fighting a war. It was a day to celebrate peace and the end of that war. Later on, the name was changed to Veterans Day to honor veterans of all American wars: World Wars I and II, the Korean War, the Vietnam War, and the Persian Gulf War.

What happened during World Wars I and II?

1914–1918
World War I

World War I was the first war involving countries from all over the world. Germany, Austria, Hungary, and Turkey formed a group called the Central Powers. They fought against Britain, France, the United States, and Russia, who were called the Allied Powers. The Allies won the war in 1918. ★

1939–1945
World War II

In the late 1930s, **dictators** in Germany, Italy, and Japan (the Axis Powers) used their armies to invade their neighboring countries. A dictator is a ruler who has complete control over a country. Britain and France (the Allied forces) declared war on Germany. The United States joined the war in 1941, when the Japanese attacked Pearl Harbor, Hawaii, by surprise. Germany and Japan surrendered in 1945. ★

★ **1910s**   ★ **1920s**   ★ **1930s**   ★ **1940s**

November

Thanksgiving

The fourth Thursday in November is a very special day for Americans. Thanksgiving is a day when people give thanks for all the good things in their lives.

- Families and friends gather together for a large meal. Some traditional Thanksgiving dishes are baked turkey, sweet potatoes, cranberry sauce, and pumpkin pie.

- Before eating, someone may give thanks for the food on the table and for being together.

The celebration of Thanksgiving began when settlers arrived in North America. The first Thanksgiving meal took place when some of those settlers gave thanks for a good harvest after a difficult winter.

When did English settlers arrive in North America? What was their life like?

1585

The first English settlers arrived in North America.

The settlers arrived on what is now Roanoke Island off the coast of North Carolina. They tried to start a colony there, but living in an unfamiliar place was too hard so they returned to England. ★

1607

Jamestown became the first permanent English colony.

The settlers in colonies like Jamestown survived because they learned how to make their own supplies and grow their own food. At first the settlers lived in homes in holes in the ground with bark roofs. Later, they used lumber to build wooden houses. They learned how to fish and dig for clams on the beaches. They hunted for deer, geese, ducks, and wild turkeys in the woods. Many settlers became farmers and grew corn, potatoes, beans, wheat, rye, and oats. ★

★ **1580s**   ★ **1590s**   ★ **1600s**

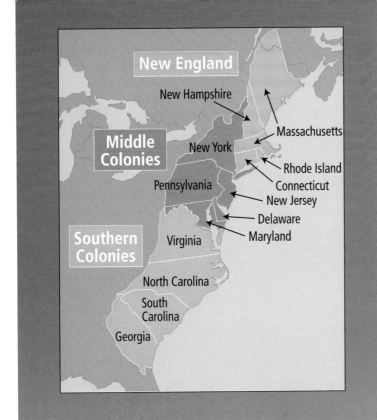

The Thirteen Original Colonies

The settlers sold things to each other and to other countries like England. Settlers in New England sold fur and lumber. People in the Middle Colonies made glass, leather, and iron tools. Farmers in the Southern Colonies sold tobacco which people said was worth its weight in silver.

1620
The Pilgrims wrote the Mayflower Compact.

Many of the settlers wanted to govern themselves. The Pilgrims who settled in Massachusetts wrote and signed the Mayflower Compact, an agreement to make and follow fair and equal laws. The United States government is based on some of the same ideas that these settlers had. ★

1621
The event which is now called Thanksgiving was celebrated in the Plymouth Colony.

In 1621, the Pilgrims in Plymouth Colony had survived a very difficult winter because a member of a Native American tribe, the Wampanoag, had taught them to fish, hunt, and plant corn. To celebrate their first harvest, the settlers had a three day celebration and invited the Wampanoag. ★

1630
The Massachusetts Bay Colony formed.

In England in the 1600s, people called Puritans formed the Massachusetts Bay Company. That company sent lots of families to New England. The Puritans took everything they would need such as farm animals, tools and clothing. They first settled in Boston, Massachusetts. ★

★ **1620s**

★ **1630s**

December

Hanukkah

For eight days in December, families celebrate the Jewish Festival of Lights, Hanukkah.

- People light a candle each night of the holiday on a special nine-branched candleholder called a *menorah*.
- Children often play a game with a *dreidl*. A *dreidl* is a spinning top with Hebrew letters on it.

Christmas

December 25 is a Christian holiday that celebrates the birth of Jesus Christ.

- During the Christmas season, many people like to sing songs called Christmas carols.
- Families and friends give each other gifts and often put them under decorated trees. Children believe that a character named Santa Claus brings them gifts if they are good.

Kwanzaa

African Americans celebrate Kwanzaa from December 26 through January 1.

- On each day, someone lights a candle in a *kinara*, a special candleholder. Each candle represents a value like unity or creativity.
- Families have a feast called *karamu*. During *karamu*, people wear traditional African clothes, play music, and dance.

New Year's Eve

On the Roman calendar, December 31 is the last day of the year. On this day, many people stay up until midnight. That's when the new year officially begins. At midnight, they throw confetti, blow horns, and wish each other "Happy New Year!"

If you want to be part of a great New Year's Eve celebration, where should you go?

Go to New York City!

One of the biggest New Year's Eve celebrations in the United States takes place in Times Square. A ball of lights slowly drops from the top of a tower just before midnight. When the ball reaches the bottom, at exactly midnight, thousands of people cheer loudly to welcome the new year.

New York City

Facts

- Over 7 million people live in New York City. It is the most populated city in the United States.

- The Empire State Building, one of the tallest skyscrapers in the world, is in this city.

- Many of the world's largest banks are here, too. That's why New York City is often called the "financial center of the world"... and it's a great place to celebrate the new year.

U.S.A. Time Line

Native America

Native Americans lived in America thousands of years before the first Europeans arrived. Each Native American tribe had its own language, culture, and way of life. ★

Europeans Explore North America

From the late 1400s through the 1600s, many explorers sailed to America from Europe. They came to find land and claim it for their countries. ★

Settlers Form Colonies

Groups of European settlers like the Puritans and the Pilgrims moved to America to build villages and towns called colonies. The colonists sold products to each other and to other countries. ★

American Revolution

By the 1760s, there were thirteen colonies that belonged to Britain. The colonists fought to be free because they wanted their own laws. They won their independence in 1783. ★

Westward Expansion

At first, most of the people settled in the East, but starting in the 1800s, the U.S. bought and fought for more land. Soon people called *pioneers* moved into the open spaces in the Midwest and the West. ★

Civil War

The people in the northern and southern parts of the United States led very different lifestyles. They disagreed so strongly about slavery and their ways of life that they fought the Civil War. The war and slavery ended in 1865 when the North won the Civil War. ★

Industrial Revolution

From the 1860s to the 1900s, many companies started using machines to make products faster. It was also a time when new inventions like the light bulb and the telephone made people's lives easier. ★

1900s

Becoming a World Leader

By the 1900s, the U.S. was greatly respected for its fine products and ability to defend itself. It had become a strong influence in the world. ★

World War I (1914–1918)

The Great Depression

When many people lost money in the stock market crash of 1929, they were left without homes or jobs. A horrible drought in the Midwest called the Dust Bowl made things even worse. The depression lasted for many years. ★

World War II (1941–1945)

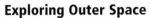

Exploring Outer Space

In the 1960s, American astronauts began journeys into outer space. The space program continues today as the astronauts help build an international laboratory in space and plan new missions. ★

Civil Rights Movement

Beginning in the 1960s, many Americans marched and demonstrated for equal rights for black Americans. Several laws were passed that helped stop discrimination. ★

Information Age

Today many Americans use computers to give and receive information. With programs like electronic mail and the Internet, people around the world are able to quickly and easily communicate with each other. ★

2000s

Grammar Practice

Sentences

**A. Choose an ending from the box to finish each sentence.
Write the sentence.**

mighty arms!	he do?
a strong man.	is Paul Bunyan.
amaze you!	he?
appearance.	famous lumberjack.

1. statement   The statue shows _____

2. exclamation   Wow, he has _____

3. question   Who is _____

4. statement   His name _____

5. command   Describe his _____

6. question   What did _____

7. command   Listen to the story of this _____

8. exclamation   The story of Paul Bunyan will _____

**B. Make up questions about this picture. Write them down.
Then trade papers with a partner and answer the questions.**

1. Is _____ ?

2. Who _____ ?

3. When _____ ?

4. Can _____ ?

5. Why _____ ?

6. How _____ ?

7. Are _____ ?

8. Will _____ ?

9. What _____ ?

10. Does _____ ?

C. Work with a partner to add a subject. Write the sentences.

1.

worked with Paul Bunyan.
subject   predicate

3.

cleared trees from the land.
subject   predicate

2.

was a lumberjack.
subject   predicate

4.

watched Paul Bunyan.
subject   predicate

D. Work with a partner to add a predicate. Write the sentences.

1.

Paul and Babe
subject   predicate

3.

North Dakota
subject   predicate

2.

Stories about Paul
subject   predicate

4.

Every morning, Babe
subject   predicate

E. Make each sentence you wrote in C and D into a question.

Example: Did your grandfather work with Paul Bunyan?

F. Make each sentence you wrote in C and D into a negative sentence.

Example: My grandfather did **not** work with Paul Bunyan.

G. Choose *and*, *but*, or *or* to join each pair of sentences. Write the compound sentences.

1. There were no more trees to cut down in North Dakota. Paul Bunyan wanted to keep working.   ___but / or___

2. Paul could stay in North Dakota and be bored. He could go west to find more trees.   ___but / or___

3. Paul and Babe decided to go west. They said good-bye to their friends.   ___but / and___

4. On the way, Paul's sharp pole made the Grand Canyon. Babe's footsteps made paths through the Cascade Mountains.   ___or / and___

5. At first, the West was full of trees. Paul and Babe cut them down quickly.   ___but / or___

6. Now Paul and Babe could quit working. They could go to find more trees.   ___or / and___

Nouns

A. Write these sentences. Add the correct noun.

Gold Room	room	Galveston	corner
man	Broadway	James M. Brown	museum

1. Luisa went on a tour of this house in _____.

2. Its address is 2328 _____.

3. It is on the _____ of the street.

4. The house is now a _____ in Galveston.

5. Luisa read about the _____ who built Ashton Villa.

6. His name was _____.

7. One room in Ashton Villa is named the _____.

8. Luisa thought it was the most beautiful _____ in the house.

B. Write the plural of each noun. Then copy the paragraph and add the new words.

1. beach   **3.** child   **5.** roof   **7.** wave

2. shell   **4.** city   **6.** half   **8.** foot

    Galveston is one of the best _____ to visit. It has many places that are fun for parents and their _____. People can visit the sandy _____. They can pick up colorful _____, too. One beach is Stewart Beach. It is behind a seawall that is 17 _____ high. At this beach, kids can play in the _____, or they can fly kites over the _____ of nearby homes. Some visitors walk through a life-size maze called "Amaze'N Texas." At the end, they make sure that both _____ of their group made it through!

C. Write these sentences, adding the red word to the blank. Make the red word plural if you need to.

kind   **1.** There are many _____ of vehicles to see in Galveston.

equipment   **2.** People go to Seawolf Park to see military _____ like a real World War II submarine.

information   **3.** At the Lone Star Flight Museum there is _____ on more than 40 restored planes.

lunch   **4.** Some people ride the Galveston Island Trolley car to the beach to eat the _____ they've packed.

time   **5.** Others ride on the *Colonel* paddle boat and imagine going back in _____ to the 1800s.

water   **6.** Many people tour the Tall Ship *Elissa* which sits in the _____ in the Galveston port.

group   **7.** The displays in the Railroad Museum are popular with _____ of people who visit the city.

lunch   **8.** These visitors often eat _____ at the Santa Fe Choo Choo Diner there.

D. Write these sentences. Add the correct word.

1. Look at __these / a__ pictures I took at Moody Gardens.

2. I went to __the / some__ Rainforest Pyramid there.

3. Inside there is __a / some__ special place to watch caterpillars turn into butterflies.

4. I got to watch __a / some__ butterflies form!

5. This picture shows __some / an__ insect called a walking stick.

walking stick

6. I spent over __an / a__ hour looking at all the insects.

7. __That / An__ walking stick was my favorite insect in the Rainforest Pyramid.

8. This is a picture of __a / an__ macaw I saw sitting in a tree.

9. __The / Some__ macaw was very colorful.

10. It was very safe in __a / the__ tall trees.

macaw

11. __Those / That__ trees were over 55 feet tall!

bat

12. __An / This__ picture shows one of the bats.

13. Later, I saw __a / the__ fruit bat, too.

14. I had __a / an__ interesting day at Moody Gardens!

E. Write this paragraph. Add _the_ where there is a blank only if you need to.

In _____ April, we went to Galveston's Grand KIDS Festival. There were lots of arts and crafts booths. My favorite booth was _____ Swedish woodcarving one. _____ woman at _____ booth even spoke _____ Swedish! We ate lots of food, including burritos from _____ Rita's Tacos. On the way home, we stopped at _____ Stewart Beach and went _____ swimming.

F. **Write these sentences.**
   Add the correct possessive noun.

1. __Luisa Rafael's / Luisa Rafaels'__ house is near the water.

2. In the front yard is her __dads' / dad's__ boat.

3. Today, her family is going on a fishing trip near one of
   __Galvestons' / Galveston's__ jetties.

4. All of the family is going, including __Luisa's / Luisas'__ two
   older brothers.

5. Catching crabs is her __brothers' / brother's__ favorite thing to do.

6. The boys have learned how to take crabs off their lines so that they
   don't get pinched by the __crab's/ crabs'__ claws!

7. Luisa likes to fish for trout with her __mom's / moms'__ fishing pole.

8. She drops the line into the __bays' / bay's__ warm water.

9. The fish start nibbling at the bait on the __hook's / hooks'__ sharp point.

10. At the end of the day, the __boys' / boy's__ bucket is full of crabs.

11. The five fish Luisa caught flop around on the __boat's / boats'__ deck.

12. For dinner tonight, the Rafaels will be eating the __world's / worlds'__
    best seafood!

G. **Write the paragraph. Replace the underlined words**
   with specific nouns about a city you know.

   Take a stroll down the street. Delicious smells come from the café.
   You can almost taste the food. Pause to look in the store windows.
   Look at all the things displayed there. Listen, can you hear music
   playing? It's coming from the shop. Have fun visiting this city!

H. **Write a paragraph about a place you have visited.**
   Use specific nouns.

Pronouns

Lisa   Jasmine   Tom

A. **Write these sentences.**
   Add the correct pronoun.

1. One day at practice, a bee buzzed Lisa.
   "It might sting __me / he__ , " she said.

2. "Just stand still," Tom said to __she / her__ .

3. Lisa stood very still, but the bee kept
   buzzing __him / her__ .

4. __I / It__ buzzed around her ears and her eyes.

5. Jasmine said, "__They / You__ will
   be okay in a minute."

6. Then the bee left as fast as __you / it__ came!

7. "Whew," said Lisa. "__He / I__ really
   don't like bees."

8. "But __it / they__ are not as scary as snakes," said Jasmine.

9. "Snakes?" asked Tom. "__We / They__ aren't scary at all!"

10. "Are you sure __you / I__ aren't afraid of snakes?" the girls asked.

11. "__I / She__ am sure," said Tom.

12. The girls didn't believe __him / we__ .

13. "__We / Us__ will see," they said to each other.

14. The girls knew a little snake was crawling toward __they / them__ .

15. Tom jumped. __He / She__ was scared!

16. "That snake is coming right at __we / us__ !" yelled Tom.

17. "Just stand still," Lisa said to __he / him__ .

18. "__You / Him__ will be okay in a minute," Jasmine said.

One	More Than One
I	we
you	you
he, she, it	they

One	More Than One
me	us
you	you
him, her, it	them

Lisa

Juan

Tom

Jasmine

Coach

B. Write these sentences. Add the correct pronoun.

1. Tom and his friends were at __their / theirs__ soccer practice. Tom and Lisa found a backpack.

2. They asked Juan, "Is this backpack __yours / your__?"

3. Juan said, "No. Ask Jasmine. Maybe it's __hers / theirs__."

4. "I've got __my / mine__," Jasmine said.

5. "Coach! Someone left a backpack on the field. Our friends say it isn't __their / theirs__."

6. "Oh! That's __my / yours__ backpack," said the coach. "I've been looking everywhere for it!"

One	More Than One
my	our
your	your
his, her, its	their

One	More Than One
mine	ours
yours	yours
his, hers	theirs

C. Write these sentences. Add the correct pronoun.

1.  Oh good, __anything / someone__ brought juice.

2.  Has __anyone / something__ seen my soda?

3.  __Everything / Somebody__ put a napkin over it!

4.  Did __everyone / someone__ get enough to eat?

D. Write this paragraph. Add a pronoun from the box for each blank.

he	him	his
it	us	their

Mr. Brown is our soccer coach. All of the Bobcat players like

_____. We practice hard, but Mr. Brown is always fair.

_____ lets everyone have a chance to play during the games.

When we win a game, he celebrates with _____. He and his

wife had a party for us after we beat the Eagles. They invited all

the players and the fans to _____ house. It was fun!

Sometimes Mr. Brown loses things. One time he lost _____

lucky cap. We found _____ right there in his pocket!

E. Write a paragraph about your favorite coach or teacher.

Adjectives

A. Write these sentences. Add the correct adjective from the box.

1. Just _____ berry isn't enough for the toucan.

2. This _____ bird gobbles up all the berries.

3. The toucan uses its _____ beak to pick them from the tree.

4. It loves berries and other kinds of _____ fruit.

hungry
one
ripe
sharp

---

5. The toucan is always squawking. It is very _____!

6. The toucan lives in the _____ rainforest.

7. Its nest is in a _____ trunk of a tree.

8. The toucan likes to sit on the _____ branches of a tree.

noisy
hot
top
hollow

B. Write these sentences. Add the correct adjective.

1. There are __many / much__ different kinds of flowers in the rainforest.

2. Some flowers are very colorful, but others have __only a little / only a few__ color.

3. The hibiscus does not have __many / much__ smell, but it is very colorful.

4. The water lily has __much / many__ petals. It smells like butterscotch and pineapple.

5. __Many / Much__ people do not like the horrible smell of the arum lily.

6. Some orchids have __several / not much__ spots on their petals.

7. Most orchids have __only a little / only a few__ leaves on them.

8. The different flowers add so __much / many__ beauty to the rainforest.

C. Write these sentences. Add *-er* or *-est* to the red adjective to make a comparison.

wet   1. Monkeys and sloths both live in the _____ place in the world. Yet, these animals have many differences.

slow   2. Of the two animals, the sloth is _____.

small   3. A sloth's tail is _____ than a monkey's tail.

big   4. A monkey has one of the _____ and most useful tails in the animal world.

large   5. A sloth has _____ claws than a monkey.

hungry   6. A monkey eats all day and is always _____ than a sloth.

quiet   7. The sloth doesn't make much noise; it is _____ than a monkey.

noisy   8. A monkey is one of the _____ animals in the rainforest!

sloth

D. **Write these sentences. Add the correct word.**

1. Ms. Steinberg's class went to the rainforest exhibit. They talked about what they liked the __more / most__ .

katydid

2. Nina said the jaguar had a __good / best__ disguise.

3. Toshiro thought that the katydid's disguise was __better / more__ than the jaguar's.

4. They both agreed that the walking stick had the __better / best__ disguise of all.

walking stick

5. Rita thought that the spotted, brown snake was the __some / most__ frightening snake.

6. Tony felt that the long, green snake was __some / more__ frightening than the brown one.

7. Everyone agreed that the sloth was the __less / least__ active animal there!

8. The toucan was pretty __bad / worse__ at keeping quiet.

toucan

9. The monkey was __worse / worst__ , though!

10. Everyone said that their __little / least__ favorite thing was going home!

E. **Write this paragraph. Add an adjective to each sentence.**

Our zoo has a _____ rainforest exhibit. Inside, the air feels _____. There are _____ vines hanging from the trees. _____ spiders crawl on the ground. You can see _____ butterflies fluttering through the air. Hanging from the branches are _____ monkeys. In the background, you can hear a _____ waterfall. This exhibit is _____!

monkey

F. **Write a description of an animal that lives in the rainforest. Use adjectives to help your readers picture the animal clearly.**

Verbs

A. Write each sentence and add the verb.

1. At first the sky _____ clear.

2. Then the clouds _____ in.

3. They _____ almost black.

4. Something _____ across the sky.

is
flashes
roll
look

5. It _____ lightning!

6. I _____ the loud thunder.

7. Then the rain _____ from the sky.

8. The raindrops _____ very cold and wet.

is
are
falls
hear

B. Write each sentence and add the verb. Then circle each helping verb.

1. The weather reporter says it _____ warmer today.

2. We _____ our T-shirts and shorts.

3. The weather _____.

can wear
is changing
will turn

4. The flowers _____ now.

5. The birds _____.

6. Spring _____!

might return
has arrived
should bloom

C. Write each sentence in Exercise B again. Add the word not.

D. Write each sentence and add the verb.

1. In winter, the sun __rise / rises__ later in the morning.

2. The sky __get / gets__ dark early, too.

3. Some people __want / wants__ winter to end.

4. They __like / likes__ the long days of summer.

5. I __prefer / perfers__ winter, though.

6. To me, cold air __seem / seems__ fresher than hot air.

7. My favorite sport __begin / begins__ in winter, too.

8. I __see / sees__ all the hockey games on TV.

9. I also __play / plays__ hockey every afternoon.

10. It __keep / keeps__ me in shape!

E. Write each sentence and add the correct form of the red verb.

say   1. The weather reporter _____ it will hail this morning.

love   2. My sister _____ the hail.

stay   3. She never _____ inside when it is hailing.

watch   4. She always _____ it from the front porch.

fly   5. She likes how the hail _____ through the air.

bounce   6. She giggles as it _____ off the street.

play   7. She even _____ in it if the hail stones are small.

try   8. She _____ to catch the hail in her hands.

catch   9. Sometimes she _____ a few.

miss   10. Most of the time, though, she _____!

F. Add *-ing* to each red verb. Then write each sentence and add the verb.

watch   **1.** I am _____ the 6:00 p.m. TV weather report.

describe   **2.** The reporter is _____ weather around the country.

form   **3.** Hurricanes are _____ off the coast of Florida.

rise   **4.** Some rivers are _____ in the Midwest.

drop   **5.** The temperature is _____ in Maine.

fall   **6.** Hail is _____ on North Dakota.

come   **7.** Storms are _____ to the Southwest.

get   **8.** California is _____ lots of rain.

shine   **9.** The sun is _____ in Texas.

hope   **10.** We are _____ for a warm day tomorrow.

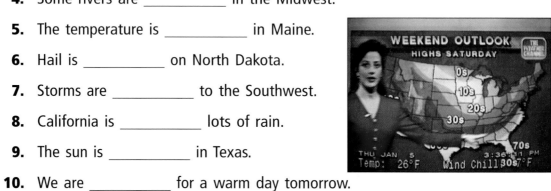

G. Add *-ed* to each red verb to make it tell about an action that happened in the past. Then write each sentence and add the verb.

visit   **1.** A TV weather reporter _____ our class yesterday.

stay   **2.** She _____ for two hours.

show   **3.** She _____ us different thermometers.

measure   **4.** Everyone _____ the air temperature.

study   **5.** Then we _____ a poster with different clouds on it.

try   **6.** We _____ to draw pictures of each kind.

create   **7.** The reporter _____ a cloud inside a jar.

clap   **8.** The whole class _____. It was amazing!

play   **9.** Before the reporter left, we _____ a guessing game about the weather.

plan   **10.** We also _____ a time for her to come back again.

H. Write each sentence. Change the underlined verb to make it tell about an action that happened in the past. Use the chart on page 191 to help you.

1. In the morning, Mr. Cruz <u>sees</u> dark clouds.

2. He <u>finds</u> the weather report in the newspaper.

3. The forecast <u>is</u> for a sunny day.

4. Mr. Cruz <u>does</u> not believe it.

5. He <u>takes</u> his umbrella just in case.

6. The sky <u>gets</u> very dark at about 4:00 p.m.

7. Mr. Cruz <u>hears</u> thunder.

8. Before long, there <u>are</u> raindrops coming down.

9. On his way home, Mr. Cruz <u>keeps</u> his umbrella over his head.

10. He finally <u>runs</u> for a taxi to get out of the rain.

I. Write each sentence. Change the underlined verb to make it tell about an action that happened in the past.

1. Lihn <u>listens</u> to a story about a snowy day.

2. She <u>thinks</u> about snow.

3. She <u>finds</u> a picture of snow.

4. It <u>looks</u> so white and pretty.

5. Lihn <u>wonders</u> about snowflakes.

6. She <u>writes</u> a poem about snow.

7. In her poem, Lihn <u>says</u> that it is cold and wet.

8. She <u>names</u> her poem, "Does Snow Feel Soft?"

9. She <u>brings</u> her poem to her teacher.

10. "Does Snow Feel Soft?" <u>makes</u> the teacher smile.

J. Write this paragraph to tell about an action that will happen in the future.

will bring	is going to
am going to	are going to go

Tomorrow _____ be hot because it will be the first day in July. We _____ to the lake. Mom and Dad _____ their rafts, but I _____ swim.

K. Write each sentence, using a contraction for the underlined words.

1. Tomorrow <u>we are</u> going to do weather projects.

2. <u>I would</u> like to make something to measure the amount of rain.

3. It <u>should not</u> be hard to do.

4. First <u>I will</u> cut off the top of a plastic bottle.

5. Then <u>I am</u> going to mark the sides of the bottle.

6. It <u>will not</u> work unless I put it outside!

7. I <u>cannot</u> forget to empty the bottle after it rains.

8. Otherwise, the measurement <u>would not</u> be right the next time it rains.

L. Write the paragraph. Replace each underlined verb with a verb that is more colorful.

The hot sun <u>was</u> directly overhead. Freddie <u>went</u> to the pool. Some people <u>were</u> in the wading pool. Freddie <u>looked</u> at the water. He <u>got</u> into the pool. "Aaah, I'm finally cool," he <u>said</u>.

M. Write a paragraph about something you did when the weather was *hot*, *cold*, *wet*, or *dry*. Use colorful verbs.

Adverbs

Mariah

A. Write these sentences. Add the correct word.

1. The gymnasts are practicing __everywhere / nowhere__ in the gym.

2. Beto always performs __good / well__ on the mat.

3. Today he jumped __higher / highest__ than he has ever jumped before!

4. Beto's muscles are getting __real / really__ strong.

5. Mariah tumbled __smooth / smoothly__ on the balance beam.

6. Then she stood __perfect / perfectly__ still.

7. She stepped more __quick / quickly__ than usual across the beam, too.

8. The gymnasts improve when they practice __often / most often__ .

Beto

B. Write a paragraph about a sport. Use adverbs to describe how the players move and act.

Prepositions

C. Where is the red dot? Write the correct answer.

1. The red dot is __under / in front of__ the line.

2. The red dot is __off / in__ the box.

3. The red dot is __inside / outside__ the box.

4. The red dot is going __around / through__ the tunnel.

D. Make more drawings of the line and the red dot. Trade papers with a partner and tell where the red dot is.

E. Write each sentence and add the correct preposition.

1. My brother Tito and I were excited about the kite-flying contest __on / in__ March.

2. It was __on / in__ the first Saturday in March.

3. __During / After__ breakfast that morning, we hurried to Grant Park.

4. The contest did not begin __until / on__ noon.

5. Tito and I wanted to practice __on / before__ the contest.

6. We got our kite ready __at / in__ 11:00 o'clock.

7. Tito flew the kite __after / from__ 11:00 to 12:00.

8. The wind blew nicely all morning __before / in__ the start of the contest.

9. __During / At__ 12:00 o'clock, there was hardly any wind at all!

10. Our kite did not fly high __during / on__ the contest, but we did win the "best design" award!

F. Write this paragraph. Add a phrase from the box for each blank.

around the kite	with a blue head	in his hand
for his birthday	to the beach	into the air

Daniel's uncle gave him a kite that looks like a red bird _____. It was a gift _____. Daniel and his uncle took the kite over _____. His uncle tossed the kite _____ while Daniel held the string _____. The sea gulls circled _____ because they were very interested in the strange, new bird!

G. Write a paragraph about a kite or something else that flies. Include prepositions to tell about time, location, and direction.

Conjunctions

H. Write these paragraphs. Use conjunctions from the box to combine some sentences.

and	but	or

1. Jungi never misses an Eagles' baseball game. He'll go to the stadium. He'll watch the game on TV. The Eagles lost their last game. They won all the games before that.

2. Robert Pérez is Jungi's favorite player. Robert is the pitcher. He is one of the best in the league. Robert could not play in the last game. Jungi thinks that is why the Eagles lost.

I. Write a paragraph about a team you like. Use the words and, but, and or at least once.

Capital Letters

A. Write each sentence. Use capital letters correctly.

1. Today i am going on a whale-watching trip.
2. My friend richard yee will join me.
3. His mother, mrs. yee, might come, too.
4. Mr. ernie vega owns the boat.
5. His helper is Alice c. Beck.
6. she is a scientist who studies whales.
7. we will learn about whales from dr. Beck.
8. dr. Beck and i will watch for whales from the top of the boat.
9. last time Mr. Vega was the first to see a whale.
10. This time i hope that i am!

B. Write these sentences. Use capital letters correctly.

1. There is a great whale-watching boat in boston.

2. It is near seaview boulevard.

3. It's across from central park.

4. The boat is called *deep dreamer*.

5. Its captain has sailed all over the atlantic and pacific oceans.

6. He used to work for a british company.

7. He often sailed around the tip of africa.

8. He has even been to the great barrier reef.

9. In fact, he has sailed most of earth's oceans.

10. Now, he doesn't go far from the massachusetts coast.

C. Write this letter. Use abbreviations for the underlined words.

472 Lincoln <u>Avenue</u>
Chicago, <u>Illinois</u> 60643
<u>Friday</u>, October 29, 2002

Captain Boris Davidov
9 <u>East</u> 15th <u>Street</u>
Boston, <u>Massachusetts</u> 02101

Dear Captain Davidov,

My family and I wanted to go on a whale-watching trip next weekend: <u>Saturday</u>, <u>November</u> 6 or <u>Sunday</u>, <u>November</u> 7. Do you have room on your boat for four people on one of those days?

Sincerely,

Claude Delors

D. Write each sentence. Use capital letters correctly.

1. The boy scouts are planning a whale-watching trip.

2. They're going during the first weekend in september.

3. It will be labor day weekend.

4. The scoutmaster told the boys, "we might see some gray whales."

5. He showed them a video, the great whales.

6. It was made by the national geographic society.

7. He also read them an article called "protecting the gray whales."

8. The boys could hardly wait for that saturday.

Punctuation

A. Write each sentence. Add the correct punctuation at the end of what each person says.

period

question mark

exclamation point

Aaron

1. Please show me the newspaper

_____

Dad

2. Would you like to see the ads

3. Here is an ad for a used bike

_____

Aaron

4. Wow, it sounds great

5. What is the price

_____

Dad

6. Call the number to find out

_____

Aaron

7. How much can I spend

8. I've been dreaming about a bike forever

B. **Write each sentence. Add commas where they are needed.**

Aaron

1. Mrs. Romero it's Aaron calling.

2. I wanted you to know that I can walk Brute

Friday Saturday or Sunday.

Mrs. Romero

3. Oh Saturday should be fine!

4. But, wait, your school fair is Saturday isn't it?

Aaron

5. As Dad always says "You have to be flexible."

6. I'm willing to take your big gentle dog for a walk anytime.

Mrs. Romero

7. I have 1000000 things to do on Saturday anyway.

8. Plus, Sunday is supposed to be a warm sunny day.

Aaron

9. OK I'll take Brute on Sunday.

10. I'll see you Sunday Mrs. Romero.

C. **Write this friendly letter. Add commas where they belong.**

251 Ramos Drive
Tucson AZ 85737
April 3 1999

Dear Mr. and Mrs. Sanchez

My mother said that you are looking for helpers for your garage sale. Can I help you set up? I can also help sell things. Please let me know if you want my help. Thank you.

Your neighbor

Jaime

D. Write this business letter. Add commas, colons, and apostrophes where they are needed.

248 Ramos Drive
Tucson AZ 85737
June 12 1999

comma

Ms. Ella Jefferson
ABC Publishers
12 Brown Avenue
Sunset NJ 07109

Dear Ms. Jefferson

I read your book *Kids Make Money* and I learned a lot from it.

I tried these ideas walking my neighbors dog helping at

garage sales and delivering newspapers every morning from

530 to 700. I would like to buy your other book *Kids Make More*

Money but I cant find it. Can you please tell me where its sold?

Sincerely yours

Jaime Santiago
Jaime Santiago

colon

apostrophe

E. Write each sentence. Add quotation marks and underlining where they are needed.

1. How can I earn some money? Aaron asked his dad.

2. His dad had seen a sign that said, Teenagers Wanted for Garage Clean-up.

3. His dad also told him to look in the magazine Dollars.

4. There was an ad for delivering the Times-Press newspaper.

5. There was also an article called Kids Can Run a Business.

6. It talked about a book called Earning Money After School.

7. The chapter called How to Quickly Earn $5 sounded interesting.

8. Aaron asked his dad, Can I borrow some money to buy this book?

underline

quotation marks

Index

P

Paragraphs
cause-and-effect, 127
main idea, 98, 125, 126, 138, 233
persuasive, 130
that compare, 128
that contrast, 129
topic sentence, 100, 101, 125–130, 138, 230–231, 233
with examples, 126
Parts diagram, 66
Parts of speech
defined, 253
See also Adjectives; Adverbs; Conjunctions; Interjections; Nouns; Prepositions; Pronouns; Verbs
Past-tense verbs, 190–191
irregular, 191
regular, 190
spelling rules, 190
Peer Conference, 90
Period, 208–209
as decimal points, 209
in abbreviations, 209
in sentences, 208
Personal narrative, 131
Play, 132–133
script for, 133
Plot
See Story, parts of a
Poems, 134–137
cinquain, 134
concrete poem, 135
diamante, 134
haiku, 136
poem in free verse, 136
rhyming poem, 137
Portfolio, writing, 157
Postcards, 109
Predicate, 165
complete, 165
compound, 165
simple, 165
Prefixes, 48–49
Prepositions, 198–199
prepositional phrases, 199
using in writing, 199
ways to use (chart), 198
See also Describing words, words that tell where; Grammar practice

Present-tense verbs, 188–189
spelling rules, 189
Prewriting, 86–87
See also Graphic organizers
Pronouns
different kinds (subject, object, reflexive, possessive, indefinite), 174–178
using in writing (agreement), 179
See also Grammar practice
Proofreading, 92
Proofreading marks, 92
Publishing, 93
Punctuation marks, 208–213
See also Apostrophe; Colon; Comma; Exclamation point; Grammar practice; Period; Question mark; Quotation marks; Underline
Purpose for writing, 86, 150–151

Q

Question mark, 208
Questions, 160–162
at the end of a statement (tag questions), 161
W-H, 162
yes/no, 162
Quotation marks
around exact words, 213, 226–227
for titles, 213

R

Realistic fiction, 141
Recipe, 103
Report, 138–139, 230–233
Research process, 220–233
alphabetical order, 224
choose a topic, 220
decide what to look up, 221
gather information, 224–227
locate resources, 221–223
organize information, 228–229
outline, 228–229
research question, 221, 227, 228
skim and scan, 225
taking notes, 226–227
write a research report, 230–233
See also Report

Two-word verbs, 54–59

U

V

W

Acknowledgments, continued

pp218, 223, and **250–253,** Reprinted with the permission of Simon & Schuster Books for Young Readers, an imprint of Simon & Schuster Children's Publishing Division from MACMILLAN DICTIONARY FOR CHILDREN, Revised by Robert B. Costello, Editor in Chief. Copyright © 1997 Simon & Schuster. Photos, pp251 and 253, courtesy of NASA. Photo of Pennybacker Bridge, p. 251, courtesy of Texas Department of Transportation.

pp222 and **235,** Cover illustration from UFO DIARY by Satoshi Kitamura. Copyright © 1989 by Satoshi Kitamura. Reprinted by permission of Farrar, Straus & Giroux, Inc.

pp222, 240, 241, and **243,** As in original. Cover photo courtesy of NASA.

p223, © 1996 Time Inc. Reprinted by permission.

pp223 and **254–255,** From THE WORLD BOOK ENCYCLOPEDIA. © 1998 World Book, Inc. By permission of the publisher.

pp235 and **239,** ARE WE MOVING TO MARS? by Anne Schraff. Copyright © 1996 by John Muir Publications, Santa Fe, NM 87505.

pp237–239, Used by permission of Innovative Interfaces, Inc., Emeryville, California.

p246, NGS MAPS/NGS Image Sales.

p248, Maps by GeoSystems from BUILD OUR NATION in WE THE PEOPLE by Hartoonian, et al. Copyright © 1997 by Houghton Mifflin Company. Reprinted by permission of Houghton Mifflin Company. All rights reserved.

p261, "Mars" downloaded from NEW SCIENTIST web site http://www.newscientist.com. Produced 1998 by Reed Elsevier Group, RBI Limited, London. Used by permission.

p269, From COLLECTED POEMS by Langston Hughes. Copyright © 1994 by the Estate of Langston Hughes. Reprinted by permission of Alfred A Knopf Inc.

p271, Robbie Short.

p274, PEANUTS © United Features Syndicate, Inc.

p274, Superman is a trademark of DC Comics © 1998. All rights reserved. Used with permission.

p274, Wonder Woman is a trademark of DC Comics © 1998. All rights reserved. Used with permission.

p275, Cover illustration from THE WIZARD OF OZ by L. Frank Baum. Published by Apple Classics, an imprint of Scholastic Inc. Cover copyright © by Scholastic Inc. Reprinted by permission.

p275, Jacket art by Garth Williams. Jacket design by Charles Krelloff. Jacket copyright 1994 by Harpercollins Publishers. Little House is a trademark Harpercollins Publishers, used by permission. of Harpercollins.

p295, Barry Mullins.

Illustrations:

Cover Illustration: Steven Durke
American Girl Magazine: p94
Doug Bekke: pp128–129 (alligator, crocodiles) pp180–183 and p315 (rainforest animal art) p190 (Galileo's thermometer) p220 (planets) p314 (monkey)
Lisa Berret: p23 (suitcase) p25 (dartboard) p28 (ice, pancake, bird, feather, pea pod) p32 (hands cutting apple) p42 (bowl, oven, cake) pp45–46 (lighthouse, coats) p48 (girl with cars)
Liz Callen: p108 (get well dog)
Chi Chung: pp190–191 (sun, desert)
Darius Detwiler: p275 (John Henry, Pecos Bill)
Steven Durke: pp10–11, pp60–61, pp84–85, pp158–159, and pp218–219 (openers)
Ray Godfrey: p40 (clocks) p66 (lifecycle) pp68–69 (raffle, rubber duck, medal) p79 (volcano) p120 (menu) p201 (baseball flyer)
Pauline Howard: p43 (boy on scale)

Beatrice Lebreton: p108 (Kwanzaa cards) p290 (Jan Matzeliger)
Claude Martinot: p65 (kites) p72 (apartments, moon) p81 (sewing materials) p82 (first place) p74 (spider) p102 (hands) p131 (hearts) pp216–217, p267, p272 (Leprechaun) p273 (Passover plate) p279 (card) p285 (gift) p296 (jack-o'-lantern) p300 (Christmas tree) p301 (confetti)
Russell Nemec: p41 (Times of the Day) p266, p276, pp279–283 (maps) p290 (shoe lasting machine) p299, p301 (maps)
Barbara Johansen Newman: p29, pp33–37 and p320, pp50–53, p147, p202 (Lucky Seas), p204 (kid and captain) pp208–213 and pp325–326, p221, p224, p226, p229, p230, p233
Winifred Barnum-Newman: pp106–107 (Stone Soup, Cinderella) p132 (the Jade Emperor) p280 (Sacagawea)
Donna Perrone: p160, p162, p320 (Paul Bunyan) p164, p165, and p305 (Babe) p168 (kites) p170 (table) p171 (umbrellas) p172 (illustrations) p173
Thom Ricks: p275 (Tom Sawyer and Huckleberry Finn)
Mary Rojas: p22 (compass) p108 (Birthday card) p135 (oak) p135 (dragon) p137(dragon)
Roni Shepard: p22 (fair)
Robbie Short: p223 (library)
Camille Venti: p40 (calendar)
Elizabeth Wolf: p19 (basketball art) p140, pp174–178 and pp311–312, pp195–196 and p321 (gymnastics) p200 (baseball game)

Photographs:

Animals Animals: p182 (parrot: John Chellman, toucan: Michael Dick, motmot: Paul Freed) p183 (motmot: Ken Cole) p184 (jaguar: John Chellman, jaguar in jungle: Partridge Productions) p185 (katydid: Patti Murray, stick insect: C. McLaughlin, katydid on leaf: Michael Fogden) p205 (whale: Donna Ikenberry), p309 (stick insect: C. McLaughlin)

Archive Photos: p111 (Wynton Marsalis: Deborah Feingold) p268 (Civil War: Matthew Brady) p269 (Langston Hughes, Rosa Parks: Georg Dabrowski) p290 (Thomas Edison, electric light bulb)

Artville: p13 (sea star) p16 (chalk, pepper, worms, grapes) p17 (celery, herbs, vegetables, pretzel, lemon, orange slices) p25 (tomatoes) p28 (gold bars) p31 (penny, clock) p32 (pear) p38 (pizza, pizza slice) p44 (hot dog) p45 (pineapple, popcorn) p49 (vegetables, pizza) p67 (hat, hot dogs, hamburger) p96 (boy) p119 (chili pepper, eggplant, lime, coconut, pineapple) p120 (shrimp bowl, burrito, salad, fruits, vegetables) p127 (present) p134 (peach, pear, pepper, pineapple) p169 (football) p179 (soccer ball) p249 (globe) p263 (hotdog, quarter, penny, baseball) p273 (basket) p276 (sailboat, Mississippi River) p282 (gold bars) p296 (Day of the Dead)

Batista Moon Studio: p234 (card catalog) p254 (encyclopedias)

California State Archives: p282 and p303 (Bear Flag Republic)

Corbis: p295 (Fransisco de Coronado)

Corel: p276 (Florida Keys)

Culver Pictures, Inc.: p270 (George Washington)

DigitalStock: p13 (present) p25 (baseball pitcher, drinking pitcher) p28 (blonde girl, two girls) p30 (bee) p32 (fish) p39 (wild) p42 (leaves, snow, flowers) p45 (rainbow) p64 (eagle) p78 (erupting volcano) p104 (manatees) p118 (blonde boy) p125 (coast) p134 (lightning storm) p138 (fish fossil) p180 (green tree frog) p183 (hummingbird, macaw) p187 (clouds) p189 and p316 (lightning) p204 (Statue of Liberty, freeway, coast, Earth, cityscape) p263 and p273 (Statue of Liberty) p276 (Redwood Forest, Rocky Mountains, Southwestern Desert, Appalachian Mountains) p293 (The Capitol) p297 (Veteran's Day) p309 (macaw)

Digital Studios: p13 (clock, hanger) p14 (watch, pencil, penny) p16 (cotton, soup) p17 (radio, orange, carrot) p21 (farm) p22 (fan) p23 (corn and cornmeal, jam, key) p24 (lamp) p25 (hammering, hand) p27 (fish) p28 (hat) p30 (flour) p31 (numbers) p38 (corks) p39 (dishes, glasses, vases) p40 (wristwatch, sundial, stopwatch, clock, alarm clock, timer, hourglass) p43 (ruler, teaspoon, tablespoon, cup, pint, quart, gallon) p44 (backpack, fingernail, flashlight, bathtub) p45 (motorcycle, seashells, shoelaces, sweatshirt) p46 (vase, pencil, sharpener) p47 (umbrellas, trucks) p49 (reused glass, vase) p55 (pencil) p58 (milk) p59 (pen) pp70-71 (can, recycling bin, pencil) p80 (pen) pp108-110 (envelope, stamps, postcard, notepad, pencil) p113 (diary, pencil) p116 (pen) p119 (envelope) p122 (pencil) p124 (notepad) p126 (stamps) p137 (fossils) pp143-145 (sketchbook, notebook) pp198-199 and p322 (kite) pp270-271 (Constitution, Three Branches of Government) p293 (Great Seal) p319 (umbrella)

Digital Vision: p220 (galaxy)

FPG International: p21 (bark) p63 (moon) p265 (The White House: Peter Gridley) p268 (Jackie Robinson) p282 (gold miners) p290 (first telephone, Alexander Graham Bell) p291 and p303 (Model T) p291 (factory, Henry Ford) p294 (John Cabot) p301 (New Year's in New York: Jerry Driendl)

Galveston Island Convention and Visitor's Bureau: p167 (family, Ashton Villa, Tall Ship Elissa) p307 (Ashton Villa)

Grant Heilman Photography: p27 (picnic: Barry L. Runk)

Image Bank: p23 (inner tube: Grant V. Faint) p75 (hurricane)

Image Club: p12 and p46 (mask) p15 (eggs)

The Image Works: p32 (boy with glasses: Bob Daemmrich) p39 (ugly landscape: John Eastcott & Eva Momatiuk)

Image Quest: p55 (cowboy) p56 (girl with violin) p57 (flying geese)

J. Barry Mittan: p69 (Tara Lipinski)

Janine Boylan: p101 (Vietnam market)

Lawrence Migdale: p23 and p264 (New Year's Day: David Young-Wolff) p277 (Mexican dancers) p289 (playing the drums) p300 (Kwanzaa)

Library of Congress: p281 (Sam Houston: F Davignon) p298 (English Settlers, Jamestown)

Liz Garza Williams: p10 (boy and girl) pp16-17 (girl) pp18-19 (boy), p20 (formal greeting) p28 (cold boy, girl singing, girl with balloon) p30 (girl with sandwich) p44 (bookshelf) p60 (girl) p70 (girl) p84 (boy and girl) pp116-117 (girls) p130 (boy) p158 (boy) p161, pp162-164 and p166 (kids and park worker) p167 (girl on bike, boy running) p168 (kids) pp170-172 (girl, woman, girl, and two boys) p192 (girls) pp214-215, p218 (boy and girl) p256 (boy)

Map Art: p21, p27, p167

Metaphotos: p16, p30 and p39 (ants) p17 (garbage, mustard) p130 (oil can) p47 (tarantula) p59 (flag) p120 (soda cup, coffee mug)

Monkmeyer: p44 (backyard: Forbert)

NASA: p83 (Dr. Franklin Chang-Díaz) p241 (Mars) p288 (Alan Shepard, John Glenn, Jr., Sally Ride) p263, p288, and p303 (Challenger)

National Archives: p297 (World War II)

Natural Selection: p44 (jellyfish: David B. Fleetman)

Newell Colour: p220 (Mars) p242 (Mars)

Norbert Wu Photography: p207 (whale)

Northwind Picture Archives: p268 (Frederick Douglass, Harriet Tubman) p280 (Lewis and Clark) p280 (Andrew Jackson) p281 and 303 (covered wagon) p282 (Homesteaders, Transcontinental Railroad) pp286-287 (Boston Tea Party, Revolutionary War, Declaration of Independence, Yorktown) p291 (Samuel Gompers, Jane Addams) p294 (Christopher Columbus) p294 (Juan Ponce de León) p295 (Don Pedro Menéndez de Avilés) p299 and 302 (Mayflower Compact)

PhotoDisc: p13 (window, sign) p14 and 46 (runner) p15 (basket) p16 (apple, sunset, basketball) p21 (dog, bat) p23 (corn) p24 (cookie, girl writing) p26 (point, pupil) p27 (scale with pumpkin) p30 (birthday girl, Ping-Pong set) p31 (first place ribbon) p32 (woods) p38 (male, female, start, finish) p39 (cat, mountains, elephant) p40 (flamingos) p42 (girls on beach) p44 (basketball) p45 (sunflower) p48 (airplane, sneakers, marbles) p49 (replaced tube) p54 (woman with pie) p56 (hand with CD) p57 (girl writing) p58 (girl) p59 (girl, pot) p113 (girl writing) p131 (girl writing) p162 and 186 (clouds) p204 (mountains) p258 (internet) p268 (baseball) p269 (gavel) p278 (Mom and daughter) p287 and 302 (Liberty bell) p300 (dreidl) p309 (bat)

PhotoEdit: p24 (kids in line: Michael Newman) p25 (plant: Amy C.Etra) p54 (people talking: Bill Aron) p81 (kids: Richard Hutchings) p100 (boys) p114 (girl: David Young-Wolff) p123 (girl: Michelle Bridwell) p127 (girl: Michael Newman) p188 (weather reporter: Tom McCarthy) p266 (Chinese New Year: David Young-Wolff) p284 (Puerto Rican Day: Robert Brenner) p285 (father and son: Myrleen Ferguson, Dragon Boats: James Shaffer) p289 (traditional dancing: Tony Freeman, jingle dress: Deborah Davis) p292 (apples and honey: Bill Aron) p293 (Uncle Sam: Bonnie Kamin)

Plimoth Plantation: p299 Photo courtesy of Plimoth Plantation, Plymouth, Massachusetts

Stockbyte: p12 (dolls) p16 (medal) p17 (rose, perfume, drums) p23 (keyboard) p30 (flower) p31 (girl with flowers) p32 (galoshes) p39 (butterflies) p44 (headphones) p45 (keyboard, toothbrush, videocassette) p46 (baker) p47 (butterfly) p48 (bicycle) p69 (duck) p80 (basketball) p82 (girl) p95 (bicycle) p110 (cassette recorder) p141 (bicycle) p288 (astronaut on moon, astronaut in space)

The Stock Market: p22 (fans: Chuck Savage) p25 (animal pen: Robert Frerch) p54 (girl with car: David Woods) p56 (boy reading: Gabe Palmer) p57 (girl with dictionary: José L. Palaez) p181 and p314 (sloth: Norbert Wu)

SuperStock: p13 (egg) p16 (fluffy clouds) p22 (sailboat) p54 (icy lake) p55 (woman) pp120-122 (family, boy) p264 (Martin Luther King, Jr.) p270 (Abraham Lincoln: The Huntington Library)

Tony Stone Images: p31 (girl listening: Don Smetzer) p38 (receive: Peter Correz) p269 (Thurgood Marshall) p275 (Annie Oakley: Hulton Getty) p297 (World War I: Hulton Getty)

Uniphoto: p21 (speaker: Mark Reinstein) p25 (tomato plant: T. Stephan Thompson) p38 (give: R. Michael R. Keller, enter: Paul Conklin, exit: Bob Daemmrich) p56 (kids and bus: Bob Daemmrich) p57 (couple eating: Jonathan Bookallil) p58 (neighbors talking: Howard Grey)

Credits

Design and Production: Andrea Carter, Command P, Darius Detwiler, Jeri Gibson, Curtis Spitler, Alicia Sternberg, Andrea Pastrano-Tamez, Edward Tamez, Teri Wilson, ZeitGraph, Inc.

Editorial: Janine Boylan, Fredrick Ignacio, Dawn Liseth, Sheron Long, Sharon Ursino

Permissions Staff: Barbara Mathewson